GHOST WHISPERER

127344

SPIRIT

GHOST WHISPERER SPIRIT GUIDE

ISBN: 9781845769352

Published by
Titan Books
A division of
Titan Publishing Group Ltd
144 Southwark Street
London
SE1 0UP

First edition November 2008
2 4 6 8 10 9 7 5 3 1

Imagery credits: opening title sequence frames pp81-85 by Maggie Taylor, storyboards pp136-137 by Ricky Lewis, GHOST WHISPERER comic cover p146 by Brian Miller, published by IDW Publishing

Visit our website:
www.titanbooks.com

Titan Books would like to thank the cast and crew of *Ghost Whisperer*, in particular Jennifer Love Hewitt
(for the wonderful Foreword, among other things), John Gray (especially for the Introduction),
P.K. Simonds, David Conrad, Camryn Manheim, Jay Mohr, Christoph Sanders, Anne Archer, Ignacio Sericchio,
and the department heads who all generously contributed both their time and material to this book.
Special thanks must also go to Risa Kessler for her tireless championing of this project and to Paula Block at CBS for her invaluable help.

To receive advance information, news, competitions, and exclusive Titan offers online, please register as a member
by clicking the "sign up" button on our website: **www.titanbooks.com**
Did you enjoy this book? We love to hear from our readers. Please e-mail us at: **readerfeedback@titanemail.com**
or write to Reader Feedback at the above address.

A CIP catalogue record for this title is available from the British Library.

Printed and bound in the United States of America.

GHOST WHISPERER

SPIRIT GUIDE

KIM MOSES
& IAN SANDER

TITAN BOOKS

ACKNOWLEDGMENTS

We want to thank John Gray, our partner and creator of *Ghost Whisperer* who is a triple threat, a great writer, director and friend, and P.K. Simonds who jumped on board in season three and is seamlessly taking *Ghost Whisperer* (and us!) to new heights. We owe a debt of gratitude to Jennifer Love Hewitt who does double duty daily as star and producer. She's the heart of the show, whose middle name best describes her. Thanks to James Van Praagh and Mary Ann Winkowski who keep us authentic without losing the fun.

Jeanine Harris did a fantastic job ferreting out research without which this book could not have been written. Bobbie Bencio's super human coordinating skills kept us marching down the field against all odds; Devra Zabot not only kept the trains running but helped stoke the engines. Nichelle Protho, our VP of Development, right hand and dear friend must be acknowledged for her hard work and patience with the Sander/Moses hydra head.

Ghost Whisperer's success is truly a tribute to the hard work and talent of our amazing cast, crew, writing team, directors, post production staff and digital media team — each contributing equal parts passion and intellect to put the best show on the air while simultaneously creating magic at the intersection of TV and the digital world.

We owe special thanks to Mark Gilbertson, our genius business partner 'shrink' for helping us create a unique blueprint and J. Moses, who taught us how to turn the 'crank' to jump start our Internet engine, catapulting us into the twenty-first century. Aaron Kaplan, Susan Brooks, Laurie Pozmantier, Brad Small, Victor Meschures and Simona Georgescu, your insight and guidance we value beyond measure.

There are no words to express the level of gratitude we feel toward CBS's Les Moonves who has been our producing godfather since the beginning of time; Nancy Tellem, who understands and champions the dynamic of digital platform roll outs to create multi-dimensional TV experiences; and Nina Tassler, clairvoyant from day one, passionately predicting what the future holds for *Ghost Whisperer*. We owe Bela Bajaria a special thanks for planting the seed that birthed the show, and Laverne McKinnon, Christina Davis and Robert Zotnowski who nurtured and guided this baby from gestation. Thank you, David Brownfield and Alix Jaffe, for keeping us on track and championing *Ghost Whisperer* through the first three years; Ghen Maynard for bridging television and the Internet with us; Quincy Smith for taking CBS and us down the web-road; Phil Gonzalez, Linda Renee, Ken Ross and their teams for helping us bust through traditional barriers daily; and Liz Kalodner and Risa Kessler who locked arms with us on this book and marched forward.

And, a special thanks to our editor, Jo Boylett, for giving us enough rope to hang ourselves, then making sure we didn't.

At ABC Studios we will be grateful forever and a day to Mark Pedowitz, who brought us in from the cold and just plain believed. We couldn't ask for a better home than ABC Studios and we thank Julia Franz, Howard Davine, Barry Jossen, Morgan Wandell, Nicole Norwood, Brian Harvey, Steve Tann, Nne Ebong, Gary French, David Goldman, Charissa Gilmore and their extraordinary teams for always helping us create the magic and find solutions.

We're very fortunate to have the guidance and support of Paramount/CBS Studio, and we thank David Stapf, Glenn Geller, and Bridget Wiley for their wisdom and generosity on this journey.

Thanks to Mark Steines at *Entertainment Tonight* for keeping his ear to the ground and this book in the *Ghost Whisperer* world.

To *Ghost Whisperer* fans everywhere old and new — without your undying loyalty and limitless fascination with the spirit world, none of this would matter.

And most important, to our sons, Aaron Gabriel and Declan Moses Sander, we love you and thank you for choosing us as your parents. 🌀

CONTENTS

FOREWORD

s an actress, I can tell you, committing to a one-hour dramatic television series is a blessing and an enormous commitment. And a single-lead show, although surrounded by a wonderfully talented ensemble, is that much more difficult. First, there are the twelve to sixteen hour days. In addition there is the responsibility of delivering a real, sometimes funny, sometimes dramatic, and always emotional performance for nine straight months (the time it takes to produce a full season of episodes). On top of all that, the commitment is for at least six years if the show is fortunate enough to be successful. As you can imagine, to do this you better love what you're doing.

When I was offered the role of Melinda Gordon in *Ghost Whisperer*, I read the script by John Gray and fell in love. I fell in love with the concept of the show. And I fell in love with the character. I was truly inspired by her strength as well as her vulnerability. I felt she was a 'super hero'. Not a 'super hero' in the comic book sense, but a 'super hero' in a very real sense. Her unquestioned love of others and her undying commitment to helping them in a purely altruistic way makes Melinda someone I can look up to.

Women in the twenty-first century often have to be 'super women'. Balancing their work — in Melinda's case it's running a small business as well as using her gift to help others — with their commitment to family — in Melinda's case her devotion to her husband Jim and her desire to have children. It is very important to me that a female-driven television show do well, and in order to do so I have to create a full person with everyday frustrations, moods, and emotions who women and men can relate to.

Over the three years we have been doing *Ghost Whisperer*, the show has evolved and grown. Just like life, we have moved from innocence to wisdom. The challenges, as we've built a mythology and confronted the dark side, have made the show, and in turn, Melinda stronger and deeper. This has been so important to my producing partners and me because

it has kept my character and the show fresh and challenging. The importance of the mystery has also grown, which is the thing that keeps the audience turning the page, so to speak.

Working with our talented cast has also been a wonderful gift for me. David Conrad, who plays my husband, is really Melinda's backbone and ballast. Aisha Tyler, who played Andrea the first season, was a great friend both on and off screen. We had so much fun on set that the crew often referred to us as "Lucy and Ethel". The supremely talented actress Camryn Manheim stepped into *Ghost Whisperer* in season two without missing a beat and we just love working together. Jay Mohr is so bright and funny and has brought a sense of humor we really need as we tell stories that are deeper and darker. He also keeps the crew in stitches no matter how long the days get. And, because we have such great guest roles, we have attracted fantastic guest stars including Mary J. Blige, Orlando Jones, Ann Archer, Christine Baranski, David Paymer, Abigail Breslin, and many more who I hope will forgive me for not mentioning them.

I also must mention the fantastic writers, directors, producers and crew. They are my true inspiration and I really love them. We are absolutely a family.

When we first began doing *Ghost Whisperer*, we and my fellow producers hoped to do a show which would appeal to those who believe in ghosts as well as the non-believers. In order for this to be achieved, we knew the show would have to be different each week. The journey is sometimes scary, sometimes funny, sometimes mysterious. Ultimately by the end, it is always emotional and inspiring.

I am so very grateful I was offered and committed to *Ghost Whisperer* and can't wait so see what the future holds for Melinda Gordon and the spirit world.

INTRODUCTION

ne of the great things about being a writer — certainly one of the most satisfying things — is that you get to create the world exactly as you would have it. No matter the genre, the period, the plot, you control what the characters think, feel and say. You control how the world works, what goes wrong, what goes right, and you (usually) know what's going to happen next. If only any of the above were even partially possible in real life… but that's another story.

Ghost Whisperer came about because an executive at CBS, Bela Bejaria, put me together with Mary Ann Winkowski, a real-life ghost whisperer living in Ohio. The famed psychic James Van Praagh had introduced Mary Ann to Bela, and Bela sensed that there might be some kind of a series based on what Mary Ann did. My first meeting with Mary Ann was a surprise… I was half expecting a mysterious, tortured woman with an Eastern European accent, who was at least as haunted as her clients. Instead I met a robust, funny, salt-of-the-earth woman from the Midwest with a great laugh, who didn't take herself all that seriously. I was fascinated by her matter of fact attitude toward her gift; and when I asked her if she saw spirits all the time, she casually pointed out that there were at least three ghosts at that moment in the Starbucks we were sitting in. She explained where each one was, who they seemed to be haunting, and how she was grateful that the ghosts hadn't yet noticed that she could see them.

Aside from my hair doing that stand-up thing on the back of my neck, I was hooked (in fact, a version of that meeting was the first scene I wrote for the pilot). I drove away thinking that this could be the perfect fusion of two genres of movies and television I love: horror, and character-driven emotional drama. It seemed to me a chance to not only do something scary and spooky, but also to look at death and grief through the lens of forgiveness and redemption… the completion of unfinished business, and the enticing, comforting notion that love transcends death.

I brought the idea to producers Ian Sander and Kim Moses, and with James Van Praagh on board, we persuaded CBS to give us a shot.

My first notion of Melinda was of a woman in her late thirties/early forties, probably still single because of the chaos her gift caused in her life. The more we discussed it, however, a new idea began to emerge: What if this person were quite young; a newlywed, just starting out in her life, struggling with finances, work, all the things people beginning their adult lives have to deal with. And, oh yeah, she sees and tries to help the dead at the same time. The original concept of her husband Jim was that he didn't know she had this gift, and she had to summon the courage to tell him before she went through with the marriage, and then we the audience would experience her abilities through Jim's not quite believing eyes.

It was the network that steered me away from that notion, and I think rightly so. Their suggestion was that Jim not only be aware of her gift, but be totally okay with it. This really clicked for us… Why not portray a marriage that works, something rarely seen on TV, in which both partners *get* each other, and support each other no matter what? Jim doesn't pretend to understand everything about what Melinda can do, but he knows her heart and he knows that what she does is important, so he's there in any way he has to be. We get a lot of feedback about their relationship from our viewers; mostly positive, but some people find the Melinda and Jim relationship too good to be true. I refer those people back to paragraph one, above.

So, that left us with a need for another character who was new to Melinda's gift, and wasn't quite sure what to do with it… Thus came Andrea Moreno. We wanted someone who could be funny and vulnerable and bring her own stories to the table; another young person starting out, but without the support system Melinda has in place.

We wanted Melinda to be starting her own

business, and after Van Praagh told us about how often ghosts are attached to their old possessions, an antique store seemed like a logical point of departure. This gave us an interesting way in to a great many stories, and a natural way for Melinda and Andrea to interact, and for Andrea — always to her great bemusement — to be involved in Melinda's adventures.

Now that we had figured out Melinda's job, what about Jim? We batted around a lot of ideas for him… Cop? Doctor? Game show host? Just kidding. (I think. There were a lot of late night discussions; anything is possible.) Finally we settled on paramedic, because of its immediacy, potential for action, and it made for a natural communion with Melinda. He tries to keep as many people as is in his power from ending up as ghosts on his wife's radar.

Add to all of the above some quirky local characters, set in the kind of small town that I have always dreamed of living in (see paragraph one again), and we felt we were off to a good start. The next step was coming up with a story for our pilot episode.

One of the cases Mary Ann told me about at our first meeting concerned a local undercover detective with whom she had worked on certain cases. This detective was killed in the line of duty, and Mary Ann told me she had encountered him in the hallway of her home. He wanted her to know and report where his body was located, as it was in a remote place that he was afraid wouldn't be found. I was struck by this story for all of the obvious reasons… and it became the genesis for the pilot.

CBS was very clear at the beginning that they were not looking for *Ghost Whisperer* to be a police-themed procedural. So I tried to figure out a way to make an emotional mystery as well as a spooky ghost story. My original thought was that a soldier from Iraq comes to Melinda, and he wants her to tell his family where his body is. However, we came to feel at that time, early 2005, that Iraq was too raw, too fresh a wound to deal with. Indeed, we wouldn't feel comfortable with an Iraq-themed episode until season three.

So we turned to Vietnam instead, using the passing of time as a theme. This opened up for me the possibility of a ghost who was killed in that war, but doesn't realize how much time has passed. He feels lost and is looking for his pregnant wife. Melinda has

to show him that his wife is long dead, and his now grown son is expecting his first child. This situation felt rich with possibilities, and seemed a good way to illustrate everything we thought the show could be. Making the pilot was a fantastic experience, particularly because of the great cast and crew we were able to assemble, and it convinced CBS (and our audience) that there was a series here worth watching.

One amusing aside, although not so amusing at the time: In January of 2005, shortly after I had handed in the pilot script to CBS and we were waiting to hear if they were going to order it made, I got a call from a friend of mine. "Hey," he began, innocently enough. "Is your show on the air already?" "Ha ha," I answered. "I only wish. We're waiting to find out if they're going to order the pilot." "Ah." My friend responded. And then he was quiet. Too quiet, as the saying goes. I suddenly felt my tongue getting a little fuzzy. "Why do you ask?" I finally managed to inquire. "Oh, no, it's nothing… It's just that I was flipping through the channels, and I saw a promo for a show where there's this woman in bed with her husband, and there's all these ghosts in the bedroom, and they want her help, but only she can see them, and she's trying to ignore them…"

I had to get off the phone immediately in order to pick up my heart, which had just tumbled onto the floor with a wet thud, and stuff it back into my chest as I crossed to the television and basically stared at it for the next two hours, waiting to see this promo. That show, of course, turned out to be *Medium*, which went on the air as a mid-season replacement just as we started shooting our pilot the next month. Fortunately, aside from having to endure some initial accusations of being copycats, once our show went on the air, the differences were obvious and both shows have coexisted happily.

Three years later, *Ghost Whisperer* continues to grow. We add new characters, new dimensions for Melinda; the network has encouraged us to add more mystery, more twists and turns. The show keeps regenerating, while keeping our basic concept intact: an emotional, character-driven horror movie every week, with a dose of humor and most likely a tear or two at the end.

A recipe, oddly enough, that also pretty much sums up our experience making each episode!
John Gray

GENESIS OF GHOST WHISPERER

LIGHTNING IN A BOTTLE

As producer-writer-directors, we birth an idea, develop it, sell it, produce it and sometimes even get it on the air. If we're lucky, viewers might tune in to the premiere of a show we're launching. If Lady Luck lingers for a week or so, viewers return to find out what happens in episode two. If she's with us for the long haul, the viewing audience builds from week to week, until the show becomes a genuine hit. In the entertainment industry, this is known as 'lightning in a bottle'. Ever try using a Coke bottle to catch a million kilowatts of electricity ripping through an angry sky? Good luck with that, right?

But that's exactly what it's like to launch a TV series and hope the audience shows up. Unless, of course, you put your heads together. Now, we're not suggesting that everyone needs a partner to make a successful TV series (although one plus one does make a thousand in our case). We're talking about enjoining the Right Brain and the Left Brain. Sander/Moses keeps the creative side connected to the business side — the Right Brain creates with the ability to think out of the box and risk failure while the Left Brain organizes, operates strategically, and executes through to success. Together they build the brand. There's never been a better time in the history of the world for Right Brain/Left Brain operators than right here right now. The multitude of digital platforms and the wide array of technical tools available today enable each and every one of us to create, and produce quality content and engage eyeballs at a quantity beyond our wildest dreams.

Not only did we develop an idea into a TV series, we also created a fan base online well before *Ghost Whisperer* premiered, then gave that fan base bridge experiences in between broadcasts of the TV series, creating an 'infinity loop', driving eyeballs from the Internet to the TV show and back again. Instead of trying to catch lightning in a bottle, we found ourselves generating it, then harnessing it to build a multi-dimensional experience and we realized there's enough here to fill a book. The convergence of this explains the timing of why we're writing the *Ghost Whisperer Spirit Guide* now. (As you read this book, we encourage you to engage with *Ghost Whisperer* by clicking on the Internet links that we've provided in every chapter.)

On a continuing basis, we give you the tools to create your own *Ghost Whisperer* experience on a variety of platforms and this helps us build a stronger creative and financial model for the show. From the beginning, our Left Brains realized that as the entertainment choices multiplied, we needed to build out your favorite on-line assets into new mediums, which created new sources of revenue to support the TV series. Doing so opened the door to allow our Right Brains to come up with out-of-the-box ideas and creative choices to attract buyers, advertisers, and viewer participants. These initiatives needed to be innovative, exciting and connected to the heart and soul of *Ghost Whisperer* so that we could compete on the ever-evolving twenty-first century playing field of digital media. The TV series, Internet initiatives, comic books and novels, music, unique Same As It Never Was merchandise, etc., are all components of engagement television, making for a richer, deeper entertainment experience for you. Some say engagement television may be the future. We say that future is now. Like the spirit world, for those who believe no proof is necessary, for those who don't, no proof is enough.

We invite you to step into the multi-dimensional

world of *Ghost Whisperer* by typing the following special code into your computer. This will link you to a special site where you can experience the *Ghost Whisperer* operation the way we do every day, test your ghost whisperer skills, and most important, share your thoughts and ghost-related experiences with us and other fans who are reading the *Spirit Guide* at exactly the same time as you.

Unlock the *Ghost Whisperer Spirit Guide* Online
www.GWSpiritGuide.com
secret code: ɓoɹpou ɯǝʃʃupɐ

'Why is the password upside down?' you ask. Flipping this book upside down is a salute to the spirit world as well as a secret signal to like-minded people. Should you find yourself walking through an airport, for instance, and you see someone flip their book upside down, know that you've got something in common with the person who's reading this book. You may choose to stop and exchange a few words about the spirit world or just nod knowingly and continue on your way. More than likely, you'll encounter each other on the special website of the *Ghost Whisperer Spirit Guide*. When you get there, we hope you'll create a little lightning in a bottle.

N THE BEGINNING

Sunday, June 1, 2008, 6:15 A.M.: We're awakened with a start by a ringing phone. Groggy from sleep, Ian puts the receiver to his ear and hears Jennifer Love Hewitt's voice piping through the line. Not a bad way to be woken up. Except she sounds alarmed. Love says she heard some "explosions" and the sky is filled with thick black smoke. She urges, "Turn on the news. You won't believe it!" When Kim punches the remote, we're greeted by news chopper video of the Universal Studios backlot (the world's largest movie production space) engulfed in vicious flames. Stunned, we blink. And look closer. *Ghost Whisperer* is burning. *WHOA!*

All of *Ghost Whisperer*'s permanent exterior sets were located on the Universal Studios backlot. The day before the fire, we were putting the finishing touches on Grandview's Town Square,

Below:
Ian Sander surveys
the aftermath of
the fire at Universal
Studios.

in preparation for the start of season four. Over the previous three years, we had put a lot of thought, time and money into modifying the world of *Ghost Whisperer*, including Town Square (which formerly was the town square in the *Back to the Future* feature films. Remember the Clock Tower?).

Back on TV, the news reports are unable to confirm what sets are burning but it does appear that a huge portion of the lot is engulfed in flames. We jump in our car and race over to pick up Love before heading to the backlot to find out, firsthand, how bad the damage is.

At the studio security gate, we're admitted but cautioned not to go too far because the fire is still not under control. As the fire rages, Love hands out bottles of water to rescue workers and we check on the status of the *Ghost Whisperer* sets. Our hearts sink when an exhausted fireman, face streaked with soot, shakes his head sadly and says, "It's absolute devastation. Everything's gone."

As the fire rages, the three of us stand inside the studio gates, tears rolling down our cheeks. Together we remember our *Ghost Whisperer* journey…

It was the summer of 2004 and Sander/Moses Productions had the good fortune to have a deal at Touchstone Television Studios to develop drama series. We were working with John Gray, a wonderfully talented writer/director of feature films and television movies, on a pilot concept with supernatural elements. We had been friends with John Gray for over fifteen years, ever since producing his first network television movie, *When He's Not a Stranger*.

11

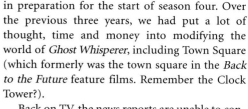

John had recently written and directed a successful movie for CBS, *Helter Skelter*. The network executive overseeing the movie told John that if he was interested in exploring a concept for a drama series about a 'ghost buster', she would introduce him to a medium and a paranormal investigator.

CBS had recently produced a successful miniseries based on the work and life of world-renowned medium James Van Praagh, and was interested in continuing to build its relationship with the psychic world. The miniseries was titled *Talking to the Dead*. James brought Mary Ann Winkowski into the fold at CBS. Mary Ann's specialty is dealing with earthbound spirits who have not yet crossed over into the Light. The slang term for her unique skill as a paranormal investigator is 'ghost buster'.

Having never done a drama series, John responded to CBS by asking if he could consult with Sander/Moses about the project (we had produced numerous series for CBS and the team there). They said they'd be thrilled if we were all interested in developing the project together.

The first thing we did when we were told of the 'ghost buster' idea was Google "talk to the dead". It turned up 60 million hits. We thought, *Now, that's a concept you can hang a series on!* (Today, if you Google those four words, you'll get 135 million hits.) Next, we met with James Van Praagh and then spoke with Cleveland-based Mary Ann Winkowski on the phone. We all agreed to move forward.

In developing the concept with John, we had additional sessions with James, more phone talks with Mary Ann, and plowed through heaps of

Above:
The iconic memorial in Grandview Town Square.

fascinating research which resulted in fashioning a story with characters that have 'legs' (TV talk for 'the ability to sustain five years or more of story-telling', which is what a series must do).

This one-hour drama series focuses on newly-wed Melinda Gordon, who has a remarkable gift for seeing spirits that are still earthbound. Before crossing them over into the Light, Melinda helps these ghosts with their unfinished business and gives closure to those they've left behind.

John wrote a pitch. Together we presented it to Mark Pedowitz, President of ABC Studios, and his amazing development team at Touchstone Television. They agreed it was wonderful and we all headed off to CBS to pitch the show. Our studio executives, John Gray, James Van Praagh and Sander/Moses were sitting in Nina Tassler's office — then Vice President of CBS Entertainment (now President) — running through the elements of the show when we put Mary Ann Winkowski on the speakerphone. Mary Ann proceeded to rid Nina's office of three earthbound spirits. It was quite amazing. The show sold in the room.

Over the next few months, we developed and John wrote the *Ghost Whisperer* pilot script. In January 2005, CBS ordered the pilot, 'cast contingent', meaning they would make it if we were able to cast the character of Melinda Gordon with an actress that excited everyone.

The Sander/Moses Productions development offices are at Disney Studios. Disney owns Touchstone Television (now ABC Studios). Jennifer Love Hewitt had recently made a pilot at Touchstone and has a development deal of her own there. Our offices just happened to be next door to each other in Walt Disney's fabulous old Animation Building.

We believe the stars were aligned for *Ghost Whisperer*, because after lining up John Gray, Sander/Moses, James Van Praagh, Mary Ann Winkowski, Touchstone Television and CBS (whew!), we were able to land Love.

Here's how the 'Love connection' worked. Over the previous six months we had gotten to know our development neighbor, Jennifer Love Hewitt, and had been talking about developing a project together. But when our pilot got ordered she was still awaiting word as to the fate of a pilot she had just completed. Love was not available for *Ghost Whisperer*. Yet!

Meanwhile, we were in the early stages of prepping the pilot. It's what's known as a 'rolling yellow light'. Even though we hadn't officially been given the go-ahead to start shooting — because we didn't have a star onboard our train — we were putting our crew together and creating 'the board'. The board is a wall in our office that we plaster with images and screen captures pulled from various sources (magazines, art books, DVDs). These images represent the look and tone that we're going for on character, wardrobe, set dressing, locations, lighting and every other aspect of the project that we're working on. As we go forward, everyone involved in the production (director, production designer, director of photography, even the production assistants) add to the board. Each day, we look at the collage of images to make sure that we haven't strayed from the vision of the show.

At this point, the search for 'Melinda' was in full throttle. We were scouring talent agencies on both coasts and in other countries. We couldn't seem to find the right actress for the role. Ironically, she was sitting in the office next door, but she wasn't available. When Jennifer Love Hewitt's pilot was not picked up, we were immediately at her doorstep asking her to read *Ghost Whisperer*. She did, and fell in love with it. We informed CBS we wanted Love for the lead. Leslie Moonves, the President and CEO of CBS Corporation and a good friend of ours, wanted to meet with Love before he would consider casting her in our show. It was quickly arranged. We had no doubt how this was going to turn out — and we couldn't imagine doing the show without her! In the meeting, they were charmed by each other and Les offered her *Ghost Whisperer*. Finally, we had our gorgeous, empathetic, accessible Melinda. And Love joined us in the trenches as a producer as well. *Ghost Whisperer* was now an official 'go'. *Yes!*

We turned our attention to 'Andrea'. Aisha Tyler had a deal with CBS to develop a comedy pilot that she was to star in. Lucky for us, they hadn't come across the right material yet, so we asked about her for the role of Andrea. After meeting with Aisha and screening tape of her dramatic acting on *CSI* and *Nip/Tuck*, everyone was sold on the idea.

The character of Jim was a bit trickier to cast. We

Above:
Jennifer Love Hewitt fell in love with the *Ghost Whisperer* pilot script.

read dozens of actors and screen tested a half dozen guys. None quite worked. David Conrad had, in fact, read for us early on but was never available to read for the studio and network during the testing process. It literally came down to the wire. We started shooting the pilot without a Jim — a gutsy move on all our part. Three days in — the day before the character was scheduled to begin work — David became available. We cast him as Jim Clancy, Melinda's dreamy husband. Fortunately, the tuxedo he had to wear the next morning for the wedding scene fit like a glove. We were in business.

John Gray directed the pilot wonderfully and it came out great (if we do say so ourselves). Before we showed the *Ghost Whisperer* pilot to the studio and network, we sat back and realized that the CBS

interact with online assets that we've created. This is *your* personal guide to a multi-dimensional experience in the *Ghost Whisperer* world. (Intersecting television with the Internet is a twenty-first century approach to TV series producing, and we're very passionate about it.)

There's a great true story floating around *Ghost Whisperer*. The ghost story in our pilot is about a young Vietnam soldier (played by the amazing Wentworth Miller of *Prison Break*) who was killed in a chopper crash. With Melinda's help, this lost soul connects with his son and together they find peace before the spirit crosses into the Light. It's very powerful, very emotional. When CBS screened the pilot for the network executives, to determine if *Ghost Whisperer* would get ordered to series, the electricity cut out in the middle of the final scene of the father-son reunion. Suddenly, the lights flickered on, revealing everyone (including the men) had been crying during the screening. Nothing like that had ever happened before or since. If the spirit world had anything to do with this, we thank them from the bottom of our hearts.

CBS saw the pilot, tested the pilot, loved the pilot and ordered it to series! It was the 'green light' we had been waiting for. We could now move forward to create the world of *Ghost Whisperer*. For the pilot, we had shot on location all around Los Angeles, Pasadena, Altadena, and the town square in Orange, California. But jumping from location

schedule was primarily made up of police procedurals. In fact, most of television at the time consisted of cop, lawyer, and medical shows. *Ghost Whisperer* did not fit in. We knew we needed to give our executives at the network and the studio a lens through which they could view the pilot.

We invited all the executives to our home for dinner and a session with James Van Praagh. The mission for James was to connect these executives to their relatives and friends who had passed away. *But will it work*, we wondered. *If it doesn't, there's plenty to lose.* We rolled the dice and issued the invites. And although the executives entered our home with healthy skepticism (and in some cases cynicism), they left intrigued, satisfied, and emotionally moved. Some (including us!) were in tears. It was great.

Leaving no stone unturned, we put together an outlook book featuring episode ideas, prospective writers and directors, statistics on how well movies like *Ghost, The Sixth Sense, The Amityville Horror,* etc. had done at the box office. We also hatched an Internet strategy for the *Ghost Whisperer* series, to brand the show and make it a multi-dimensional experience for you, the viewer. As you make your way through this book, you'll see how it works. Use it as a road map to go to the designated links to

to location when shooting a series isn't practical — it's too expensive and too time-consuming. For the series, we landed the Universal Studios backlot as our home base and built exteriors and interiors of the permanent sets we needed to tell the stories.

Going to work every day on the Universal lot is a dream come true for us. Each morning as we're waved through the front gate by our man George in the security booth, our adrenaline kicks in. We navigate the winding James Stewart Avenue to our sets, weaving around members from other TV shows and feature films as they push racks crammed with gorgeous costumes, carry key lights and camera equipment, and herd elephants and camels. You never know what's going to greet you on any given day when you enter the studio gates. What you do know is no two days will be the same. It's truly magical...

So here we are, back where our story started, June 1, 2008 — inside the Universal backlot gates. But now, there are no crew members or exotic animals or equipment. There's only charred, twisted metal and burned out skeletons of trucks and cars, black smoke and rubble everywhere. The fire is so hot that the pavement pulverizes when we step down on it. As we look across the remains of what was Grandview's beautiful Town Square, the iconic soldier memorial located in the center, although scorched, stands proud, silhouetted against the flames.

We look at each other mournfully, and comment on how lucky it was that no one was seriously injured and that our interior sets had not been affected, nor had the historic house Jim and Melinda live in (formerly Atticus Finch's house in *To Kill a Mockingbird*). We also ponder the irony of the episode we were prepping to shoot on the burning sets just one day before the fire broke out. The title: 'Firestarter' — about a ghost that starts fires... As always, truth is stranger than fiction.

We also talk about how *Ghost Whisperer* is a dream come true for us. Every day we work on film that tells a universal tale — people having one last chance to reconnect with a loved one who's died. We have the most gifted cast, amazingly talented writers, the best damn crew in the business, and great partners at the network and studio.

In show business, the saying goes, "Making a feature film or a TV movie is like running a marathon, and making a TV drama series is running 'til you're dead." Perfect for *Ghost Whisperer*, don't you think? We vow to take the fire in stride, to look ahead to rebuilding and improving, to reach out further to our fans online and all other digital platforms, as well as with print media from graphic novels to novelizations and original novels, and, most importantly, we vow to celebrate the spirit world as we keep moving forward to make the future of *Ghost Whisperer* better than ever. ◎
www.fansofgw.com
ghostwhisperer.tumblr.com

MELINDA'S
SPIRIT GUIDE

HOW TO BE A MEDIUM

id you know that each of us is born with the ability to see spirits? Then as we start to grow older and embrace convention, our capacity to communicate with the other side diminishes. Mediums are different — they retain and hone those abilities so that they can continue to communicate with the spirit world. Melinda Gordon's Grandma helped her develop her abilities from when she was a small child. Likewise, paranormal investigator Mary Ann Winkowski's grandmother worked with her on her abilities as a child, helping her to perfect the skill of mentally conjuring up the Light so she could cross spirits over.

According to Dr Joseph Kim, PhD, "Humans are limited by their five senses and they only look at things they are curious of. Therefore, their perspective of the world is limited." Kim encourages us to think about the world from other perspectives. "An eagle has vision so superior, it can spot a bug two miles from where it is perched. A fly has extreme peripheral vision. Because of their super powers, the frame of reference these creatures have of the world is very different from each other and from us." Likewise, mediums have a unique range of reference, due to their psychic abilities.

According to medium James Van Praagh, author of *Ghosts Among Us: Uncovering the Truth About the Other Side*, "Not every psychic is a medium. But every medium is psychic." As a medium, you must first have a strong foundation of intuition. James assures us everyone has intuition, but to varying degrees. A medium's intuition is extremely heightened. James says, "Every psychic has the ability, but not everyone can raise the vibration that a medium can." The more you pay attention to the energy and develop it, the stronger your abilities will become.

Mediumship involves the cooperation between two individuals: a person in the world of the living and a spirit from the other side. When a connection between these two entities is established, two types of phenomena can occur: communication, and the manipulation of energies and energy systems. Mediums act as human instruments for: discarnate spirits (those still roaming the physical world); spirit personalities, for the purpose of presenting information; causing paranormal activities; channeling specific energies or manifesting themselves, for objective examination or identification.

Mental mediumship and physical mediumship are the two types of communication that mediums use when interacting with the spirit world. Mental mediumship involves relating information through communication, through transference or mental telepathy. Mental mediumship takes place in the consciousness of the medium.

In mental mediumship, the medium is hearing, seeing and feeling the spirit's communication. It's the medium's job to relate that information, with as little bias or personal influence as possible, to the recipient of the message (known as the 'sitter'). According to James, mental mediums are most common.

Physical mediumship, on the other hand, involves the manipulation and transformation of physical systems and energy. Physical mediums cause something to happen within the dimension in which we exist. What actually happens varies with the style of mediumship involved, but the results can be seen and heard by those who don't necessarily have the ability to communicate with spirits. A type of physical medium is healers.

James Van Praagh says that through his mental mediumistic abilities, he receives messages from spirits and feelings about their presence that provide "detailed evidential proof that a loved one survived death."

www.fansofgw.com/quiz/

AN INTERVIEW WITH
JAMES VAN PRAAGH

What type of medium are you?

I'm 'clairvoyant', that's a French word meaning 'clear sight'; I can see spirits, images or scenes that spirits project in my head. I'm also 'clairsentient', another French word, meaning 'clear sensing'; I sense spirits' personalities and emotional levels. And, I'm 'clairaudient' — 'clear hearing'; I'm able to hear the thoughts of spirits.

Clairsentient — does that mean you can experience the five senses of a ghost?

For me it's a total sensory experience. So, yes. A ghost will project an image into my head, but along with that image may come emotion (of a lost son or daughter, say). In my case, talking to the dead is a multi-sensory experience

And physical motion related to a ghost, do you feel that?

In regards to the 'death condition', absolutely. One of the first things I'll pick up when communicating with a spirit, is his or her last memory — we call that the 'death memory'. The first thing I pick up is how the ghost died. If shot in the head, I feel sharp pain in my head. If he hung himself, I'll feel that. I'm a 'survival evidence medium' — my job is to bring through evidential details to prove that life goes on, that the consciousness survives. For example, at one of my recent book signings, a lady unknowingly had her mother's spirit sitting behind her. The mother asked me to tell her daughter she's with her all the time. She said she was with her daughter the previous week "when she put the butterfly tattoo on her left shoulder with my name underneath." I couldn't possibly have known about that because the lady at the book signing was wearing a long-sleeve shirt. The specific details about the tattoo experience were

GHOST
WHISPERER

brought through to me by the spirit.

So how does it work?

To communicate with spirits who have gone into the Light, I raise my vibration — energy level — through meditation to a higher level. And the spirits in the Light slow down their vibration and intersect with the third dimension so we can communicate. I'm a medium between the two worlds.

While Mary Ann Winkowski's vibration is very much of this Earth (she sees an earthbound spirit standing in the room), mine are very fast. I've learned to raise my energy level higher, so I can get glimpses of spirits. It's like standing next to a freeway with cars passing by at 50 mph and someone yells out the back window. I have to figure out what they're saying. Their emotion comes in slower, which is nice.

And ghosts look like what?

I see them solid, like I see you. I can tell visually that they're spirits because they have a light around them.

Ever meet a spirit you didn't like?

When you go into the Light, there's a complete opening of consciousness. Think of it like ice cubes in a tray. Each is separate and singular, like humans when we're on Earth. Turn up the heat, and the ice cubes melt. You're no longer able to differentiate one from the other. In the Light, there's a oneness, a full complete spiritual being. A soul awareness. These spirits are enlightened — they know there's more to

Above:

Melinda watches Dr Martin Schaer go into the Light in 'Cat's Claw'.

Previous Page:

James Van Praagh with Jennifer Love Hewitt on set.

life than what was on Earth. So, what's not to like?

Ever been frightened by a ghost?

Never. I'm more afraid of the living than I am of the dead — at least with the dead I know what I'm getting. I'll tell you something interesting, though. Dark spirits are around. They're very prevalent in prisons and seedy areas where there's lots of negative energy. Lower vibratory spirits — these are the ones that are earthbound — hang out at bars and clubs. They were most likely alcoholics and drug addicts when they were in the world of the living. They miss the sensation so they hit those areas to pick up the vibe.

What's your mission as a medium?

I think of it as service to humankind. I'm able to provide information to open people's hearts and minds to a new level of awareness. It's the reason I do *Ghost Whisperer* — to open people up to their spiritual selves. My job is to change people's perception that they are a *spirit* having a *physical experience*, not the other way around. I want people to understand that they should measure the world from a spiritual point of view, not a physical point of view. You have to be aware and mindful that you're a spirit with physical experiences. I think that is the show.

How old were you when you realized you had the gift?

I used to see lots of spirits when I was little. At school, I was an outcast because I saw things others couldn't. Once I was with some children at a local cemetery, and I saw two other children running around a headstone — they were maybe three or four years old. The kids I was with thought I was crazy. But when we went over to check out the headstone, everyone saw the names and dates engraved on it. It was a marker for two children, three years old, who died young, twins.

Does anyone else in your family have the gift?
My older sister Lynn has mediumship, but it takes the form of spirit photography. She'll take a picture of someone and there will be a spirit next to the person — not an orb, but a very clear image of the spirit. My grandmother on my father's side read tea leaves and my grandfather on my mother's side was psychic. They didn't call it that back then, but he just knew things. He'd tell my grandmother to set an extra place at the table because there would be unexpected company. Even though she was doubtful, she'd do it, and sure enough, the knock would come at the door.

Is your day jam-packed with spirit encounters?
It's very much like a radio: turn it on, tune to the frequency, turn it off. I open up to communicating with spirits when I'm ready. When I'm finished, I turn them all off by taking away the awareness and the power. Sometimes they do reach me when I'm not paying attention. If they're extremely pushy, they'll come through. Once, I was working out with a trainer and this spirit came through, asking me to give the trainer a message about oatmeal. I was not happy. I told her I paid for the session so this was my time not hers.

What's one of your most powerful experiences?
I did a reading for a couple who had lost their son in a suicide. He came through and insisted that it wasn't a suicide. He claimed he was killed by his best friend over a drug deal gone wrong. The parents went back to the police, the case was reopened. The truth was discovered and the perpetrator was prosecuted. He's in prison. This gave the mother, the father and the son peace.

Give us your take on death.
There is no death. There's only life. For over twenty-five years I've been doing this work and I've come to realize that life comes in all different forms — energy does not die, it simply changes form. All death is, is leaving the shell of the body, the encasement. It's a car your spirit drives. When the car wears out and stops working, you leave that car and eventually get a new one.

Tell us something we don't know about spirits.
When you go to sleep at night, your spirit leaves your physical body and you travel to the astral world, the fourth dimension, where you see your loved ones, spirit guides and friends who have passed. This happens when you have an out of body experience as well.

Speaking of OBE, explain the 'silver cord' (that Melinda encountered in 'Dead Man's Ridge').
The 'silver cord' connects the soul to the physical body. At the time of death, that tether is severed and you're open to this new consciousness.

When someone is in a coma, as was the case in 'Dead Man's Ridge', the spirit is very aware. It hears everything. Many times the spirit will leave the body and be right there hanging out nearby. When my father was dying, he slipped into a coma. While everyone was in the room, he whispered to me that it was time to go. He said, "I'll go, but I just don't want you kids fighting over the house." I told him it was his time to go and that we wouldn't fight. He died within five minutes. Later that day, he came back and told me that I got it right. My father had always been skeptical of what I did. He wasn't sure if it was real or not, so when he said that to me, it was a pretty amazing thing.

Are the *Ghost Whisperer* sets haunted?
Definitely. Most studio lots are because of all the energy created by the activity and drama. Mary Ann Winkowski and I have worked the *Ghost Whisperer* sets together. She makes sure that the ghosts don't disrupt production and I help cast and crew connect with their loved ones. It's a great partnership.

What's your favorite part of being a medium?
Helping people realize that there's more to life after death.

Anything you want to share about the 'afterlife'?
You create your heaven and hell based on how you live your life. The good that you make is what you take with you. ✆

www.jamesspiritworld.blogspot.com/
www.vanpraagh.com/

IS YOUR HOUSE HAUNTED?

ouse hauntings are only done by earth-bound spirits (as opposed to spirits that have already crossed into the Light). When a person dies suddenly as the result of natural causes or an act of violence, they are usually in a confused state, like the soldier in *Ghost Whisperer*'s pilot episode. Many times, spirits are not aware that they are dead, which is why they attach themselves to a familiar location — often it's a house. Other times, spirits are so attached to a particular place emotionally, they stay on even after death. Either the house they're haunting happens to be their own or it's one that strikes a specific cord in regards to unfinished business.

At home, you might all of a sudden smell your deceased loved one's favorite perfume or the cigar he smoked. Or someone might say something that only your loved one used to say. Cold chills is another way you can tell you're not alone in the house. Having thoughts that aren't yours can be a sign as well. And if there's a lot of fighting at home or your kids are constantly getting colds, then chances are you've got a ghost or two affecting the energy.

Spirits don't use electricity, but if they're close to a source (like a computer, TV or fuse box), they'll disrupt it. And they're masters at ringing doorbells. Also, they move things. It's because spirits like to cause problems. If what they're doing aggravates you or causes you stress, look at the amount of energy you're putting out that they can feed on.

According to medium James Van Praagh, "Sometimes spirits transfix their images onto other people's faces. You look at them and think, *she looks like my daughter, my father*, etc. Then it's gone."

The early signs of a haunting can vary. It depends on what type of haunting you're having. If the spirit seeks to get the attention of the living occupants at or in the location, that's known as the 'annoyance factor'. This is when spirits do things that are a nuisance, similar to a child seeking attention. In these situations, the spirits may be looking for assistance to pass over or to accomplish certain tasks. It's also been documented that the spirit can simply be seeking company from the residents, or even from the investigators themselves.

The following are signs of a haunting. The frequency of these events normally escalates as the haunting progresses:

Things That Go Bump: Knocking, banging, rapping, scratching, creaky footsteps, doors opening and shutting when no one's around. Except for the scratching (which may very well be rodents), the others are pretty good indicators that there's more there than meets the eye.

Hide, You Seek: Ghosts like to frustrate you by shifting stuff around (like your car keys). *Ghost Whisperer* creator John Gray said his daughter, Caitlin, once left a puzzle on the kitchen table. He looked away for a second, and when he turned back, the puzzle pieces were rearranged. A bit unnerved, John reassured himself that it was his imagination. A couple of months later, while Mary Ann Winkowski was ridding John's house of wayward spirits, she discovered the culprit responsible for the puzzle prank, as well as lots of middle-of-the-night doorbell ringing — a ghostly mischief maker who used to live next door. Mary Ann sent the naughty spirit into the Light.

Touchy Feel Icky: If something brushes past you, touches your hair or puts a hand on your shoulder, but when you look over, there's nothing there, it's likely to be a spirit trying to connect. Ghost buster Mary Ann Winkowski shared with us how she once was in a movie theater and people walking along the aisle were stumbling slightly as their popcorn flew into the air. While everyone (her husband included)

thought a crease in the rug was causing these people to lose their footing and their popcorn, Mary Ann knew better. She could see a prankster ghost tapping the bottoms of people's popcorn boxes as they walked by.

Shadow People: If you see shadow movement or silhouettes independent of living, breathing humans, beware! A good visual reference for shadow people is the scene in 'Love Still Won't Die' in which Melinda steps out of the shower only to realize she's being watched by ghostly shadow people…

Psychokinetic Phenomena: If your best china slides across the table unassisted or pictures fly off the wall or furniture shimmies across the floor, you've got visitors from the spirit world. Check out 'Ghost Bride' for a bead on how this works.

Spirit Orbs: If when you take photographs inside your house there are ghostly shapes or glowing spheres in the photos, you've got company.

Name Calling: When alone, do you hear someone calling your name? If you do and your Beatles CD is

Above:
Cold chills taken to extremes in 'Dead Man's Ridge'.

not playing backwards, the name calling is a pretty good indication that your house is being haunted.

Night-Vision: If you're waking up in a cold sweat night after night because you're having freaky nightmares, you may be experiencing nocturnal visits from the other side.

Animal House: If your pet behaves strangely, barking or meowing at something unseen, or if it cowers without apparent reason, or refuses to enter a room it normally hangs out in, you've got a problem. Or if your pet is walking around something that isn't there, most likely it's a ghost. Animals have sharper senses than humans and their psychic abilities may be more finely tuned. Bob the dog's behavior in 'Children of Ghosts' is a good example.

Child Talk: If you have a small child in the house who seems to be talking to someone but there's no one there, they may have a new playmate — not of this world.

Hide 'N' Seek: If you have the strange sensation that you're being watched but the curtains are drawn

and your partner's not home with you, it's possible you're under the prying eyes of a nosy earthbound spirit. Ghosts are usually glimpsed in mirrors — as with Bloody Mary in 'Don't Try This At Home' — on staircases, peering into or out of windows, perched on chairs, and in hallways. 'The Collector', 'Bad Blood', and the pilot all feature such occurences.

If you're experiencing one or more of these events on a regular basis, you should first check, then re-check for logical explanations. If you find no plausible explanation, don't panic. Activity of this nature is generally non-threatening. Many times spirits are there to warn you or to let you know they still love you or that they miss you. Generally, they're trying to influence you in a positive way. However, since the ghost is most likely feeding off the energy of you and your household, you may want to act.

We don't recommend garlic, holy water, or the so-called 'shoe remedy' (an old wives' tale which says placing your shoes at the foot of the bed, one pointing one way and one pointing the other, confuses ghosts so they hit the road — *not!*) If you truly believe your house is haunted, do NOT engage with the spirits — you'll only make them stronger. Get yourself some quince seeds and call

Above:
A ghost watches Melinda in 'Last Execution'.

an expert. A good place to start are Mary Ann Winkowski's and James Van Praagh's websites.

Once you've found a paranormal investigator you're comfortable with, ask him or her how long they've been doing this and about their past investigations, particularly those involving private homes. Find out if the investigator is affiliated with national organizations. Being affiliated with a group that has a good reputation can help you make a wise decision about allowing the ghost buster into your home. You might also call the organization for additional information.

One final thing that may prove valuable (and interesting) in determining what's going on in your house is that a home's history can often explain a haunting. You could be amazed at what you discover. The most efficient way to research the history of your haunted house is to go to your local municipal building and speak to the Registrar of Deeds. If they can't help, they'll refer you to the right person. In the end, even if your digging does not reveal anything related to the haunting, doing research still has psychological benefits because you'll have a sense of being proactive.

Good luck! 🖐

RECOGNIZING GHOSTS

he term 'ghost' describes a phenomena that usually consists of a form of energy that can generate dim light and affect photographic sensors, cause temperature drops, produce electromagnetic effects, and is typically the 'spirit' or 'soul' of a dead person or animal. Simple, right? Not quite…

Just as every fingerprint is different, so too is every ghost. Ghosts have differentiating visual characteristics. A ghost can appear 'diffused', looking like a bright spot with no discernable edges. Or it can have a 'hard' look, with well-defined features and sharp edges. A 'soft' look is one that's visually undefined and fuzzy. And, sometimes, ghosts appear random and cloud-like, with no discernable shape whatsoever.

Mary Ann Winkowski, author of *The Truth About Ghosts*, says, "Ghosts do not always announce their presence with scents or sounds. And, I can't say that I have ever identified the presence of an earthbound spirit by detecting slime or any other kind of sticky, oozing substance." To her, ghosts look human, except they don't appear solid.

Ghosts can, however, take on different forms:

Orbs: The most common form of ghost phenomena. An orb is a spherical form that usually shows up in photographs. Orbs are translucent and usually range in size from about an inch to the size of a basketball (similar to the ones Melinda and Professor Payne see in 'The Collector'). Orbs are believed to be the natural form of ghosts. When photographed in motion, orbs exhibit trails, almost like comets. Sometimes, overlapping orbs create a strobe-like effect, and the number of spirits present can be determined by counting the overlapping images contained within the frame of the photo. Swarms of small orbs are sometimes referred to as 'sparklies' and can be indicators of large amounts of 'ghost energy' present when the photo is taken.

Humanoids: Ghosts that look like humans. They may appear soft- or hard-edged. They usually wear the clothes they were wearing when they died. In *Ghost Whisperer*, you never see a spirit dressed in anything other than what it died in — even if it died in the nude, as in 'Delia's First Ghost'! You will, however, see the ghost's clothes in various stages of disintegration. If, for instance, the ghost died in a fire, as he did in 'A Grave Matter', the first time you see him,

his clothes are burned and tattered. But as Melinda helps the ghost find resolution, his clothes become more pristine, which symbolizes the healing that enables the ghost to go into the Light.

Demonoids: Ghosts with a head, two legs and arms, but they absolutely do not look human. Usually these ghosts are projecting some image other than themselves. Two *Ghost Whisperer* examples are 'Horror Show', when the ghost frightens Melinda under the bed sheets, and issues #2-4 of the new graphic novel, where a ghost projects the image of Osiris.

Necroforms: The scary, scary ghosts usually portrayed in horror movies. They appear as rotting corpses, as in the *Ghost Whisperer: The Other Side 2* web series, or skeletons, like the ghost in 'Speed Demon'. This is a rare form of manifestation.

Dendrites: Branching forms. There may or may not be symmetry in their formation. And they sometimes have sparking energy, similar to that featured at the opening of 'Delia's First Ghost'.

Streaks: Thread-like forms that look like rapidly moving light streaks. Check out the camping

Above:
Wide Brim Hat Man makes a fleeting appearance in 'Friendly Neighborhood Ghost'.

Opposite:
A fiery ghost makes a dramatic appearance in 'The Night We Met'.

Previous Page:
The prophet ghost follows Melinda in 'Delia's First Ghost'.

scene in 'A Vicious Cycle', where Melinda does battle with what she thinks is a sheet but turns out to be ghost streaks.

According to Mary Ann, "Ghosts can't walk through you, and you can't walk through them. However, I never rule out the possibility of something that I've never experienced before." (Good, because it's something you see in *Ghost Whisperer* and we love the visual sensibility of it!)

Ghosts make their presence known in many ways, but they can only do as much as their energy will let them. A ghost with a relatively high amount of energy can create chaos, while a ghost with low energy can do very little and is usually focused on finding an energy source. Depending on the level of energy a ghost has, it can generate a slight sense of presence in humans or, at the opposite end of the spectrum, is capable of interaction with the world of the living. Check out the highly spirited ghost in 'Ghost Bride' who gives Melinda a real run for her money.

Mary Ann confirms, "It's not possible for ghosts to draw energy from other earthbound spirits. They need the emotional, metaphysical energy *generated by the living* to fuel their existence. So when you are experiencing lots of negative events at home, it may very well be an indication of a spirit presence, siphoning energy from your environment."

The manifestation of ghosts may be seen, it may be felt. The simplest is a feeling that a ghost might be present or that you're being watched. Out of your peripheral vision, you may see movement or hear voices or get a cold feeling that's not registering on a thermostat.

A more aggressive manifestation is the image ghosts leave on photographs. We say aggressive because ghosts are invisible, so for them to leave an imprint in the world of the living, it takes a whole lot of energy.

The next level of manifestation is audio — a phenomenon that is usually recorded and verified by experts (*see* Ghostly Sights & Sounds, p101).

"I've never encountered ghosts who have announced their presence by rattling chains and saying, 'Boo!'" Mary Ann chuckles. "I have, however, seen some earthbound spirits deliver a resounding

kick to a home's furnace, resulting in a serious *boom* that could scare you right out of bed!"

The most aggressive manifestation is the movement of objects, whether directly or those objects being discovered in new positions when no other person or thing could have moved them. Professor Rick Payne experiences this type of phenomena in his office during 'Cat's Claw'.

At the extreme level of manifestation are apparitions, which range from slightly transparent to truly solid. This is very rare, but it does happen. In some cases the ghost doesn't appear until the apparition vanishes. An example occurs in 'The Ghost Within', when ornaments that Melinda comes across at a flea market disappear and reappear in her antique shop.

Mary Ann implores us to keep in mind that ghosts do not have super powers like Superman or Spider-Man. "Ghosts are just regular folks — who happen to be dead. However, with enough energy, some spirits are able to move objects or create sensations of a physical presence to get your attention." ✌

www.youtube.com/watch?v=iAACVG_u3_Y

27

THE LIVING

THE LIVING

he world of the living is a three dimensional existence that takes place on Earth. As you know, this is where humans, plants and animals exist. If you break humans down into groups by gender, race, occupation, zip code, etc. you'll eventually get to the sub-sub-sub-groups, one of which is 'believer' and 'non-believer' relative to the spirit world.

Philosophers, theologians, and even scientists (string theory and parallel universes) will tell you that beyond the third dimension where we, the living, exist, there are fourth, fifth, sixth dimensions, and beyond. The behavior or actions of those dimensions can impact and affect the living.

As a member of the world of the living, if you're not sure which subgroup you belong to, believer or non-believer, take this quick quiz. If you already know where you stand, feel free to move on:

1. Are you afraid to die?
a) Who wants to stop living?
b) Not so much. I kinda know what's going to happen next.
c) Oh yeah. I don't want to leave my loved ones alone.

2. I feel like someone's watching me and I believe it's because…
a) I may have a peeping tom.
b) A loved one could be present from the other side.
c) I'm sooo paranoid.

3. There are these orb shaped lights in photos that I've taken at my home. I think…
a) I need a new camera

b) Ghosts are present and their energy has been captured on camera.
c) Somebody punked my pictures.

4. Have you ever seen a ghost?
a) Only through Melinda's POV on *Ghost Whisperer*.
b) No, but I'm not a medium or paranormal investigator, otherwise I probably would.
c) Yeah, and he looked like Bruce Willis.

5. Do ghosts actually exist?
a) Only in the dark corners of our imagination.
b) Paranormal phenomena are alive and well because the physical world isn't all there is.
c) Nope!

If you chose (b) as the answer to each question, then even though you're in the world of the living, you've got the right idea about what comes next in the world of the departed, and this makes you a believer. If you chose (a), (c) or (d) then you're a non-believer. And that's alright too.

Based on their behavior (and the above quiz, of course), we did an analysis of the *Ghost Whisperer* characters operating in the world of the living — who are believers and who are not. See if you agree…

Melinda Gordon is not only a believer in the spirit world (big time!), but she's also an enabler, as her mission in life is to use her gift to help wayward souls into the Light.

Melinda's husband, Jim Clancy, wondered all his life what happens to someone who dies. Once he became a paramedic, and began grappling with life and death on a daily basis, that question became even more prominent. Since hooking-up with his beloved "Mel", Jim finally understands how life, death and the fourth dimension really work. Jim's a believer, no doubt.

Professor Rick Payne is an academic trained in critical thinking, so for him, seeing is believing. Then he encountered an authentic ghost whisperer. Through his friendship with Melinda Gordon, Professor Payne has experienced more than he ever could have imagined in terms of the spirit world. So, Payne started as a non-believer, but now he's a confirmed believer.

With Melinda's mother, it's very much a gray area. Beth Gordon is a believer; she has to be because she has the same gift as her daughter. However, Beth is also a non-believer because she's immersed herself in denial about the spirit world. While in the world of the living, Beth will keep convincing herself that ghosts do not exist. That way, she doesn't have to deal with them when they come calling. Unfortunately for Beth, it's not that simple. For now, Beth straddles the line between believer and non-believer.

Melinda's evil brother Gabriel definitely has the gift. That automatically puts him into the believer category. The fact is, Gabriel's passions and beliefs in the spirit world are so strong that he spends much of his time and energy among the living trying to tip the scales in favor of the dead to empower the dark side.

Delia's adorable teenage son, Ned, typifies teenagers everywhere in that he's psyched about the spirit world. The bonus for Ned is he actually knows an amazing woman named Melinda Gordon who randomly connects with the dead right before his very eyes. It doesn't get more believable than that!

Finally, we have Ned's mom, Delia Banks. For two seasons, she's come down hard as a non-believer. Even though Delia loves her dear friend Melinda, she thinks Melinda's just "a little nuts". But that's only through season three. Wait until you see what happens in season four...

Everyone in the world of the living loves a great ghost story and our job here at *Ghost Whisperer* is to deliver that from week to week. You don't have to be a believer to enjoy the show, but it certainly doesn't hurt.

When *Ghost Whisperer* was launched in its first season, we didn't know how the living would embrace the departed coming into their homes week after week through their TVs to tell their stories. What we discovered is that the world was (and still is) in such a precarious state that people are looking for hope anywhere they can find it. Viewers tell us *Ghost Whisperer* provides hope that there's more to life than what's right in front of them in this crazy world of the living. 🕊

www.fansofgw.com/grid/thelivingandthedead/

MELINDA GORDON

"We're in the life business. Death is just a part of it."

y name is Melinda Gordon. I'm married, live in a small town, and I own an antique shop. I might be just like you, except from the time that I was a little girl I knew that I could talk to the dead. "Earthbound spirits" my grandmother called them — they're stuck here because they have unfinished business with the living, and they come to me for help.

What was required to launch Melinda Gordon's character in season one was for the audience to relate to her as a real, grounded person, and at the same time, accept the conceit that she has the otherworldly gift of communicating with the recently departed. And no one except **Jennifer Love Hewitt** could have struck that perfect balance for portraying her. Love is the quintessential beautiful, sexy twenty-first century girl next door, with a great deal of empathy. Women want to be her and men want to be with her.

"I was really lucky to be offered the part of Melinda Gordon. As soon as I read the [pilot] script I was hooked. I knew I had to play her," says Jennifer Love Hewitt of why she jumped at playing the ghost whisperer. "I was so inspired by her undying belief, strength, empathy, and unquestioning love for others that is given with no need for love in return. She is someone I look up to. We should all help people the way Melinda does. I believe she does it not because of her gift, but because it's who she is. I was given a true gift by being cast in this show and will be forever grateful."

All my key memories are marked by ghosts — I'm guessing that's different from how you grew up. But

Grandma always reassured me my abilities are what make me special. ('Special' is a much better word than 'different'. It took a long time for me to really appreciate that.)

When I was in elementary school, my classmate, Sarah Applewhite, passed away. But she didn't 'cross over'. When her spirit showed up at school and I told my teacher I could see her, no one believed me. They probably thought I was crazy. (I don't blame them. It's hard for some people to embrace the unconventional.) The principal called my mother to come get me. When mom picked me up, she said she didn't want me to admit to anyone else that I see ghosts. But then Grandma said it was just fine and I should embrace my gift. I always take Grandma's advice. I even got to help my little friend Sarah reconcile her unfinished business with her parents and go into the Light.

On the first day of shooting, the first scene of the day was up, and we were standing at the monitor with John Gray, who wrote and directed the pilot. Usually, as a producer, you try to schedule a few simple days at the top of a pilot so the actors have the opportunity to take it slow, work out the bugs, find their rhythm and get their confidence on the set. Unfortunately, circumstances dictated that we shoot Jim and Melinda's wedding reception early in the schedule. It was a giant set-piece with our entire cast plus guest actors, tons of extras, a band, dancing and all the trappings. Lots of pressure for the first actor to be lensed — who was Love. All the actors took their positions on their marks, John yelled "Action!" and Love started her lines. About two lines in, the three of

us turned and looked at each other with our mouths gaping — Jennifer Love Hewitt *was* Melinda Gordon. With any other actor playing that role, we're sure the three of us would have been doing our usual mental notes about how to make the film work — cut here, adjust there, do a pick-up right here, adjust the actor's motivation here… Not this time. Those first moments of film were extraordinary. We remember thinking as we stared at our lead actress on the monitor, "This is way more than any producer or director has a right to wish for."

"I just really wanted the audience to connect with Melinda," Love recalls. "For the ghost believers to have a hero and for the non-believers to wonder why they don't believe and maybe want to. I wanted a female driven drama to do well on television for women everywhere. For myself, I wanted the challenge of creating a full person every day, who could change and grow with the series. I wanted people to understand Melinda's need to be who she is and love her for it. I wanted to be able to touch our audience's hearts. I wanted to be able to do what I love every day, and also have it really matter and make a difference for people. I hope we have succeeded and thank the audience so much for watching."

Over the years I've crossed over lots of children. I find myself particularly attached to these experiences. Maybe it's because I really love children. In fact, Jim and I hope to have children some day. I believe we will. Anyway, I remember a little boy, Kenny Dale, who was hit by a train. At first Kenny didn't realize he was dead, so I had to convince him of that. (This happens a lot with ghosts — they don't understand that no one can see or hear them.) In addition to helping Kenny, I had to convince his mom that it wasn't her fault he died. That's always a tough one. But I did it and Kenny was

a great little partner in doing so. One thing I discovered while helping Kenny and his family, which I hadn't realized before, is young children often see ghosts. That's where I believe imaginary friends come from.

Another reason kid ghosts' memories are so powerful to me is because many times they teach me something about myself and my childhood. I once helped an angry young ghost and came to the realization that I was afraid of having children of my own in case they inherited my abilities. I remember how isolating it was growing up seeing ghosts, and I didn't want my children to go through the pain of being different…

When I helped the spirit of a little girl who had drowned, I was reminded of my own father who, when I was her age, would visit me. This was after my mom and dad split up. He would leave me gifts, which I was afraid to use because I knew it would upset my mom. Eventually, I came to terms with it.

We use lots of children in *Ghost Whisperer* because they bring so much heart to the show. And Love is always patient and sensitive when playing scenes with young actors. "I started acting when I was ten," Love explains. "I really have learned to do it along the way. I just try to give as much of myself and my heart as I can every day. I can't imagine doing anything else." And because of her experience growing up in this business and the way she has always conducted herself, Jennifer Love Hewitt is a great role model for young actors working on *Ghost Whisperer*.

Just like lots of people, my family history is complicated. After dad left home, I had no idea what happened to him. For the longest time, I thought he took off because of mom and me — because we talk to ghosts. I didn't realize until much later that mom never told him about her gift. When I look back now, I realize we've had issues partly because mom always resented how I used my gift. And she resented my relationship with Grandma. (Grandma passed when I was a teen, but she still connects with me in lots of ways. Maybe you've had a similar experience.) Anyway, as you can imagine, all this family history affects how I approach relationships with other people. It's the good news and the bad news of life, right?

In season one, Melinda's husband Jim surrounds her with security, love and understanding. He is the most important person in Melinda's life. Jim never doubts what she says and is always ready to step in and protect or help her. This support system enables

Above:
Melinda wears the locket Tom Gordon gave her.
Opposite:
Delia, Melinda and Jim in Iraq War episode 'Haunted Hero'.

Melinda to forge ahead with helping earthbound spirits and those they have left behind. "Melinda and Jim are a perfect fit," observes Love. "She is the hero for so many people every day, and when she gets home Jim is her hero. It isn't easy to be married to Melinda and all of her ghosts, but Jim is always there trying to understand. He really is her backbone."

Jim's greatest concern in watching his wife work through her spirit encounters is that because her compassion is bottomless and she is unwilling to give up on spirits, no matter how angry or obstinate, it often puts Melinda in danger.

I'm never going to deny that dealing with the dead takes its toll. It's extremely emotional, and at times, physically taxing. Sometimes a spirit will put me in

35

jeopardy. There's no way around all this since I feel a deep responsibility to ghosts — they need my help. Maybe if the world was filled with ghost whisperers, I might feel differently. But for many, I'm their only hope. I could never just turn them away or ignore them like my mom has. Grandma helped me understand that I was given this gift for a reason and I need to make the most of it every single day.

Melinda has encountered danger from the spirit world and the world of the living many times. In 'On the Wings of a Dove', Melinda comes face to face with the ghost of a criminal and refuses to back away when the murderous spirit threatens Jim's safety. In the end, Melinda helps the lost soul find peace. In 'Voices', the electronic voice phenomenon (EVP) of a deceased mother makes Melinda extremely ill. Feeding off the emotions of the spirit, she is overwhelmed with nausea and blinding headaches, but pushes through the near-debilitating physical ordeal to heal the emotional scars of a father and son.

However, for Love, "The scariest moment by far was the episode where a man was hung and took Melinda on that journey with him. I had to put on shackles, so I couldn't move my arms and legs, and then a dark hood, so I couldn't see." In the episode, 'The Last Execution', the increase in spirit interaction is highlighted when the earthbound soul of a hanged man jumps into the body of another person, causing the living being to experience the hanging. Then, suddenly, the spirit turns on Melinda. One can only imagine the dedication it took for our star to play those scenes, particularly since she's a bit claustrophobic.

But Love is nothing less than the consummate pro. Case in point — the tunnels under Grandview during the shooting of 'Weight of What Was'. Love dedicated herself to making sure we got every bit of film we needed before she surfaced from the dirty, cloistered set. "They built the set with a removable wall, because they are really nice people. So that helped a little," Love says. "It was hard though. The good thing was that Melinda had to be really scared. So no acting required! But after fifteen hours, I was ready to get some air."

What keeps Love going when the going gets tough on set day in, day out?

"I often see Melinda as a modern-day Joan of Arc. I also think she's a bit of an angel. She's my hero," she

Above:
Melinda helps Kenny Dale in 'The Crossing'.
Opposite:
Melinda is reunited with her first ghost.

replies. "Heroes are so brave — they deal with the good, the bad and the ugly, no questions asked. That's what Melinda does every week!"

Love's favorite aspect of her character is "Melinda's non-judgment of anyone and everyone she meets. To be honest, I worry for her sometimes; I worry that it will make her look weak, because she's always so willing to let the door slam in her face, or be called a freak. But then you get the sense that it's all okay, that although it affects her, it also rolls right off. Being able to combat anything and anyone with compassion is a true gift.

"Every moment with this cast, the crew, our writers and directors is amazing. They are my constant inspiration," Love continues about what motivates her. "I love them all so much. We laugh together, cry, get tired, emotional, all of it. I wouldn't do it and couldn't do it every week without them. They are what make this show special. What you see every week, that you love, is them; their hard work, their hearts."

Though having this gift can be isolating and a burden, losing it would be even worse. A while ago, I took a horrible fall and hit my head and was seriously injured. After having a near death experience I was visited by the spirit of my Grandma. She gave me the strength and will to not die. But when I came to, my gift seemed to vanish. I could no longer see spirits. I no longer felt special. Fortunately, the gift returned just in time for me to battle and defeat the forces of the dark side.

Midway through season one, Melinda realizes the spirits that are coming to her for help are getting stronger, becoming more interactive. She senses a shift in the spirit world and realizes that her communication with earthbound spirits is changing. That's the up side. The down side is revealed in 'Fury', when Melinda discovers dark spirits are keeping book on her. Their increased power makes them more dangerous. Melinda realizes spirits can now hurt people, maybe even kill them.

Melinda learns the implications of the spirit world's growing strength in 'Friendly Neighborhood Ghost', when a ghost injures her. And the ante is upped dramatically when a dark spirit, Wide Brim Hat Man, makes his presence known. He projects such powerful negative energy that as he haunts Same As It Never Was, even Melinda's best friend, Andrea Moreno, senses his presence.

We call him "Wide Brim" because when this dark spirit first started appearing to me, I could only make out his silhouette, and the shape of his hat was his most distinguishing detail. It took a while for me to figure out what he and his sidekick, Laughing Man, were up to. But with the help of Professor Rick Payne, my paranormal advisor and dear friend, we cracked it! Wide Brim's real name is Romano and he's what we call a "soul collector". He manipulates and lies to keep earthbound spirits from crossing into the Light so he can

draw from their energy to further his dark cause. Wide Brim even tried to claim the spirit of my BFF, Andrea.

During the whole Romano business, I was faced with crossing over more than 200 souls — something I'd never done before. But it worked! The energy during the cross over was so powerful that Jim was able to witness a sliver of it. It was extraordinary for all of us. And served as a major setback for Romano.

Love acknowledges that Melinda has been through a lot. "The first season Melinda was still learning her gift; how it affected her, her friendships, her marriage and her safety. She was learning how to be a wife and find the right balance in order for her marriage to grow. Also owning an antique store was a lot. She spent a lot of time hiding or apologizing for her gift and scared of who she was. Then the dark side really started to take over her life and that tested her strength. Although they didn't win, what they took from Melinda was unforgivable. I really believe in the plane crash of the season one finale, they not only killed Melinda's best friend, Andrea, but the dark side killed her innocence. They changed Melinda forever."

Season two kicks off with the unfinished busi-

Above:
Melinda is faced with the prospect that she has lost her gift, but her mother (Anne Archer) is not sure that's a bad thing, in 'The Vanishing'.

ness of dark spirit Romano and the need to release Andrea's soul so she can cross over into the Light. Together, Melinda and Professor Payne figure out a key spirit equation: Melinda is a light spirit, a protector of souls, and if a dark spirit like Romano can take the soul of a light spirit like her, then he becomes invincible. Melinda knows that Romano can't force Andrea to stay earthbound. This empowers her to help Andrea by reuniting her with her brother. Once the siblings' relationship is healed, Andrea goes into the Light — which puts the kibosh on Romano.

Melinda is grateful to Payne for his help in saving her best friend. "Professor Payne is the Robin to Melinda's Batman," says Love. "At first, it was a weird and beautiful relationship. The info he gave her about the supernatural was not only helpful, but exciting. Very quickly he became her best friend. They would do anything for each other. She would protect him with her life and I feel like he would do the same. They are truly kindred spirits."

Aside from the new relationship with Payne, Melinda also gets a new friend in Delia, who has a teenage son, Ned. "Delia is a great person in

Melinda's life," Love says, her eyes lighting up. "She is the solid ground under Melinda's feet. Though Delia doesn't believe in ghosts, she believes in Melinda. And though Melinda wants Delia to understand, she respects her disbelief. They make each other laugh and for Melinda to have such a good friend is so important. And Ned is like the little brother Melinda never had. His excitement about the ghost world is something Melinda experiences with no one else, other than Payne. But she is always respectful of Delia's feelings and parenting. She also has to make sure that Ned is safe."

Once, while visiting Andrea's grave — it's what I do when I miss her — something strange happened, a ghost appeared claiming he was buried in the wrong grave. (I say "strange" because spirits don't usually hang around cemeteries — there's so little human energy there.) Interacting with this lost ghost stirred up some painful emotions about how it felt to be abandoned by my dad. By solving the cemetery ghost's mystery, I was able to heal the relationship between him and his daughter. And seeing how this brought them peace made me decide to do the same for myself.

Although anxious about what she might discover, Melinda becomes determined to follow the leads about her father, Tom Gordon. But before she gets to the next level of her investigation, she receives an eerie warning from the spirit world: "Five signs and death will come." Later, the threats from the dark side hit too close to home when a haunted message appears scrawled across Jim's back, "srom itcelid", making Melinda fear her gift is putting the people she loves in danger.

Furthering this sense of impending doom, in 'The Curse of the Ninth', Melinda tries to cross a spirit over but fails when he chooses the dark side. Before vanishing, the spirit tells Melinda, "Think you're the only afterlife game in town? There are others around here, people who are dying to meet me." The manner in which the spirit is sucked under does not bode well. And Melinda encounters another dark omen when she tries to help a ghost named Randy in 'The Cradle Will Rock'. Randy refuses to cross over, saying he's made his deal, but he has another message for Melinda: "The dead will walk." Then Melinda meets another ghost whisperer, Gabriel...

I decided to take a chance on opening up to

CHARACTER TIMELINE

- Grandma teaches Melinda how to use her gift.
- Mom rejects Melinda's gift.
- Dad abandons Melinda as a young child.
- Mel's best friend and her boyfriend in college reject and betray her.
- Mel meets Jim during a building collapse.
- Melinda moves to Grandview and opens Same As It Never Was.
- Mel and Jim get married, move into a fixer-upper house.
- Andrea goes to work for Melinda at the shop.
- Andrea dies in a jetliner crash.
- Melinda crosses Andrea over.
- Melinda has a near death experience.
- Mel meets Delia and Ned Banks.
- Delia goes to work for Melinda at Same As It Never Was.
- Ned discovers Mel's gift.
- Melinda meets Professor Payne, and reveals her gift to him.
- Melinda reveals her gift to Delia.
- Melinda meets Gabriel, then discovers he's working with the dark side.
- Melinda encounters Tom Gordon.
- Mel discovers the town buried beneath Grandview.
- Melinda and Jim want to have a baby.
- Melinda realizes Tom Gordon is not her father, Paul Eastman is.
- Melinda learns Paul Eastman always loved her.
- Melinda reconciles with her mom.
- Melinda realizes there are only five shadows but six loved ones in her life — doom pending.

39

Gabriel, especially about the shift I was seeing in the power of the spirit world. It was exciting to meet someone my age who has the same abilities as me. And it made sense for us to compare notes. So I was horrified to discover Gabriel is a soul collector. Different from Romano, and possibly more dangerous, because unlike

Romano, Gabriel operates in the world of the living. Who knows how powerful Gabriel's effect on the spirit world will be.

In the season two finale, when a bolt of lightning causes a monument to fall on Melinda, her spirit leaves her body and encounters a man who tells her she has a brother. When she wakes up from her near death experience, Melinda tells Jim she spoke to her dead father, who told her she has a brother. And that brother is Gabriel.

According to Love, "As Melinda came back for season two, she was a little jaded and full of fear. I feel like season two was a ticking clock for Melinda. She was on a mission to protect those around her and show the dark side that light will always prevail. Then finding out she had a brother and getting closer to solving the mystery of her father, Melinda's world once again turned upside down. When the dark side was able to kill Melinda for a few minutes at the end of season two, she not only saw her father in the Light, but saw how truly vulnerable and at risk she is at any given moment."

Below:
Melinda with husband Jim, her "backbone".
Opposite:
Andrea, Melinda and Jim attend a wedding that almost didn't happen in 'Ghost Bride'.

The inaugural episode of season three, 'The Underneath', opens with Melinda in the hospital being treated for a concussion from the monument accident. And Gabriel is nowhere to be found. But when an image of a man appears on the x-ray of Melinda's head, she wonders if her father is trying to send her a message. Melinda soon dreams of her dad, who explains even though he had to go, he didn't want to and that she'll understand someday.

When Melinda confronts her mother about Gabriel, Beth assures her daughter that she never gave birth to another child, but observes, "Who knows what your father was up to."

Melinda continues to help lost spirits and the living — from a ghost who was stalked, to a lost soul from the Iraq war, a fake medium, and a ghost that's haunting Jim — while uncovering the truth about her family. In the process she also unearths (literally!) secrets about the history of Grandview, and finds that the two are inextricably linked — and both have strong ties to the spirit world.

Gabriel, meanwhile, continues to menace

Melinda out of jealousy and spite. In 'All Ghosts Lead to Grandview', Melinda confronts him with a choice — they can work together and free all the souls under Grandview or he can continue on his evil path. But Gabriel tells her he's picked another horse that's much faster than her and that she has a choice too. "Don't be so sure you have all the answers," he warns Melinda before he walks into darkness.

Eventually, Melinda uncovers the dark truth about Tom Gordon. He is not her father. Another man — a spirit, actually — who's been haunting Melinda's dreams, is her biological father, Paul Eastman. But there is lots more to the long sought after truth about Melinda's parentage.

Love believes, "When season three began, Melinda was ready to fight. She was tougher, more scared, and more than ever ready to ask a lot of questions. What the heck is the Grandview underground — this city below us — who is her brother, and once and for all, what is her mother hiding and who is her father? But was she ready for the answers? My favorite thing about season three was Melinda

solving the mystery surrounding her father, not only because it was fun to act, but at the end of all the hell, she got the father she always wanted. He was proud of her, loved her, and best of all, didn't abandon her. I feel like a huge part of her healed in this season."

One day, while waiting for a lighting change on set during filming on season four, Love shared with us the secret of how she approaches her character. "I try every day to make Melinda as real as possible. Moody sometimes, frustrated, over emotional, sensitive, hungry, high and low, scared, damaged, all of it. And then I add the patience of a saint, invisible wings of angels, the strength of a Greek god, the love of a mother, and the empathy of someone untouchable. I try to make her a best friend, a good wife, a great listener, and a great woman. I try to show her imperfections as much as her perfections. To me a truly great person is flawed. The true beauty of someone is in there, good and bad. She tells me who she wants to be every day, I then mix that in with myself, and Melinda comes to life."

With all that I've learned on my journey so far, I

FUN FACTS

« Melinda's middle name is Irene.

« Melinda loves anchovies on her pizza.

« Melinda didn't know how to cook when she met Jim.

« Melinda bought her first car with the babysitting money she made in high school.

« Melinda graduated from Hillridge High School and went to college in Washington State.

« Melinda played field hockey in high school and wore braces when she was seventeen.

« Melinda likes chick flicks and horror movies.

« Melinda had a red umbrella turn inside out on her first date with Jim. He replaced it on the fifth anniversary of that encounter.

« Melinda knows nothing about sports!

« Melinda is allergic to Ho-Hos.

« Melinda doesn't like her birthday or Halloween, but loves Christmas.

« Melinda's biggest fear is being studied for her gift.

« Jennifer Love Hewitt had her home ghost busted by Mary Ann Winkowski.

« Jennifer Love Hewitt is afraid of bats.

42

have more confidence and greater clarity about life, death and my special gift. Part of my strength and wisdom comes from my loving husband, Grandma, my spirit guides, and my family and friends, like Professor Payne, Delia and Ned. And part of my strength and wisdom comes from you, my dear friends. I'm eternally grateful that you are right here with me each week as I face new challenges. Together, let's continue to discover the parallels between two worlds: the world of the living and the spirit world.

www.facebook.com/profile.php?id=1152894437&ref=ts/
www.jenniferlovehewittonline.com/
www.melindasdiary.com

Q&A With Jennifer Love Hewitt

Clearly Melinda is the heart and soul of this show. How difficult is it to bring that level of emotional energy to the scenes?

I think if you can understand Melinda's passion for what she does, then the crying is easy. When we do the cross over scenes, that is her truest self; she is taking her gift and healing people. How could you not cry? I'm also very inspired by the guest actors we have. They really give their hearts to us in those scenes, and that is really beautiful.

What are the biggest similarities between Melinda and yourself? Biggest differences?

Melinda is much smarter and braver than me. She's much better on a computer. I'm a good cook and she's not. We both would do anything to help someone. I'm very emotional and sensitive like her. I can't wait to be a mom, and she's a little scared. We both love clothes and antiques. We both worry all the time. We both believe in ghosts. The only difference is I won't go into dark alleyways, basements, morgues, or onto bridges late at night for the fun of it. I'm afraid of scary things and she's not. I wonder about her sometimes.

What's been your favorite *Ghost Whisperer* moment?

My favorite moments are when I get to work with children. They make me so happy and their energy is so pure it makes you feel cleansed. The funniest moments are any time I get the giggles, just because it always gets the other actors going.

It must be difficult to work on a show that confronts fears every week. How do you cope with the barrage of scares?

I don't always like having to face my real fears on the show. But once you face them they are gone. So that's great!

How does it feel being named *TV Guide*'s Sexiest Actress on TV?

The crew joked that now everything we do has to be sexy. It was a great honor, and I will try my hardest to live up to the title!

How do you think Melinda's look has changed in the last three seasons?

First of all we've enlisted new people on the 'Glam Squad' in season three. Antonella [Renyer] is my makeup artist and she truly is an artist; Michael Reitz now does my hair and it is lighter, hipper, and more sophisticated; and Dorothy Amos is the new costume designer and, along with my on-set dresser Di[ane Charles], we are now dressing Melinda in a more youthful style.

Your on-screen marriage is the envy of TV audiences all over the world, why do you think that is?

I think what's great about Jim and Melinda's marriage is they truly are partners. Even when there is conflict, it's done with respect. They are always on each other's side. It's fun to play something so positive. We hope Jim and Melinda inspire other real relationships!

In 'Friendly Neighborhood Ghost', you met a special guest star — can you tell us about him?

We had a guest star come on, Ross McCall. An ordinary day at work changed my life forever! When we met I knew instantly that he was special. The show has brought me so many wonderful things, but Ross has been the most amazing thing.

What direction would you like to see Melinda take over the coming seasons?

I would like to see her kick some dark side butt! It would be great to see her as a mom. I would love for her to be able to truly inspire more people who might have her gift. It would be cool for her to get possessed by the dark side for a moment. I would like for her to be able to have a good relationship

Below:
Melinda is faced with crossing over more than 200 souls in 'The One'.

with her mom and maybe help her step-brother find the light instead of the dark.

Rumor has it you'll be directing an episode of *Ghost Whisperer* this season. Has this always interested you?

I am so excited! I've been wanting to direct for a while and can't wait to do it on a show that I'm so passionate about. It will be fun directing Camryn, because she will joke with me and make me laugh. I hope everyone likes my episode.

What are your beliefs about the paranormal and how does that effect the way you portray Melinda?

I definitely believe spirits are out there. Maybe not like the ones Melinda sees, but their energies. It's so great to think that our loved ones might be able to still watch over us. I think Melinda has a great gift.

There is talk that the *Ghost Whisperer* sets are haunted. Have you experienced any strange occurrences?

We've had ghosts make appearances on film. We've had lights explode that weren't on or hot. We've had lights move on their own as we were looking at them. We've had crew members feel ghosts around them. It's cool. We like that they visit. It's their show after all!

43

JIM CLANCY

"I'm holding you right now. I love you right now. What else matters?"

After a life-threatening accident, Jim Clancy regains consciousness in a hospital bed, his wife Melinda at his side. Jim glances around the room, asks, "Am I *dead*?" When Melinda shakes her head, no, Jim replies, "Never know with you." It's an odd exchange. Odd for anyone, that is, except the man who's married to a ghost whisperer.

"Jim is the closest view into Melinda's world," **David Conrad** explains of how his character works in the show. "In some sense, Jim provides the TV audience with a reflection of what it must be like to stand right next to someone who can see the supernatural and still treat that person as a regular human being. Like being next to the magic trick on stage and still believing."

For that reason and more, Jim Clancy has amassed a huge fan-base even though he's got no direct connection to the spirit world. Jim's a regular guy and the *Ghost Whisperer* audience loves him for it. They also love how sexy, how romantic, how real Jim and Melinda are together. They're like two peas in a pod, and yet they're opposites in lots of ways. Mel loves anchovy pizza; Jim's a pizza purist. Jim digs deep when pondering the meaning of life: "I mean, are we the puppets, or the puppet masters?" Mel takes it as it comes: "Never question the Cosmic Law of French Toast." Jim saves lives; Mel saves souls.

Let's take a beat and rewind back to the pilot where viewers first fell in love with Jim Clancy. We're at Jim and Melinda's wedding reception where they're dancing romantically and Melinda spots something outside the window. Jim whispers in her ear, "Don't tell me. You see something?" When Melinda shakes her head, Jim whisperers, "Good, because it would be nice to keep the celebration, you know, among the living." That's it, right there! Viewers get Jim's awareness of his wife's ability to see and speak to the dead, the respect he has for her and her extraordinary gift. And, he looks dreamy in a tux.

When Jim's brother Dan stops by to celebrate the couple's nuptials, it becomes clear he's only there in spirit. Dan is a ghost. He claims he wouldn't miss the wedding for anything in the world. Even though it's Melinda's first encounter with her brother-in-law's spirit, she confides in him that she's worried about her new husband having trouble on his job as a paramedic. Recently someone Jim was trying to save died — that's never happened to him before. Dan assures Melinda that his brother can handle it, he knows how to take away other people's fear. Jim just needs to understand "he can't save them all."

Jim's job as a paramedic is the counterpoint to Melinda's calling as a ghost whisperer. Even though it's a dichotomy in their lives, they have similar pressures. Jim tells Melinda, "I just can't stand us both being like this... both having to deal with who's staying and who's going. I have to find something different, or someday I'm gonna make a mistake and the next one won't come back. At least not to me." The earnest questioning of

capabilities, coupled with knowing that his father never supported his career choice (primal male stuff), makes for a crisis in confidence that Melinda helps Jim through.

And yet, Jim performs extraordinarily well as a paramedic. Whether it's saving a dying woman in the apartment above Andrea's in 'Mended Hearts', or tending to 200 victims after a jetliner crashed outside Grandview, during which he finds the sole survivor (in 'The Gathering'), Jim is always heroic.

Our favorite Jim Clancy hero moment is in 'Weight of What Was', when he busts through a tunnel wall in the underground to rescue Melinda. "Jim's no hero," says David. "He's just willing to take his vows, both professional and marital, seriously. He reminds me that both are sacred — a word we don't pay much attention to these days."

What makes Jim so accessible is that he's less than perfect. For example, he prides himself on his handyman skills, but the quality of his work around the house is hit or miss. And Jim knows it.

Above:
Jim in action.
Opposite:
Jim and Melinda enjoy a moment together, but they're not alone, in 'Miss Fortune'.

When a visitor admires some of his work, Jim replies, "Thanks. Just don't look too closely at the electrical wiring… or the plumbing… or the roof."

Living in a place that's being slowly remodeled by the man of the house does try Melinda and Jim's patience (the remodel is threaded through season one). Eventually it causes the couple to contemplate selling. But, on the same day, at the same time, they come to the same conclusion — although far from perfect, they love their home. It's a keeper.

Like most people, Jim is on the outside of the spirit world, hoping to someday get a glimpse of what Melinda sees and hears. In 'Hope and Mercy', and again in 'Wings of a Dove', Jim has an encounter with a ghost that's way too close for comfort. The spirit puts an angry spin on Jim, affecting his words, deeds and attitude. Unaware of what's going on, Jim thinks he's suffering from anxiety and depression. Melinda knows better. She reveals there's a spirit attached to Jim and it's not a good one. She describes the ghost that's haunting Jim as being covered in strange tattoos. BOOM! This hits Jim like a ton of bricks. Tattoo Man was the victim of a vehicular accident that Jim was involved in. Tattoo Man was a dangerous criminal in the world of the living and now his spirit is back with a vengeance.

Once Melinda and Jim unravel the mystery of Tattoo Man's unfinished business, Melinda is able to convince him to detach from her husband and go into the Light. This bizarre experience with the ghost causes Jim to question his role in fate and destiny. Mel assures her husband that the *accident* cost Tattoo Man his life, not *Jim*. "Accidents are a

necessary part of life," she says. Jim takes in the otherworldly wisdom of his wife, but ponders what reason could possibly justify a man's death.

On the lighter side of ghost life, Jim gets a kick out of some of the experiences he and Melinda share. He loves that Homer the ghost dog takes up residence at the Clancy household. He finds it amusing when a little boy ghost randomly pops in while his mother, Faith, visits for the weekend. Like most people in Jim and Melinda's life, Faith is unaware of Melinda's abilities. It takes some fancy footwork on the couple's part to cover for the mischievous little ghost.

It's a challenge keeping Melinda's gift a secret from the outside world, but it's the challenge that Jim takes most seriously. Not because he's ashamed or embarrassed by Melinda's unconventional abilities, but because Jim wants to protect his wife from those who don't understand. He intervenes when Ned discovers Melinda's unique communication skills and makes Ned understand the importance of keeping Melinda's secret. "In these situations, I try to imagine my wife as the center of my world," explains David.

In 'Deadman's Ridge', only Melinda knows (thanks to a spirit) where a missing man is trapped in the mountains. No one believes her — no one except Jim. He takes on a group of skeptical Rangers who are searching for the man. "She's my wife. And she's right," he tells them. "It doesn't matter how, I'm telling you, she's right. Just deal with it and have a little faith. You'll see." And they do.

A truly magical ghost moment for Jim happens when he arrives at a haunted orphanage (in 'The Lost Boys') and peeks around a corner. Melinda is reading *Peter Pan* to a seemingly empty room. Jim is so moved, his heart so full of love for his amazing wife, that he accidentally bumps a chair, scaring off the three young ghosts who had been listening, spellbound by Melinda.

David Conrad's favorite episode is "the one with the flashbacks to Jim and Melinda's first meeting." In the 'The Night We Met', Jim is helping evacuate a collapsing building when he spies Melinda losing a slipper as she steps over a puddle. Jim picks the slipper up and tosses it back to the beauty — in a twenty-first century twist on Prince Charming. Melinda tells Jim that someone is in danger and he

acts on the tip even though she has no proof. To Jim's amazement, Melinda (and the ghost who told her) turns out to be right.

Later Jim bumps into Melinda during a rainstorm that turns her red umbrella inside out. He invites her to dinner at the "Umbrella Room" — a hotdog stand in the rain. During this highly romantic scene, in which Jim tenderly wipes mustard from Melinda's lip, they discover they have nothing in common. That's all it takes to launch them into a wonderfully magical, complex relationship that straddles the world of the living and the world of the dead.

As perfect as the marriage is, Melinda and Jim do have ups and down just like any contemporary couple. Jim gets frustrated because at times Melinda has her head too into the ghost world.

Below:
Jim and Melinda
have their ups and
downs.
Opposite:
Jim's love for
Melinda brings her
back from the
brink in 'The
Vanishing'.

"Sometimes I think I'd see you more if I were dead." And sometimes Melinda pushes back because, in certain circumstances, Jim is just too damn protective of her. In 'Friendly Neighborhood Ghost', Jim suspects their new neighbor is dangerous. Conversely, Melinda is convinced he's merely haunted, and reminds her husband there's a difference between caring and controlling.

A pivotal moment in their relationship occurs during 'The Vanishing', when Melinda has a head injury that puts her into a coma. Jim, fearful that he'll lose the love of his life, desperately whispers, "Stay with me, baby. I love you so much." What he doesn't know is, at that exact moment, Melinda is having a near death experience and is about to go into the Light. Jim's intense love and need for Melinda is what brings her back from the brink.

Jim's compassion and support are endless. When Melinda is in pain because of her family history, Jim holds her close and tells her, "I hate that you had to go through that. I wish I could go back in time and make that little girl feel better." And when it comes to protecting his wife, Jim's courage is pretty endless. He confronts Melinda's father, Tom Gordon, in no uncertain terms when he endangers Melinda.

First and foremost, Jim Clancy is a family man. He looks forward to the day when he and Melinda have a baby. Even though Melinda has her doubts, Jim believes she'll make a great mother. She voices concerns that their child might inherit her abilities and she fears the child will struggle as she does. Jim assures Melinda it'll be fine, "we'll handle it."

In 'Deja Boo', when this possibility seems like it's about to become a reality, Jim and Melinda check the results of her pregnancy test — negative. When Melinda wonders if she'll ever get pregnant, Jim assures her he's ready to go down any road with her, through any door.

That's exactly how Jim Clancy's fans feel about him.
www.facebook.com/profile.php?id=1185354644&ref=ts
www.cbs.com/primetime/ghost_whisperer/bio/
david_conrad/bio.php

Q&A With David Conrad
How'd you end up married to the most beautiful and unusual woman on television?
I auditioned for the role of Jim really early on and

didn't hear anything. Then the producers called again as I was about to leave LA and do a play in Pittsburgh. I tested, heard nothing, and decided, *well, let's go do the play*, jumped in my car and got as far as Oklahoma before they called me and said, "You got the job." I did the pilot on the proviso that they'd make space in the shooting schedule for the play. Did both. The rest is… well you know.
Your brother is a real paramedic. Does he influence how you do your job on screen?
I call him way too much to ask advice about procedures and about how medical people talk, their shorthand with each other. He's really the model for Jim. He has a way of crossing his arms that his friends make fun of. I do it on the show sometimes and they call me and laugh.
Share the biggest similarity and the biggest

difference between you and Jim.

The biggest similarity is our love of the kitchen. Our biggest difference — his patience.

As a heartthrob and one of *Extra*'s Most Eligible Bachelors, do women approach you on the street?

I can't take that stuff seriously. I mostly have a good laugh with anyone who comes up to me to talk about the show. It's actually mostly guys who want to know about Jennifer Love Hewitt, "Dude tell me… is she that hot in person?"

Is she?

Yeah. And beautiful. And smart. And talented. And kind.

How's the evolution of your character going?

In the beginning, Jim was mostly a strong-man-of-few-words type. It's been good that they let him be funny once in awhile and that he gets to put out a fire on occasion. I like that he likes to cook. I like that he likes his wife's friends. That won't change. I'd like to see him grapple a little more with the issue of having kids.

Word about is you rescued a crew member and saved a bee's life in the process.

(Laughs) I don't remember saving anyone's life but I'll go to great extremes to make sure a bee or a spider gets away from a trampling or whatever danger. As I've gotten older my sense that any creature has a soul, however simple, has gotten stronger. But bees especially — I have a thing about them. Bees are like little furry cats that fly. And they do so much to enable us to grow food. Without them we'd have a pretty miserable diet. Hard to believe that an insect can be endangered.

As for the crew, I can't say enough about them as a group of people. They're the best bunch I've had the pleasure to work with. I do so little compared to them. They labor to make me look good and they always have a smile for me even when I show up hours after they've been at work. They are the best part of working in the TV industry.

You're a Pittsburgh guy who commutes between Hollywood and your hometown. Is Grandview typical for a small eastern town?

The folks in Grandview are kind of Anywhere, USA… Not in a bad way but in a way that people can pick up similarities the nation over. One of the East Coast qualities I enjoy in the show is the way all the police and fire guys seem to know each other, which is fun to play.

Are you a believer?

I don't believe there's a ghost named Frank Conrad who haunts me (that was my great-grandfather), but I do think there are ties between people that don't go away simply because the physical body of the person passes on. I'm inclined to think the Native Americans have a good take on this vision of life.

Have your beliefs changed since you've joined *Ghost Whisperer*?

Not really, but I am moved by the number of people who come up to me who have lost loved ones. The need people have to reach out to those they've lost is stunning.

Have you had any strange experiences?

Mostly out in the woods, or on stage where one would imagine ghosts to be. Kind of easy for them to get to you then.

Do you believe in karma?

I believe in karma but not as a payback system. It's not like you earn karma credit. It's not gas in a tank. There's no karma ref.

Angels?

I hope there are angels, at least the better ones of our nature… or the ones with swords, racing down to save someone from the battlefield on occasion.

Possession?

It might be the only odd thing I do believe in. But its not just ghosts who can do possession — lovers, characters in a play long dead… That'd be nice to be possessed by them.

CHARACTER TIMELINE

- Jim's brother dies.
- A rift develops with his dad when Jim chooses to become a paramedic instead of a lawyer.
- Dad dies.
- Jim meets Melinda.
- Jim learns about her gift.
- Jim and Melinda marry.
- They move into the house Jim surprises her with.

50

DELIA BANKS

"And he smiled, and he said, 'What's one day compared to being married to you every single day?'"

When we were casting for the part of Delia Banks and **Camryn Manheim**'s name came up, we were told "Nobody does it better." And that couldn't be more true. Camryn is smart, talented, lovely to behold in front of the camera lens and is an Emmy-winning actress with more fans than she knows what to do with. She embodies the character she's playing like nobody's business.

"After I finished eight years on *The Practice*, I wanted to spend some solid time with my newborn son," Camryn Manheim explains of her decision to join the *Ghost Whisperer* cast. "I did a few films and then realized that television is actually the most conducive to raising a family. In feature films, you may be required to work in different cities and countries, and it is difficult to bring a family with you. When I was approached by the creators and producers of *Ghost Whisperer* to play Delia, I decided it had all the elements that I was looking for to maintain a happy, healthy and creative life." Smiling broadly, Camryn nods, "It was the best decision I ever made. This is the most loving and supportive atmosphere to work in, and since Jennifer Love Hewitt does all the heavy lifting, I have plenty of time to spend with my son."

Like Camryn, Delia Banks is very grounded. She's a single working mother whose beloved husband, Charlie, died four years before (he had stopped at an ATM and was shot during a random robbery). Now, Delia is raising her son Ned on her own. After Charlie's death, Delia kick-started a career as a real estate agent, but it's never been her passion. When she was younger, she was very much an artist. That's

why, given the choice between closing deals on houses or finding and selling gorgeous period paintings, estate jewelry and fabulous antiques, Delia opts for the latter and goes to work at Melinda's Same As It Never Was antique shop. Occasionally, Delia moonlights in real estate — mainly because it's a great way for us to do haunted house stories like 'Bad Blood'!

Delia steps into the *Ghost Whisperer* world at the top of season two when Melinda (who's an acquaintance) contacts her about a couple of collector's edition Grateful Dead tickets that were stolen from the shop. The culprit? Delia's son, Ned. Although they're two very different women, it's clear from the start that Melinda and Delia are destined to be best friends.

Unbeknownst to Delia, Ned's 'five-finger discount' is the result of a 'Deadhead' ghost who's using subliminal messages to make sure his rock 'n' roll memorabilia goes to "worthy people." Every night, as Ned is falling asleep, the ghost whispers in his ear "take the tickets." Once Melinda discovers what's going on in Ned's dreamstate, she's faced with finding a resolution that does not hit Delia's radar, because Delia's a hard-core ghost skeptic.

Camryn says of Delia's attitude, "I think it's important to have a skeptic on the show because it answers a lot of questions for people who aren't convinced that ghosts exist."

Delia continues to keep a toehold in real estate, which brings Melinda into the haunted housing market. Like the time the new owners of a house that Delia sold start having trouble with their plumbing

51

and electric. Melinda tags along just for the fun of it. Almost immediately, she discovers the house is haunted. Ironically, the owners have their suspicions as well. But, in her pragmatic way, Delia thinks the whole thing is ridiculous — all they need is a good handyman. (In this case, the handyman is poor Jim!)

Melinda's need to keep Delia in the dark about her gift begins to take its toll. When Delia senses that Melinda is pulling away, Delia asks her to stay connected, telling her she feels like everyone else has their entire life ahead of them. With Charlie gone, she feels like all she's got is the past. Melinda realizes that with the loss of Charlie and trying to handle Ned, who's on the cusp of becoming a teenager, Delia is overwhelmed. Melinda is so supportive that Delia becomes convinced Melinda is her guardian angel — figuratively speaking, of course.

All dressed up, looking fabulous in a pirate costume, and with somewhere to go, Delia invites Melinda to a Halloween party during *Ghost Whisperer*'s first Halloween episode. When Melinda rolls her beautiful fawn eyes at the prospect of celebrating Halloween, Delia teases, "Ghosts are fun." If Delia only knew! For the first time in their friendship, Melinda shares a bit of ghost insight: "Each year, on this particular night, the veil between the living and the dead gets thinner." Delia doesn't quite know what to make of it.

Delia is dismayed to find, as she prepares to honor her late husband's birthday, that Ned refuses to participate in this annual event for the very first time. It makes her feel that in addition to losing a husband, she's also losing her son.

In 'Dead to Rights', the audience meets another member of Delia's family — her glorious (giant) dog, Bob. This canine (named in honor of creator John Gray's dearly-departed pup) is trained as a therapy dog and Delia brings him to the local hospital where they work with patients. In keeping with the volunteer spirit, Melinda and Delia donate items to a silent auction. But when Ned tries to sneak his dad's stuff into the donation trunk, Delia and Ned have their first real fight. Ned confesses he dumped dad's stuff because he hates that his mom cries every single day over the loss of Charlie. Touched deeply by her son's misguided gesture of love, Delia realizes it's time to let go and move forward with life.

Now that Delia is committed to taking a big step

forward, she has to figure out how. For starters, she flexes her flirting muscles with Tim Flaherty, Jim's sidekick at the fire station. Melinda and Jim get in on the act by playing matchmaker. They slyly give Delia and Tim tickets to the Little Broadway Theatre in the heart of Grandview. But when Delia turns up on opening night looking gorgeous, Tom is a no-show.

Delia's hesitation about dating is a universal one for women who have lost their spouses. Nobody delivers that kind of accessibility better than Camryn. In a very vulnerable state, Delia asks Melinda, "If I start dating, will Charlie slip little by little from my memory?" Melinda assures Delia that letting go and forgetting are two very separate things.

During a trip to the local jewelry store in 'The Cradle Will Rock', Delia and Melinda's lives are in jeopardy when they become victims of a heist. Delia is devastated when the antique art deco emerald ring that Charlie gave her is stolen by the perps. When Melinda returns the ring (with a little help from her ghost friends), Delia is overjoyed, but her suspicions of Melinda's "uniqueness" are also aroused. When she asks Melinda how she knew specific information, Melinda does a pretty good job of bluffing. But Delia's not totally convinced.

Finally, in the 'The Walk-In', Delia learns why Tim bailed on their date at the theater. He claims their relationship was happening so fast, he freaked out. After doing lots of thinking, and getting grief from Jim, Tim realizes that Delia's an amazing woman, so he decides to go after her, romantic guns

53

CHARACTER TIMELINE

- Delia's husband Charlie dies.
- Delia gets a job in Grandview real estate.
- Delia meets Melinda, starts working at the antique shop.
- Delia has a falling out with Melinda when Charlie's spirit turns up.
- Delia is almost killed by electrocution.
- Delia discovers Ned is not a skeptic.
- After much conflict, Delia repairs her relationship with Ned.
- Delia tells Melinda she'll try to open up to the spirit world.

blazing. Tim's efforts to win Delia back start with an endearing song/sign combo, "I'm sorry." And Tim keeps at it until Delia realizes he's not going away. Finally, she meets him halfway — in the middle of Town Square where they reboot their relationship.

Then, just as Delia gets her dating life on track and Ned straightened out, Bob goes off the rails. In 'Children of Ghosts', Delia has a close encounter with *Dog* Whisperer Cesar Millan. (*Ghost Whisperer*'s John Gray is married to *Dog Whisperer* executive producer/director Melissa Jo Peltier.) Cesar gives Delia advice about Bob being territorial but hesitates because there's something amiss that he can't quite see. Only the ghost whisperer knows for sure, and she can't tell a soul — Bob's rowdy behavior is being caused by Homer, the ghost dog. As Melinda tries to cross Homer into the Light, Bob chills.

A huge milestone for Delia occurs in 'Delia's First Ghost'. Although she likes Tim very much, Delia decides she's going to make him work to prove he's

'the one'. She multi-dates a couple of guys at once and strange things start happening to her and to Ned. *Simultaneously.* After one freaky date, Delia returns home with the heel of her shoe broken and red wine and axel grease all over her beautiful lavender dress. Believe it or not, she got the better end of the deal — her date caught fire and got a flat tire!

Although the identity of the ghost haunting Delia and Ned is not revealed, it turns out this ghost is haunting Tim as well. When Jim realizes, he tells Melinda it's time to tell Delia what's going on.

Anxious about how this will affect their friendship, Melinda gingerly tells Delia she's got a ghost attached to her. That ghost is her husband Charlie. Delia's response is strident to say the least, "You're kidding right, that's insane. Why would you tell me that?" When Melinda bravely stands her ground, Delia turns on her in one of the most powerful scenes of the series, "How many times did I walk in here and see you talking to yourself or acting all jittery… and I never said a word… I thought you were just 'quirky'. Now I know you're nuts. And by the way, I quit." Delia slams out of the shop. Melinda is absolutely destroyed.

When Delia gets home she finds herself under siege from Charlie's ghost, which sends her back to Melinda for help. The twist is that Charlie's not trying to break Delia and Tim up. In his own misguided way, he's trying to get them together. And he's not terrorizing Ned. He's actually trying to teach his son a lesson that will keep him out of trouble.

Once Delia and Ned understand Charlie's true intentions, they are able to deal with their feelings of love and loss. Charlie lovingly says goodbye to his family and crosses over. Delia and Melinda reconcile, agreeing they are too important to each other to not continue being friends. But Delia has a caveat; when it comes to ghosts, she's not ready to go there yet. Melinda respects her friend's standing but from her POV it's "Love me, love my ghosts."

In regards to her character taking this amazing journey, Camryn says, "Although I'm a skeptic in real life, since joining the show, I'm not so quick to disregard people's feelings about the paranormal. I'm much more interested in their stories and accounts."

Melinda and Delia's relationship of "don't ask, don't tell" reaches another milestone in the season two finale. The fifth clue of the mythological Five

Signs (*see* Spirit Symbolism p76) from the spirit world, "Death of a loved one", is still unanswered when, having barely survived a series of haunting accidents, Delia is hospitalized. During a visit with Delia, Melinda confides that exactly one year earlier, Andrea's life was in jeopardy. Melinda feels responsible in part for Andrea's death and knows that the dark spirits are trying to hurt the people she loves. Delia does believe Melinda can feel and see things, but she's having trouble believing ghosts can change the course of our lives. Melinda tells her that in order to be safe, this once Delia needs to believe. Delia concedes, setting the stage for great growth in season three. Camryn embraces this. "I like the idea of Delia opening her mind a little bit so she can really experience something new and meaningful and not just take Melinda's word for it."

Delia finds herself being increasingly protective of her friend. Two great examples are when a stalker shows up at the shop and when Melinda disappears in the tunnels below Grandview. While Melinda is

Above and Opposite:

Melinda and Delia manage to stay firm friends, despite Delia being a a hard-core ghost skeptic.

trapped in a small underground air pocket, Delia joins forces with Jim and Professor Payne to save her. During this race against the clock, Delia has her first physical encounter with a ghost — it brushes against her arm. She is amazed. But, Delia being Delia, she's not quite convinced it was a paranormal experience.

In need of extra income, Delia continues dabbling in the real estate market. When Delia finally gets papers signed by the new owners of a house, Melinda tags along to the "most beautiful haunted house in Grandview." Delia's not buying the "haunted" bit and for once, neither is Melinda. However, slowly Melinda begins to change her mind, causing her and Delia to square off again. Delia wants Melinda to back off. Melinda claims she doesn't look for ghosts and it's not up to her to leave them alone — it's up to the ghosts. Stalemate.

The two women come to a resolution when Delia admits that there is a default switch in her head that always resets to "that can't be." Melinda reasons that she hates to see Delia so closed off — there are tons of things in life we take on faith that we can't see. Why can't Delia do that with spirits? In what may be the most significant development in their relationship, Delia responds: "I can. I will... I'm gonna try."

And while she's trying to balance out the ghost/no-ghost thing, Delia struggles with parenting issues tied to a son who's now a full-blown teenager. Of how she brings her real-life parenting sensibilities to the relationship between Delia and Ned, Camryn says, "There are some relationships on screen that remind you that you're acting. When I play a doctor, I never really believe I'm a doctor, or when I played Gladys Presley, I never really believed I was a middle-aged Southern woman who was the mother of the King of Rock 'n' Roll. But when I play Ned's mother, nothing could be more organic and natural. I find myself asking Christoph what he did on the weekend, and if he's dating, and if he's eating well. I remind him not to drink and drive, and to register to vote. A few weeks ago, he came over to hang out with me and my son Milo," Camryn adds. "Now, if you ask Milo if he's an only child, he says 'No, I have a brother, Christoph.'"

Below:
Delia's job at Same As It Never Was perfectly suits her artistic nature.

www.cbs.com/primetime/ghost_whisperer/bio/ camryn_manheim/bio.php
www.camryn.com/
www.facebook.com/profile.php?id=1380416341

Q&A With Camryn Manheim
What was your initial take on Delia Banks?
I was really impressed that the creator of the show wanted to incorporate a character who'd never had any paranormal or otherworldly experiences. Because both Melinda and Jim were already past the stage of questioning Melinda's abilities and had accepted them, I was happy to introduce a character who was more skeptical and had yet to fully accept Melinda's gifts.
Any hesitation in taking the role?
Are you kidding? I was thrilled to be offered the part, especially after hearing raves about how lovely and kind Jennifer Love Hewitt was. I can tell you after working with her for two years, all those rumors were true.
What do you love about Delia?
There is nothing not to love about her. Delia is warm, kind, funny, a good friend, and a good mom. Right

now, I'm really enjoying the fact that Ned is growing up and becoming an adult. The complicated relationship a mother and a son have when he moves out of childhood to being an independent person is what makes my job interesting, by showing the human condition in its purest form.

The biggest similarities between Delia and yourself? The biggest differences?

Similarities: She needs proof and evidence before she believes in something. She is devoted to her friends and her family. She is a joyful person and enjoys her life day to day.

Differences: She is a simple woman and loves living in a small town and having a very regular life. She has an underlying sorrow because she lost her husband and still grieves for her loss.

What are your beliefs about the paranormal and how does that effect the way you portray Delia?

My father was a mathematician. He believed that you need proof and evidence before you should believe in something. I guess his philosophy on life rubbed off on me. I believe ghosts exist, I have just personally never had a paranormal experience. Well, let me rephrase that. It's very possible I've had a paranormal experience, but I didn't recognize it as such. Ultimately, all things are left up to interpretation, and given the choice to perceive a situation as paranormal or just unordinary, I usually go with the latter. I've had some bizarre and questionable experiences, but I choose to think of them as strange and unanswerable occurrences.

You're lots of fun behind the scenes. Wanna share?

My favorite part about shooting is when they let the camera roll after the director has yelled "Cut" and the cast just starts goofing off and saying whatever they want. They usually take those little bits of film and make a gag reel and show it at the Christmas party. It's hilarious.

The crew of *Ghost Whisperer* is unbelievable. You can't imagine the skill it takes to execute all of the special effects on our show. They do it with such precision that they almost make it look easy, it's mind-boggling. I have so much respect for them.

But the truth is all of the fun that we have is the result of two things: the producers and Jennifer Love Hewitt. Without their passion for the show, and their easygoing nature, it would probably be a nightmare working on *Ghost Whisperer* because of how much

---

FUN FACTS

- Delia loves anything lavender, especially roses.
- Delia is an artist at heart.
- Delia loves Halloween, her parents made a big deal out of it when she was a kid, decorating the house like a movie set.
- Delia's favorite song is 'Every Breath You Take' by The Police.
- Delia used to love going "clubbing" in her younger days.
- Delia likes wearing beautiful jewelry.
- Delia always dreamed of owning her own shop.

---

we have to accomplish each and every day.

What's your favorite episode so far?

I love the episodes when I was dating Tim, a) because it's fun to date, b) because I got to show the emotional side of Delia, and c) because I got to get out of the store and have a storyline that didn't involve ghosts.

Are you *Ghost Whisperer*'s resident skeptic?

You decide. I don't believe in crystal balls, tarot cards, palm readings, exorcisms, possession, curses, psychic rituals, séances, ouija boards, automatic writing, pendulums, dream visits by spirits that have crossed over, the Light, earthbound spirits, angels, totems, apports, karma, reincarnation, past lives.

One last thing. What made you want to become an actor?

When I was nine years old and away at summer camp, a camp counselor asked if I'd like to be in the play *The Lion, the Witch and the Wardrobe*. I'd never been in a play before and it sounded fun, so I agreed. I loved the camaraderie of the cast, I loved the attention of the director, but the thing that hooked me was the applause. After the play was over, everyone rose to their feet and applauded the cast. And all the older campers wanted to be my friend. I remember thinking, "I'm going to be an actor and have all the friends in the world." And though that was my original reason for wanting to become an actor, over time as I studied the craft I fell in love with the power that theater has to change the way people view and interpret the world.

PROFESSOR RICK PAYNE

"I like to think of myself as truth serum without the needle or CIA."

rofessor Rick Payne, played by the love-able **Jay Mohr**, was introduced as a guest star in the premiere episode of season two, 'Love Never Dies'. Payne was brought on to the show to provide an encyclopedic knowledge of the spirit world, as well as genuine concern for Melinda Gordon's safety as she puts herself in greater danger to protect those she cares about.

Jay's hilarious razor-sharp insight has earned him the nickname "Slam Man" on the *Ghost Whisperer* set because he never holds back. When asked about taking the role of Professor Payne, Mohr grins, "I think I made a mistake once… yeah… it was only once. It had nothing to do with *Ghost Whisperer*." Jay is a wonderful actor who is fun to work with for the exact reasons he's fun to watch. Executive producer P.K. Simmonds confirms, "Jay brings humor, energy, creativity and spontaneity to the set and to his role. He also brings sports commentary and sometimes doughnuts."

Jay's lightning-fast rat-a-tat-tat speak is exactly what we were looking for when John Gray created the Payne character. The delivery of technical exposition required to ground the *Ghost Whisperer* mysteries from week to week has become imperative in the storytelling as we push out further and further into the ghost world. When asked how he feels about the spirit realm, Jay launches into his killer impersonation of Christopher Walken (in a skit titled 'Christopher Walken's Psychic Hotline', made famous on *Saturday Night Live*) which reflects his

bizarre in-studio spooky happenings.

Jay Mohr's character was launched when Melinda seeks Professor Payne out at Rockland University, looking for help with the dark spirit tormenting earthbound spirits of Grandview. In the first scene of the season two opener, Melinda learns that Payne is considered a leading expert in the field of Parapsychology. Payne combines his studies of other-worldly phenomenon with modern day psychology. He wants to believe in the paranormal, but as a scientist he is skeptical because of a lack of concrete evidence.

Though Melinda keeps her gift a secret, it doesn't take long for the hyper-kinetic Professor Payne to go from curious to suspicious about her probing questions and odd behavior. When Melinda shares with him the few clues she has on Wide Brim Hat Man, Payne experiences a phenomenon from the dark side that shakes his skepticism. At first, Payne thinks he's being punked by his fellow professors. Once he rules that out, Payne realizes the pictures and evil symbols plastered all over his walls and ceiling along with warnings to "stop or die" are an actual haunting. Most anyone else would be terrified. Not Payne. Psyched about the incident, he calls Melinda, wanting to know what's going on. What is she after and how does she know so much about the spirit world? But Mel stays mum.

Payne is immediately intrigued by this first haunting, because the reality of parapsychological phenomena and the scientific validity of

parapsychological research is a matter of continued dispute. Unbeknownst to Melinda, Payne begins recording her interactions with the spirit world.

In 'The Ghost Within', Payne is drawn further into Melinda's world as he teaches her about apports. When Payne holds the object in question, an ornament, he sees nothing but the object. When he finally convinces Melinda to take it in her hand, she experiences a vision. Payne is mesmerized by this. He wants to run more tests on Melinda, who clearly has no intention of being his lab rat — regardless of how passionate the professor is about empirical proof. His interest conversely piqued by Melinda's rejection, Payne exclaims (as only Payne can), "You baffle me, you little minx."

While Payne is trying to figure out the Rubik's cube that is Melinda Gordon, Melinda Gordon is learning to trust the strange but charming professor. And, for *Ghost Whisperer* fans, the popularity of their bantering chemistry goes right through the roof.

After guiding Melinda in the area of spirit symbolism (*see* Spirit Symbolism, p76), Payne actively tries to figure out what exactly Melinda is hiding. In 'The Night We Met', Payne visits Same As It Never Was for the first time and meets Delia Banks. When Delia takes off, Melinda asks Payne more questions about symbols tied to the spirit world — specifically the number five. Ever the negotiator, he assures her he'll answer her questions if she answers just one of his… You know what's coming, right? Payne wants to know if Melinda's got supernatural powers. She confides that sometimes it feels that way. Payne is blown away by her. His area of expertise involves research that does not fit within standard theoretical models accepted by mainstream science. And right before his eyes stands a living, breathing human who clearly is connected to the spirit world. The professor is astonished by his good fortune.

When Payne tries to get more out of Melinda, she cuts him off, informing him that he got his one answer; she's awaiting hers. True to his word — and not one to pass up an audience — Payne launches into what's practically a treatise on the number five.

With each episode, Payne becomes more intrinsic to solving ghost mysteries that Melinda encounters. His wealth of knowledge is invaluable. In 'The Curse of the Ninth', Payne helps Melinda understand why a certain ghost sound is so disruptive — it's a frequency that is so low we can't hear it but we can feel it big time. And when ghosts want to make their presence felt, they use that frequency. Payne advises that a Low G on the musical scale neutralizes it. Payne adds that many great composers died after completing their ninth symphonies — known as 'The Curse of the Ninth'.

The next significant phenomenon that Payne experiences begins in his office, when a small African mannequin is teleported several times between his desk and the bookshelves. Understandably a bit creeped out, Payne heads home. But when he stows his briefcase in the hallway, seconds later, when he glances back, the briefcase has been moved. Freaked, he hits the (beer) bottle.

By the time Payne shows up on Melinda's doorstep, he's drunk, and the dam breaks — Payne confronts Melinda and his own belief system. Frustrated, he tries to make sense of everything in his

But Payne being Payne — an absent-minded professor — he can't find his car keys. As Melinda steps outside to help, she sees blood trickling from his mouth which matches a spirit vision she had earlier. Melinda knows immediately that Professor Payne is being possessed by a spirit. And Payne's reaction? "That's romantic — in a *Dawn of the Dead* kind of way."

This is a turning point in Payne's journey. He now knows the truth about Melinda's abilities to communicate with the dead. And while all this is going on, Payne's wife, Kate, returns from the dead to haunt him.

Professor Payne being in the know about the ghost whisperer completely shifts the dynamic of their relationship. Payne is no longer just a resource for Melinda, he's her friend and confidant. Their blossoming friendship leaves Melinda feeling like she has to warn him that being connected to her can leave him open to destruction and heartache, just as it did her friend Andrea Moreno. But Payne is too excited about astral projections, out of body experiences and other spirit-related phenomena which he's encountering through Melinda to care about the

Below: Melinda and the professor look into the Bloody Mary urban legend in 'Don't Try This at Home'.
Opposite: Payne and Melinda, a great ghost busting team.

life. He tells her she's probably just smoke and mirrors anyway, and the next thing he's expecting her to do is pull a rabbit from her hat! Before storming out, Payne lays it on the line: There's not enough give and take in their relationship, and he may be drunk, but at least he's honest. After claiming he never wants to see Melinda again, Payne slams out of her house.

possible dire consequences.

Not only do Melinda and Payne explore the strange and cryptic side of the spirit world together, but they also explore the soulful aspects as well. Melinda helps Payne understand that when someone dies, the soul is pure. And he enlightens her about reincarnation.

Another milestone for Payne in the spirit world is when Melinda lets him haul his special ghost-tracking equipment into her house. He uses Cerulean cameras and electromagnetometers to detect hot spots and measure the brain activity of a young girl being haunted. During this unusual session, Payne finally sees a ghost — even though it's in his machine. It's an extraordinary encounter.

Payne gathers more hard evidence when, in 'The Collector', he trails Melinda's brother to the Grandview jetliner crash site and records images of countless spirits surrounding him. Any lingering doubts about the spirit world that Payne had dissipate during his surveillance. So when Kate manifests and passes a message through Melinda to her husband telling him to read her journal, he takes it all very seriously. He is heartbroken when, in his wife's journal, he discovers she cheated on him before she died. Kate asks for forgiveness, but Rick rejects her —

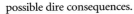

Above:
Payne and Melinda investigate another ghostly mystery.

he says there's too much pain. Furious, Kate threatens him and Melinda from the grave.

Overwhelmed by the revelation of his wife's infidelity, Payne tells Melinda that he's leaving on sabbatical. He's determined to leave it all behind. But as he's packing his office and trying to sell his house, Melinda's powerful visions about the spirit world intensify and Payne halts what he's doing to help decipher the meaning of her visions.

Payne cracks one Melinda vision by interpreting the symbolism that represents a prophet ghost. He explains prophet ghosts are very common in mythologies, and even appear in Charles Dickens' work. In thinking it through, Payne realizes darkness is building in Melinda's world, and not wanting to abandon the bravest person he's ever known, he cancels his sabbatical to stay and help her.

Payne's assistance in interpreting the events that are converging on Melinda culminates in the season two finale, 'The Gathering'. He knows a single trigger can dangerously affect the world, throwing everything out of balance — this could cause a huge shift between light and dark spirits. Payne's insight leads Melinda to protect four children from the evil her brother Gabriel and the dark side are planning.

In the opener of season three, Professor Rick

Payne's true feelings for Melinda are revealed. While sitting alone at a restaurant waiting for her, he practices what he would really, *really* like to say to her: "You know, when I was standing there, and I thought you were dead, I thought you had died right in front of me, it was as if… I don't know, like everything inside me just dropped. Like all these things I felt — things I know I shouldn't ever say, couldn't say — now I'd never have a…" But before he gets it out, Melinda interrupts by slipping into her chair across the table from him. And they're back to business.

The first time Payne shows interest in the opposite sex, other than Melinda or his late wife, is in 'Double Exposure', when he sets his sights on a fellow professor. But it turns out the lady in question is being haunted by a former lover. Melinda and Payne solve the mystery, but spooked, he backs away from the relationship before it ever gets started. Payne figures he's got enough complications in his life with a ghost wife and a ghost whisperer, he certainly doesn't need a haunted girlfriend too!

Melinda and Payne's friendship hits a serious obstacle when she finally discovers that he's been making notes about her. He explains that he recorded everything she said or did because, well, after spending a lifetime studying the paranormal without a shred of real evidence, along comes Melinda Gordon. He wanted to make sure that her encounters with the spirit world were all real, that he wasn't dreaming them. And besides, he's an academic, his job is to write down what he observes. She asks if he has given any consideration to what this would do to her life, because once it's out, scientists like him would want to make her an experiment, put her under a microscope. And if that happens, she won't be able to help the ghosts that need her most.

The final milestone for Payne is the result of a chance encounter with an old girlfriend (played by Jay's real-life wife, Nikki Cox). This meeting leads him to believe that he's the father of her child, which ignites the jealousy of his dead wife, as she badly wanted to have a child with Payne. Unfortunately, he put it off. A few weeks later, she died. Melinda helps Payne understand that the child is not his and he needs to do some work on his marriage, regardless of the fact that his wife is no longer in the world of the living. Emotional flashbacks reveal the circumstances of the Paynes' marriage, along with

CHARACTER TIMELINE

- ❦ Payne tells his wife Kate that he's not ready to have kids.
- ❦ Kate dies.
- ❦ Payne meets Melinda Gordon.
- ❦ Payne figures out Melinda's gift and his outlook on the world is changed forever.
- ❦ Melinda tells Payne his wife is haunting him.
- ❦ By reading a journal, Payne discovers his wife cheated on him.
- ❦ Payne thinks he may have a child but then learns the boy isn't his.
- ❦ Kate crosses into the Light.
- ❦ Payne witnesses supernatural events
- ❦ Melinda almost dies.
- ❦ Payne notices that one shadow is missing from the group in the season three finale.

the need for them to deconstruct the layers of anger and frustration that have built up over the years.

When Melinda helps strip it all away, Payne and Kate are able to get to the root of their problem, reconnect, and examine their feelings for each other. They both agree to move on — even though they finally admit they are still profoundly in love.

Payne is eternally grateful to Melinda for saving him from the vicious haunting that he was being treated to by his angry wife, and for enabling him to do the one thing that everyone in the world wants to do, have one last heartfelt conversation with the person you love most who has departed the world of the living.

www.cbs.com/primetime/ghost_whisperer/bio/jay_mo hr/bio.php

ghostwhispereroncbs.wetpaint.com/page/Jay+Mohr's+ Ghost+Whisperer+Tie+Challenge

A Crash Course on Spirit-Related Terminology With Professor Rick 'King of Non-Sequiturs' Payne

We know that an apport is an object sent from beyond to the living with symbolic meaning. Help us out with 'psychometry'.

Easy! Psychometry is visions of the past that you get

63

from touching apports. [As in] "My old girlfriend had a couple of apports I tried to get my hands on."

How about 'infrasound'?

A frequency that's so low, we can't hear it, but human beings can feel it. It rattles our bones, makes us sick…

Everybody knows an OBE is an out of body experience. Tell us something we don't know.

To be sure, OBE is when the energy of the body carries the consciousness of the physical body. It results in astral projection — that's the visual manifestation of the energy of a person during an OBE.

Sometimes you talk so fast it seems like you're having a brain fragmentation. Is that anything like 'soul fragmentation'?

Ah-ha! That means "no" in professor speak. Soul fragmentation is when, during the process of reincarnation, the memories of past lives stay with a person. Another term for it is 'soul residue'.

While we're on the subject, what about an announcing dream?

Souls are assigned and this type of dream lets the expectant mother know when a soul is ready to be incarnated. Had my mother had an announcing dream about me, she might have thought twice about moving forward.

Parapsychology, the Study of:

Telepathy: The transfer of information on thoughts or feelings between individuals by means other than the five human senses.

Precognition: The perception of information about future places or events before they actually happen.

Clairvoyance: The obtaining of information about places or events at remote locations, by means unknown to current science.

Psychokinesis: The ability of the mind to affect time, space, matter or energy by means unknown to current science.

Reincarnation: The rebirth of a soul or other non-physical aspect of human consciousness in a new physical body following death.

Haunting: A phenomena often attributed to ghosts in association with places or items connected to the deceased in some manner.

What do you know about zombies.

Zombies are Earth souls put into corpses and usually controlled by voodoo priests. Zombies are rare indeed, but once, working a case with Melinda Gordon, I saw a 'dead man shopping'. Not a pretty picture, but clearly an example of what we're talking about here. And if you plan on encountering a zombie, I recommend a 'spirit jar'.

And that is?

A candle blessed by a Haitian voodoo shaman that will guide an Earth soul to it when lit.

Ever encountered a poltergeist?

Every morning when I walk into my bedroom closet to find something to wear… We're talking about the supernatural, though, aren't we? By the way, that's what my wife used to call some of the outfits I wear. Except now she's 'supernatural' 'cause she's a *ghost*… Where were we? Oh, right, poltergeist. A poltergeist is actually a supernatural event caused by human agents. Nine out of ten times it is a girl going through horrible trauma.

Can you tell us what an 'aura' is?

Come on! You don't know what an aura is? It's a gas ionization of moisture molecules around an organism. And ectoplasm is a form of bio-energy that is the by-product of psychic phenomena. And you can record all this electromagnetic activity with a device called an electromagnetometer. I own one. It rocks!

'Imprint haunting', is that something new?

No, no. Imprint hauntings have been around for centuries. It's basically Groundhog Day for ghosts. That's when a ghost is stuck in sort of a time-loop, doing the same thing over and over.

How about 'oppression'?

Now that's something I've never been accused of. Oppression, in relation to the spirit world, is when a ghost controls the body of a person without ever entering inside of it. The spirit does all its influencing from the outside.

Here's a tough one, 'spectral displacement'.

You're joking, right? Spectral displacement is an advanced iteration of the possession phenomenon where the visiting spirit doesn't control the host body's consciousness, but instead gives it the old heave-ho, creating what is called a displaced spirit.

Tell us something we don't know about Payne.

I *kill* at Ghost Charades. ☺

NED BANKS

"I know what you're thinking. You never should have taught me about ghosts, because now I'm seeing them everywhere."

U sually on a TV series, when a kid acts out it's because of family or friend issues, drug or alcohol problems, or teen angst. Not so in *Ghost Whisperer*. During Ned Banks' debut (played by **Tyler Patrick Jones**), in 'Love Still Won't Die', he acts out because of a haunting. A ghost has attached itself to Ned and is influencing him to shoplift Grateful Dead memorabilia from Same As It Never Was. Melinda nabs Ned. And the ghost! After getting to the root of the problem (and bonding with Ned's mom, Delia), Melinda agrees not to press charges. Instead, she crosses the ghost over, and cuts a deal with Ned — he gets Melinda's Deadhead collector's items in exchange for putting in hours at her shop.

The bonus for Ned comes when he witnesses Melinda doing the extraordinary — talking to the dead. The novelty of her gift wears off quickly for Ned, however, when he learns Melinda cannot see his father (who died three years earlier). Ned gets so angry, he threatens to reveal Melinda's secret. But Jim intervenes by bonding with Ned and becoming a role model for this young guy who's on the cusp of becoming a teenager.

In 'Dead to Rights', Ned makes up his mind he's going to participate in Melinda's spirit journey, so he tries to convince her to let him be her sounding-board, someone she can bounce spirit stuff off since he knows her secret. Uncomfortable that Ned knows way more about her abilities than his mom, Melinda shuts him down, but knows this is not the end of it.

On the home front, Ned and his mom struggle with coming to terms with his dad Charlie's death

and Ned growing up. In 'Speed Demon', Ned sneaks out of the house and hangs with a tough crowd that's involved with the "Midnight Circle", an illegal street-racing group that is being threatened by an angry spirit. When Melinda discovers what Ned's up to, she infiltrates the secretive group to protect Ned and give closure to the ghostly speed demon.

In 'Delia's First Ghost', the loss of Ned's father and Melinda's abilities collide. Charlie has not crossed over and is, in fact, haunting Ned. Melinda gets to the bottom of it, reuniting Ned, his mom and his dad so they can be together one last time before Charlie moves into the Light.

In 'Slam', **Christoph Sanders** steps into Ned's shoes at sixteen years old. Cast to play the older Ned because the writers needed to tackle more mature storylines, Christoph says, "My favorite aspect of Ned is that he's genuine. I think that's really important in a person. Having so much backstory on film made coming aboard easy in some ways and hard in others. Easy because I already have so much to work with, and hard because I'm already committed to all the choices that Ned has made in the past episodes."

Season three opens with Ned at a new high school. He enlists Melinda's help when he suspects

one of his classmates is being haunted. Unlike in 'Delia's First Ghost', Melinda asks permission from Ned's mom before involving him in her ghost investigation. Although fearful about Ned's participation, and still skeptical at her core, Delia gives the okay for Ned and Melinda to move forward together into the intersection of the living and the dead.

Christoph only has good things to say about his TV mom, played by Camryn Manheim: "Camryn is a wonderful woman, and an outstanding mom on and off the set. I think it's important to surround yourself with people who have something to teach, and Camryn fits that to a tee."

In addition to the new high school and encountering his first ghost, Ned's life in full-blown teendom is chock-full of other firsts — his first girlfriend (she's haunted by a menacing spirit), his first car accident (fender bender), and his first real face-off with his mom about becoming independent.

Out of all the episodes that he's done so far, Christoph says 'Home But Not Alone' is his favorite. "It was my second episode, so I felt more a part of the show, not like this was just going to be a one-time thing."

A one-time thing? Not by any stretch of the imagination, Christoph. Not a chance.

Q&A With Christoph Sanders
For such a young dude, you've been acting for a long time — how'd that happen?

FUN FACTS
- Ned finds out Melinda can see ghosts before Delia does — by eavesdropping.
- Ned and his dad used to build models together.
- Ned digs vinyl records.
- Ned completely trusts Melinda.
- Ned starts at a new school in season three.
- Ned has his first girlfriend — it makes mom uncomfortable.
- Ned plays on his high school basketball team, second string.
- Ned thinks Delia is over-protective — Jim and Melinda agree.

 66

Above:
Ned seeks advice from Melinda when he thinks his girlfriend might be haunted in 'Home But Not Alone'.

Opposite:
Ned is concerned about events at his new school in 'Slam'.

I grew up in Hendersonville, NC. When I was nine, I tried a theater acting class at the Flat Rock Playhouse, the State Theater of North Carolina, and really liked it. My first show in front of an audience was *A Christmas Carol* when I was ten. At twelve I got my first agent, and auditioned for film and TV for about four years before I got a job doing a series of commercials. After that, I decided that acting was what I really wanted to do for a living. I continued auditioning and doing as much theater as I could, and when I turned eighteen I graduated from a theater conservatory program that I had been involved in for four years. That summer I got cast in an independent film, during which I talked to a few people in the film and a friend already out in LA about the idea of moving there.

With everyone's help, I lined up a place to stay and got in contact with my now manager. The following January my family helped me move out to LA. I started auditioning almost as soon as I got here. I was fortunate enough to book a couple of small roles, and then in November of '07 I booked the returning and older role of Ned Banks.

How did you step into Ned's shoes?
I got a chance to watch a few episodes with the younger Ned before I started to film my first episode. I realized Ned's a good-hearted, smart guy, and I did my best to come up with a character that would fit that and still have some room to grow.

Ned's had a lot of growth already — where do you want it to go from here?
There are several directions that I would like to see Ned go — start getting more involved in helping Melinda with the ghosts, or... *(Grins)* maybe going to the dark side for a while. Who knows?

Is Ned anything like you, really?
Ned is a great guy, and I can only hope to be as good as he is most of the time. I like to think that I'm a pretty adventurous guy and I think the same of Ned — I like to camp and surf, but I think Ned would rather hunt down a ghost and search for clues.

How do you feel about ghosts?
Being from western North Carolina, I grew up hearing a lot of ghost stories, so I've always believed in the idea of spirits. Growing up I spent a few weeks out of the year at my grandfather's house, which is about six hours from Hendersonville in Roanoke Rapids, NC. It was a big house with a barn and several acres. At night, it was a spooky place. We would play with the ouija board, and we would always be hearing strange sounds when it was real quiet. I miss that place.

Anything else you wanna share about the spirit world?
I believe in the human ability to channel energy; as far as the use of cards and crystal balls, I'm not ruling them out, I just haven't been swayed one way or the other. I do think that there are forces in the world that have yet to be explained, which is extraordinary because it allows us all to form our own opinions on what it means.

BETH GORDON

"He gets to be the hero and I get to be the evil mother."

eth Gordon is one *tough* mother and her relationship with her daughter Melinda is rocky because of it. So for the part of Beth Gordon, we needed an actress who could play strong yet, beneath that, carry a vulnerability which would eventually surface. And visually, the actress had to resemble Jennifer Love Hewitt to sell the mother-daughter relationship. That was a pretty tall order. Because of her extensive body of work, **Anne Archer** was our first choice, but we couldn't imagine she would do a TV series. We were thrilled when Anne signed on to play Beth Gordon.

Anne says she joined *Ghost Whisperer* because "I thought the premise of the show was interesting and fun, and Jennifer was really quite lovely and it would be fun to work with her. Also, so many people mentioned they were hooked, completely hooked on the show."

Beth rejected Melinda's gift from when she was a child, and it made Melinda feel ashamed and embarrassed about communicating with the dead. What's so amazing is that Beth has the same gift. When Melinda discovers this in 'Melinda's First Ghost', it rocks the foundation of her world. She always believed her ability had skipped her mother's generation, coming from Grandma directly to her.

Melinda believed all her problems with her mother could be traced back to this specific rejection. When Melinda finally confronts her mother about it, Beth says, "I've never learned to deal with them, not the way your grandmother could, the way you do. I just can't stand to feel their pain, it stops me

68

cold. You feel their pain and you help them anyway."

In pushing the ghosts away, Beth pushed Melinda away too. This dysfunctional behavior is one of the reasons Melinda harbors concerns about having a child. She does not want to repeat her mother's mistakes.

In 'The Vanishing', Melinda awakens from a coma and no longer sees ghosts, so she turns to her mother for advice. Beth assures Melinda that her life is better off without spirits. Once again, she imparts a cynical life lesson to Melinda — she never told Melinda's dad about her gift, but he abandoned them both anyway.

Melinda's estranged father, Tom Gordon, is a persistent bone of contention between mother and daughter. When Melinda talks about him, Beth admonishes her to "stop romanticizing him, he doesn't deserve it."

In 'The Underneath', after receiving a message from Tom, Melinda tracks Beth down and confronts her. She tells her that spending her whole life denying she can see spirits has turned her life into a house of cards riddled with secrets. Beth's response? "You want the truth? You need to leave Grandview. It'll hurt you. It's not a good place for people like you and me." Melinda, however, insists she is not running away, not from what she can do and not from her home. The core difference between mother and daughter is embodied when Melinda observes, "The difference between you and me, I can't live with a lie." And Beth replies, bleakly, "You'd be surprised what you can learn to live with."

In her search for truth, Melinda digs deep into her family's history and is stunned at what she discovers — Beth lived in Grandview at one time and played a role in the death of a woman who resided there. With the help of an angry ghost, Melinda investigates the circumstances surrounding the death and realizes Beth was not responsible. Eventually, Melinda is able to make her mother understand the death was the result of an unpreventable accident.

Much of the theme that interconnects Beth and Melinda is how revelations can heal damaged relationships. In 'Stranglehold', Melinda discovers that her father, Tom Gordon, is still alive, and Paul Eastman, the man who is haunting her in her dreams, is dead. Melinda knows that somehow these two men are connected through her mother.

Above:
Anne Archer and Jennifer Love Hewitt on set between shooting scenes for 'The Underneath'.

When Melinda digs up the bones of Paul Eastman from the basement of a house in Grandview, it turns out the house was Melinda's childhood home. Beth finally admits to her daughter that she was in love with Paul Eastman — they were engaged to be married when he was wrongfully imprisoned for the murder of a young boy. Tom Gordon framed Paul Eastman for the murder while misleading Beth into believing he was searching for evidence to exonerate Paul. Tom's motivation? He had fallen in love with Beth and wanted Paul out of her life forever.

Finally, Beth reveals to Melinda the last and most important piece of the puzzle: Paul Eastman is Melinda's real father. Beth was pregnant with Melinda when Tom Gordon came into her life. She also believes that Paul died in a prison fire.

FUN FACTS
ɕ Beth Gordon hates Halloween.
ɕ Beth was jealous of Melinda's relationship with her mother.
ɕ Beth claims migraines when ghosts try to communicate with her.

When Melinda connects with Paul's spirit, she discovers one more truth — Paul did not die in the fire. He escaped, but when he showed up on Tom Gordon's doorstep to confront him about the past, Tom killed him and buried the body.

Bringing the dark family secrets that Beth Gordon harbored all those years into the light gives Melinda tremendous insight into her mother's character. And during a reunion of Melinda, Beth and Paul Eastman's spirit, Paul gives his daughter another new perspective on her mom. He says Beth always loved Melinda, put her first and tried to protect her. Before he crosses over, Beth asks Paul for forgiveness. Now that her hidden past has been exposed, her relationship with Melinda can be healed.

www.annearcher.com/

Q&A With Anne Archer

What is it like to play such a tough mother?
Great fun... Actors love to have something meatier to act!

How is it working with Jennifer Love Hewitt?
She is a doll — gracious, grounded, and a fine actress.

What is your favorite scene?
The first scene I shot in the series where Melinda

Below: Beth and Jim discuss Melinda's head injury in 'The Vanishing'.

CHARACTER TIMELINE

- Beth accidentally causes the death of a woman when she tries to use her gift.
- Beth is duped into marrying Tom Gordon.
- Beth hides the true identity of Melinda's father.
- Beth hides her gift from Melinda.
- Beth tries to protect Melinda but ends up alienating her.
- Beth finally tells the truth.
- Beth talks to Paul again.
- Beth reconciles with Melinda.

and I see each other after a number of years.

Do you believe in ghosts?
I certainly know we are a spirit and we inhabit a body.

Ever encounter one in real life?
I am afraid that has not happened to me.

Where would you like Beth and Melinda's relationship to go from here?
I would like to see them work together to help ghosts cross over.

GABRIEL RANCE

"We're blocking the light, Melinda; soon no one's gonna get through. These aren't your grandmother's ghosts any more."

gnacio **Serricchio**'s first *Ghost Whisperer* audition was for a one-episode guest star role as the Naked Ghost in 'Delia's First Ghost'. Because of the type of role he was auditioning for, we really got to *see* Ignacio. Afterwards, we talked about how well he plays mystery, what a great fan base he's got (he played Diego Alcazar on US daytime drama *General Hospital*), and of course, how gorgeous he is. It made much more sense to cast Ignacio in the reccurring role of Gabriel.

Starting in season two and continuing into season three, it is a slow reveal that Gabriel is Melinda's half-brother on her father's side of the family — and he's up to no good. Like Melinda, Gabriel can communicate with earthbound spirits, but he chooses to use his gift for a darker purpose. Ignacio loves playing the flip-side of Melinda. "Gabriel's 'dark' deeds contrast with Melinda's 'light' deeds," observes Ignacio. "If you don't have contrast all the time, you will lose the audience's interest. Having another character with the same powers as Melinda Gordon, but using them for evil, is the ultimate contrast." He adds, "Is it too obvious that I like working on *Ghost Whisperer* and want to come back? It's thrilling to experience evil, even if it's not real, because it opens your eyes to what happens in real life, how much power we have as humans to inflict pain and suffering. And, of course, as an actor, it's a challenge to control the dark side and never let it take over."

When Melinda first encounters Gabriel, she is

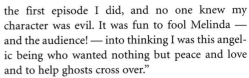

CHARACTER TIMELINE

- Gabriel is the illegitimate son of Tom Gordon.
- Gabriel was placed in an asylum because of his gift.
- Like Gabriel, his mom was put into an asylum because of her gift.
- Gabriel found out Melinda was his half-sister.
- Gabriel learned to hunt and collect souls, creating the family he never had.
- Gabriel's relationship with Tom fueled his hatred for Melinda.
- Gabriel's father dies.

thrilled to meet someone who shares the same abilities and she can't wait to trade stories about their experiences with the dead. Both Melinda and Gabriel have noticed a shift in the spirit world, as though they are getting stronger. But jealousy and resentment secretly fuel Gabriel's behavior toward Melinda. From his point of view, Melinda Gordon has lived a perfect life. (Little does he know!) Gabriel believes that while growing up she was surrounded by a warm, loving family — while he was raised in an insane asylum. Sadly, he was institutionalized because he talked to the dead.

In 'The Collector', Melinda is shocked to discover Gabriel is not crossing spirits over into the Light, but rather collecting them. When she confronts him, Gabriel says they're all getting ready for what's coming. Referring to Melinda's earlier observation about a shift in the spirit world, Gabriel says the earthbound spirits he's helping to collect are the ones who are blocking the Light. He threatens, "Soon, no one's going to get through."

Gabriel tells Melinda they are two sides of the same coin; he wants her to leave her life and partner up with him — together they'll be unstoppable. Horrified, Melinda flees, but returns to Gabriel's creepy house with Jim and Professor Payne. Although Gabriel is long gone, they search the house and are stunned to discover evidence that Gabriel has been stalking Melinda and her loved ones.

'The Collector' is Ignacio's favorite episode. "It's the first episode I did, and no one knew my character was evil. It was fun to fool Melinda — and the audience! — into thinking I was this angelic being who wanted nothing but peace and love and to help ghosts cross over."

Gabriel resurfaces throughout seasons two and three, conspiring with the dark side to put Melinda in peril. After his motives become more overt, Gabriel locks eyes with Melinda in 'The Gathering' and wickedly ticks off The Five Signs on his fingers — the fifth being "Death of a loved one".

"We all have a dark side, some very deep down and some are more connected to it on a daily basis," Ignacio explains. "My mother will tell you that I am a nice kid and I'd like to think I am, which makes playing a bad guy more fun. It gives me a chance to get away with anything without really hurting somebody. I can do things that I would never do as Ignacio."

www.facebook.com/profile.php?id=1328457328

www.tvguide.com/celebrities/ignacio-serricchio/240656

Q&A With Ignacio Serricchio

What direction would you like to see Gabriel take over the coming seasons?

I think Gabriel and Delia should hook up. *Kidding!* It would be very interesting if Gabriel pretends to be reformed by Melinda and once he gets close to her again, he uses one of his many evil spirits to take over Melinda's body and then she turns a little evil herself.

Can you give us the similarities between you and Gabriel? The differences?

The similarities between us are that we are both Aries and enjoy long walks on the beach. The differences are that I actually smile 24/7 and Gabriel is in dire need of one of my jokes.

What are your beliefs about the paranormal?

What I love about this show is that it gives people hope that there is something better waiting for us in the afterlife. The whole idea of spirits sticking around because they have unfinished business is almost a relief for those who have lost loved ones like myself.

Have you experienced any strange occurrences on the *Ghost Whisperer* sets?

One night I was walking back to my trailer and I

heard a noise coming out of another trailer. When I opened the door, there it was… Jay Mohr changing! Scariest sight ever. Thanks to that experience, I now believe in werewolves.

Do you believe in ghosts?
I've yet to see one, but other people say they have and I believe them.

Curses?
I've never been able to touch my toes with my mouth and I blame it on a guy who was doing yoga and I went up and tickled him, which made him fall. I think he put a curse on me.

Dream visits from spirits that have crossed over?
YES! YES! YES! My cousin and my uncle visit me every once in a while in my dreams and it makes me happy to see them, happy wherever they may be.

Angels?
I work with children with cancer who have more appreciation for life than anyone I've ever met. That's a big YES.

Karma?

Above:
Melinda has a dangerous encounter with Gabriel in 'Weight of What Was'

I've experienced it myself. That's why I try to be nice all the time and do not lie as much.

Reincarnation?
I hope so. I'm dying to come back as a monkey. ☺

FUN FACTS
- Gabriel is actually Melinda's step-brother, not her half-brother, because Tom Gordon is not her biological father.
- Gabriel's mother has the gift too.
- Gabriel does his father's bidding.
- Gabriel's mother lives in a halfway house.
- As a child, Gabriel's playmates were ghosts and he would cry when they left.
- Ignacio was born in Buenos Aires, Argentina.
- Ignacio is the complete opposite of the dark character he portrays.

MELINDA'S
SPIRIT GUIDE

SPIRIT SYMBOLISM

Although the main thrust of what happens on *Ghost Whisperer* from week to week is about Melinda Gordon and the spirits she encounters, the underpinnings of the journey are based on mythology and symbolism tied to the spirit world.

While watching *Ghost Whisperer*, you can catch glimpses of important symbols or hear Melinda and Professor Payne banter back and forth about glyphs. These mythological references are integral to the storytelling. Take the number '5', for example. Five is tethered to the spirit world because it corresponds with the fourth dimension. Five also represents the world of the living — it is the number of the human being (the human form makes the shape of a pentagon when arms and legs are outstretched). And the five-sided pentagon is considered perfection.

Five is a very powerful symbol indeed. Therefore, the message of "The Five Signs" that Melinda receives from the spirit world must be reckoned with. In 'The Night We Met', Melinda shares the five cryptic messages with Professor Payne. Payne explains the number five has significance in many religions and cultures: 5 is the unification of 2 (the feminine element) and 3 (the masculine element); the Pythagoreans considered five to be a symbol of marriage and synthesis; the hand has five digits; we have five senses; Christ had five wounds; there are the five pillars of piety in Islam.

In 'The Prophet', Payne tells Melinda that the first four visions she's had point to the fifth accident, which is yet to come. Unfortunately, they don't have a clue when or how the accident will happen. Melinda races against the clock to discover what the final accident will be so she can try to prevent it from happening.

www.fansofgw.com/claymation/

The Five Signs

1. The Death of a Dove: The dove is immortalized as a symbol for unconditional love and purity. The flip side is, doves are tied to the otherworld and death. Great misfortune is said to accompany the death of one of these graceful creatures.

In 'The Curse of the Ninth', Professor Payne explains to Melinda, "The death of a dove, symbolically speaking, indicates misfortune, and the death of a dove near someone's house means the impending death of someone in that house." The second reference to the dove is visual. In 'Free Fall', a dove slams into Melinda's bedroom window and drops to the porch below. Melinda mournfully wraps the dead dove in a red bandana, then goes back inside the house. When she returns minutes later, the dove is

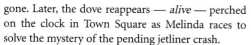

Right:
A bee flies in 'A Vicious Cycle'.
Opposite:
Melinda cradles a dead dove in 'Free Fall'.

gone. Later, the dove reappears — *alive* — perched on the clock in Town Square as Melinda races to solve the mystery of the pending jetliner crash.

Doves are considered messengers of departed souls that have come back to guide those soon to die. The dove Melinda found on her porch foreshadowed what was to come. The jetliner crashes outside Grandview and Melinda is inundated with lost souls looking for guidance. One of these spirits is Melinda's best friend Andrea, who died in the crash.

BEWARE...

...if a dove enters your home. It can mean either an imminent death or the arrival of an important message in the near future.

...if a dove taps on your window. It is an omen of the impending death of one of the house's occupants.

...if you hear the call of a dove while walking or riding downhill. Misfortune will follow.

2. The Bee: The bee is believed to be the sacred insect that bridges the natural world and the underworld. *Ghost Whisperer*'s opening title sequence features the bee because it symbolizes the soul, death and the release of a spirit.

In the last scene of 'A Vicious Cycle', a bee lands on the railing of Melinda's front porch. Droplets of blood from nowhere splash the bee. In 'Cat's Claw', Melinda is mesmerized by a bee that turns in a circle five times. The bee's death-dance takes place in a drop of blood. These strange bee sequences represent a soul trying to escape the mortal world, bypassing the Light, and traveling to the underworld. This is the journey Andrea's spirit embarked on until Melinda rescued it from the evil Romano. Other spirits on the same dark path are: Brandon ('Curse of the Ninth'), Randy ('The Cradle Will Rock') and Shane ('No Safe Place').

BEWARE...

...if a bee turns five times in a drop of blood. Your soul is destined for the dark side.

...if two bees are headbutting. A soul nearby is

up for grabs.

...if a bee flies. A soul will rise.

...if a bee vanishes. Sound the alarm — there's serious trouble at hand.

3. Death of a Loved One: In 'Dead to Rights', Melinda sees writing on Jim's back, "srom itcelid". The phrase is backwards and in Latin. Flipped, it reads "mors dilecti". Professor Payne translates the phrase into English as "Death of a loved one". The misdirect is that after reading this spirit message, Melinda looks at Jim, believing his fate is connected to the message. In hindsight, Professor Payne's translation suffers from a slight wrinkle. The Latin word *dilectio* translates to 'brotherly love', *amor* translates into 'romantic love'. Jim is most definitely Melinda's romantic love. Therefore, Jim is not in mortal danger.

In 'The Gathering', Melinda fulfills the prophecy herself by dying for a brief time. But five sensitives — children who survived near death experiences and operate at a higher consciousness — bring Melinda back from the dead.

BEWARE...

...if you discover writing on your back. The spirits are using you as a notepad to get messages through to the living.

4. The Dead Will Walk: In 'The Cradle Will Rock', this is the message that Randy, the ghost who refuses to cross over, gives Melinda. In the next episode, 'The Walk-In', a ghost possesses a corpse in order to

Did you know?
Since the words on Jim's back were written from the inside, the letters should be mirrored and appear from right to left instead of left to right. (Perhaps there is a deeper meaning here?)

attend a high school reunion. Clearly, the spirit world is getting stronger.

BEWARE…

…if you see a dead man hanging around looking for something to do. It's likely a 'walk-in', meaning a spirit has taken over a body that's been vacated by its soul.

5. When the Forgotten Return, Death Will Be Closer: In 'Children of Ghosts', Melinda discovers this message inside Cesar Milan's book. Then, in 'The Collector', ghosts from the past, including Reggie, Jared, Randy and Amy the flight attendant, return from the dead. Their spirits are being collected by Gabriel. He's helping the dark side build an "army of souls".

BEWARE…

…if you think someone is collecting souls. It's because that person wants to make the dead stronger than the living.

…if you see a dead man walking. It means the veil between the living and the dead is getting thinner.

The Number Five

In 'The Gathering', Melinda and Professor Payne discover the four disasters that they're investigating occurred on May 11, and they assume that the fifth will too. Each features the number five:

1. Rome, Italy, May 11, 2003. Bridge collapse kills 111, plus 2 on the ground. 1+1+1+2=5

2. Moscow, Russia, May 11, 2004. Subway tunnel collapse kills 32 people. 3+2=5

3. London, England, May 11, 2005. Ferry *Mary O'Connell* capsizes, killing 311. 3+1+1=5

4. Grandview, USA, May 11, 2006. Plane crash in Grandview kills 230. 2+3+0=5

They don't know what will happen or where the fifth event will be. Payne tells Melinda that the five children who survived the May 11 disasters have all been touched by the Light. This suggests the fifth accident will be disguised as something small but will have a huge effect on the world.

To Melinda's horror, the fifth accident hits close to home. The location: Grandview. The date: May 11, 2007. The circumstances: During a ceremony to honor those who died in the jet crash exactly one year earlier, a deadly storm blows in and causes Melinda to die. But disaster is circumvented when the five sensitives save Melinda by bringing her back from the dead. The children's near death experiences allowed them to foresee the future. This, coupled with their extraordinary pureness of spirit, is what saves Melinda from the prophecy of "The Five Signs".

Did You Know?
1. The number five formed the first counting process from which all else came.
2. The number five consists of two unequal parts, two and three. The diversity brings evil and misfortune.
3. Five is a circular number as it produces itself in its last digit when raised to its own power.
4. The number five symbolizes meditation, religion, versatility.
5. Pointing up, the five-pointed star depicts individuality, spiritual aspiration and education. Pointing down it represents witchcraft and is used in black magic.

Beetles and Cats

In ancient Egypt, the Scarab beetle was associated with change, transformation and resurrection. In the present day, the appearance of a beetle in a dream can represent different things, depending on the feeling it evokes in the dreamer. Masses of crawling black beetles will likely inspire fear, while a beautiful metallic-green beetle may be something to admire and wonder at. In regards to cats, they have been associated with religion and the spirit world since ancient times. In Ancient Egypt, cats symbolized beauty and fertility/birth.

In 'Woman of His Dreams', beetles and cats haunt Jim's dreams while Melinda is out of town. When she returns, Melinda and Professor Payne join forces to decipher the meaning behind what turns out to be Egyptian symbols sent from the spirit world. Payne explains that the beetle signifies the need for change to reach the next stage in one's life. And the cat represents the all-knowing who are mute, so they cannot influence decisions made by humans. After successfully putting together the pieces of this mystery, Melinda realizes the ghost of a beautiful model is sending these symbols to Jim as an SOS. She needs help saving her sister from a deadly lifestyle.

BEWARE...

...if you see a black cat crossing by moonlight. It means a deadly epidemic.

...if you are responsible for ending even one of

Below:
A distinctly uncuddly ghost cat in 'The Woman of His Dreams'.
Opposite:
Melinda receives a disturbing message in 'Dead To Rights'.

> **Did You Know?**
> In Greek mythology, the five (there's that crazy number again) rivers of Hades are Acheron (the river of sorrow), Cocytus (lamentation), Phlegethon (fire), Lethe (forgetfulness), and Styx (hate), which forms the boundary between the upper and lower worlds.

a cat's nine lives. You will be haunted by that cat for the rest of your life.

...if you hear the noise of alley cats in your dream. This is a warning to avoid an indiscreet acquaintance in your immediate circle.

...if you stand in the path of a scarab. The single-mindedness of a scarab beetle trying to overcome an obstacle has to be seen to be believed.

Sacred cats kept in sanctuaries in ancient Egypt were carefully attended to by priests who watched them day and night. The priests interpreted the cats' movements (a twitch, a yawn, a stretch) to foretell future events.

The River Styx

In Greek mythology, the River Styx formed the boundary between Earth and the underworld. The Styx was guarded by Phlegyas, who ferried souls from one side to the other.

In 'The Prophet', Professor Payne explains a vision that Melinda had about a ferry. He believes this ferry and the water it's on symbolizes the River Styx. Translation: Melinda's vision is about the ferrying of souls to the afterlife.

BEWARE...

...if you enter the Greek underworld by crossing the river Acheron. The far side of the river is guarded by Cerberus, the three-headed dog of Hades.

Bridges

In many cultures, bridges represent the journey of the dead to the otherworld. By the same token, bridges are associated with the return of the dead to the land of the living. One can travel across a bridge from one land mass to another, but while on the bridge, the traveler is neither in one place or the other.

In 'The Prophet', Professor Payne explains to Melinda that bridges can symbolize the connecting of two worlds

BEWARE…

…if crossing bridges in the living world. Like all crossing places, they are dangerous, and many are known to be haunted.

…if crossing bridges in the spirit world. It is the final test, and can lead to paradise or an underworld with punishment and dissolution.

Tunnels

Tunnels are perceived as transitional places, like bridges — a place between two worlds. This is particularly relevant to near death experiences (NDE), where once the spirit leaves the body it passes through a psychic tunnel that ends in another world.

In 'Weight of What Was', 'All Ghosts Lead to Grandview', 'The Gravesitter', and 'Pater Familias', Melinda navigates the tunnels beneath Grandview. She does so to help ghosts that have unfinished business tied to the underworld. Payne tells Melinda that tunnels are classic symbolism for crossing over.

BEWARE…

…if you have the sensation of moving through a bright tunnel of light or passage way. You are having a near death experience.

…if you have the sensation of being pulled or drawn through a dark tunnel at great speed. You are dying.

…if you are given a life review, then reach a border or boundary. You are about to cross over.

…if you have a sense of being dead. You most likely are.

Mirrors

Many cultures believe that mirrors are a veil between our world and the other. Mirrors are considered portals.

'Don't Try This At Home' introduces mirrors into the *Ghost Whisperer* mythology. Payne explains to Melinda that Queen Elizabeth I had her own personal magician who used a mirror to scribe the future. The Greeks thought that any reflective surface would do — the unsuspecting

Did You Know?

"In dreams, a mirror can symbolize the power of the unconscious to 'mirror' the individual objectively — giving him a view of himself that he may never have had before."
— Jung, 218

could even be pulled into the underworld by evil spirits lurking beneath water. Thinking this through helps Melinda realize she must outwit a scary ghost who's doing her haunting through the looking glass.

BEWARE…

…if a mirror has no reflection. It means nothingness.

…if you are gazing at your own reflection. You could lose your soul in the process.

…if you know of an urban legend that is played out in front of a mirror. Forget about it!

Flies

Flies have often been used in mythology and literature to represent agents of death and decay. In contemporary times, flies are used primarily to introduce elements of horror.

'Horror Show' introduces a number of mythological symbols used in notorious horror films, but the use of flies is probably the most historically significant (remember the fly sequence with the priest in *The Amityville Horror*?). When a swarm of flies causes a young college co-ed to go crashing through the plate glass door of Same As It Never Was, Melinda and Professor Payne add up the clues and discover a ghost is creating his horror film — from the grave!

BEWARE…

…if your basement is blanketed in flies. You either need a ghost buster or an exterminator. Or both!

…if you don't have the budget to CGI the required number of flies into your next film. Real flies stick to any surface, including *you*!

…if you dream of flies. The spirit world may be trying to tell you that you've surrounded yourself with unreliable, untrustworthy people.

OPENING TITLE SEQUENCE

et's start with the title itself. All through the development season that spawned *Ghost Whisperer*, we were encouraged to come up with a more specific title for the project. At the time, *Ghost Whisperer* was simply the 'working title'. We put together lists of hundreds and hundreds of titles — everything from *R.I.P.* and *Nearly Departed* to *Melinda Is Nuts* (Kidding! But the challenge was making us nuts).

We even held a contest with our cast, crew and staff during the making of the pilot to see if anyone could top *Ghost Whisperer*. Nothing quite fit. When we walked out on the floor of Carnegie Hall minutes before President and CEO of CBS Les Moonves and President of CBS Entertainment Nina Tassler announced CBS's 2005 Fall Schedule, we whispered to our CBS exec settling into her seat across the aisle, "What's it gonna be?" She nodded firmly, "*Ghost Whisperer*. It's perfect." We were thrilled. When we got back to LA, we burned our title lists in effigy.

Because *Ghost Whisperer* was such an unusual TV series for CBS when it launched in fall 2005, we

believed it paramount that the opening titles embrace the show's uniqueness. Rather than creating the traditional TV titles with footage featuring each main character/actor intercut with fancy graphics and showy transitions, we went for art manipulated with ghostly movement. And, since the main character, Melinda Gordon, was youthful, we felt we had a shot at connecting with a younger demographic. Therefore, giving the opening titles the vibe of a CD cover, made a lot of sense.

To brand the show *Ghost Whisperer* (very important in twenty-first century TV producing), we used the title sequence to stake a claim in the mythology of the spirit world.

Erin Sarofsky and her very talented team at Digital Kitchen in Chicago came aboard to work with us. They used Maggie Taylor's unique art as a base. Each frame Maggie creates is a digital photo collage. Starting with objects she finds on eBay, in flea markets, and in her own environment, Maggie uses a flatbed scanner, Adobe Photoshop and an Iris printer to produce images of surprising beauty and emotional impact. We love Maggie's style, and the images she creates are rich in metaphor, implying that the world the viewer is entering speaks to a transcendent life experience. Maggie's images helped us tap into the relationships between life, death, spirits and the symbolism of bees.

Bees were chosen as the iconic symbol in *Ghost Whisperer*'s title sequence because, in ancient times, bees were considered a symbol of the soul, of death and the release of a spirit. When bees fly, a soul will rise. (For everything you could ever want to know about bee mythology, check out the beautifully written *The Secret Life of Bees* by Sue Monk Kidd.)

When you look closely at our opening titles, you'll notice the background in each frame is *gently* moving and evolving, and the transitions are magical.

leaves on Melinda's dress rustle. The background of the frame is dead — a grove of trees that are bare.

Panel 4 (opposite top): This sequence is tied to Melinda's identity — she's married and she has an antique store. In the series, some of the antiques that come into Same As It Never Was have ghosts attached to them, which is represented by the period male and female suits in the frame. Positioning the suits side by side alludes to the partnership of their marriage. Notice that Jennifer Love Hewitt's name casts a shadow because she's from the world of the living. Conversely, the antique clothes, representing spirits, have no shadows. (In the TV series, the ghosts never cast shadows. Got any idea how

Panel 1 (above): Start on the sky with moving clouds — pull back to reveal —

Panel 2 (right): An unconventional cemetery with Melinda standing in the foreground, because what Melinda does is unconventional. First one spirit rises, then another, and then a fire, which symbolizes energy, an important factor in the ghost world. A bee rises from the grass and passes through frame which transitions to —

Panel 3 (below): About growth. Melinda is torn between two worlds, the world of the living and the world of the dead. The foreground is alive with richly colored flowers blooming. The vine on the right side grows before your very eyes and the

JENNIFER LOVE ❀ HEWITT

we do that?) The floating feather symbolizes ghostly antics that take place in the world of the living.

Panel 5 (left and below): A woman holds an egg, which represents beginning a piece of business. Her ghost is holding the bird, symbolizing a completed piece of business. This ties to the premise of the series — ghosts have unfinished business which Melinda helps them complete. The ghost has a slight moving energy, the bird winks, the dark clouds roll out, the woman disappears off the chair and butterfly wings drop from the sky. Footsteps on the ground travel through frame as it begins to rain.

Though one of the most beautiful and complex sequences, this was deleted from the titles in season

DAVID ✦ CONRAD

fire in the lower corner burns. This is a clue to the man's unfinished business. The people in the background moving very fast represent the living. As the fire starts to die out, we push in on the photo of the old woman.

Panel 8 (bottom): This represents the underworld (which is explored in season three). The camera tracks up the ladder from darkness into light — into the world of the living.

Panel 9 (opposite top): In the middle of a beautiful field is a suitcase. The suitcase symbolizes Melinda's journey each week. It cracks open and a bee (representing a spirit) flies out. The bee moves towards the camera as if it is entering the

one because it tipped the scales on making them "too period", and because they were running too long.

The house represents Melinda and Jim's home. The light in the window is a beacon for spirits.

Panel 6 (above): Through the rain and clouds, Melinda and a child are revealed. The child is a ghost. Melinda crosses him over —

Panel 7 (right): Reveals a man holding a picture. He represents an earthbound spirit in search of unfinished business. The reason you can't see his face is because, like many earthbound spirits, he's confused — he does not know who he is. The picture he's holding flaps slowly back and forth as the

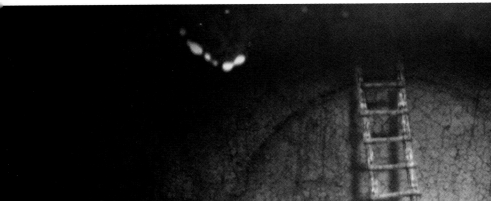

CREATED BY JOHN GRAY

she added the head of a young girl from a nineteenth century black and white photo. Maggie then scanned images of real carpenter bees, found in her studio, into her computer, duplicating them and transforming them into a dress-shaped swarm. She added the background, which was sourced from a photo of an Irish bog. Then she added the flower and tweaked the overall colors. (For more amazing insider tips check out *Maggie Taylor's Landscape of Dreams* by Amy Standen.)

Panels 11 (p81) and 12 (below): The bee settles on the *Ghost Whisperer* logo and the gorgeous Jennifer Love Hewitt is revealed. Ⓑ

www.fansofgw.com/grid/mythology/

85))

viewer's world.

The art piece used as the foundation of the suitcase sequence is titled Strange Case. Very appropriate for *Ghost Whisperer* because each ghost story is a strange case. Strange but wonderful.

Panel 10 (above): The bee enters frame and lands on a beautiful girl blanketed in bees. Like Melinda Gordon, this girl has no fear. She signifies hope, closure, and peace. In the final beat of this sequence, a different bee leaves her and flies toward camera. This symbolizes a spirit crossing over into the Light.

The body is a picture Maggie Taylor took of herself. She added a mottled texture to age it. Next,

THE LOST

THE LOST

now what we love most about the lost? Their randomness. These earthbound spirits are aberrant — you never know when they're going to pop-up.

Ghost Whisperer's aberrant ghosts started out as experiments. Then, when they began to get traction with fans, we fed the frenzy. Whenever the lost ghosts make an appearance in the show, the audience senses they're being tipped off in some way that Melinda's world is about to get scorched by negative ghost energy. They couldn't be more right.

Frankly speaking, almost every ghost that appears in *Ghost Whisperer* starts out as a member of the lost brigade. But through Melinda's great work of figuring out what's keeping these spirits earthbound, most of the lost souls join the departed by crossing into the Light. But every once in a while, one of the lost will get sucked into the dark side and continue to wander the world of the living, wreaking havoc wherever they go.

The ghosts featured in this section have not crossed over. And since they are still hanging around, we were able to get one of them to describe how he came to the realization that he was no longer in the world of the living.

I suddenly found myself standing by the road, staring down at my own body, lying by my feet. For a second, everything was eerie... quiet. Then I realized I was no longer me, but something separate. I didn't feel any pain and, believe it or not, I felt no confusion either. I was just there, staring down at myself, completely emotionless. In an instant, my reasoning kicked

in. I wasn't afraid, not in the least bit — but I was curious. Then anxiety began to creep up on me. I thought, What should I do? I dropped to my knees to get a better look at myself. My body was face up on the gravel and appeared almost serene, as if I were asleep. The one thing I did find disturbing was the blood.

I thought, How can this be? Why am I suddenly divided into two people? *When I looked around, there were shapes in the distance, human shapes that were out of focus. They were standing in a bright Light, but they didn't seem to be able to communicate with me. By the same token, the people gathering around my lifeless body on the road seemed oblivious as I shouted and waved, as if I wasn't trying to communicate with them. It was the oddest sensation.*

I glanced back at my body. It was like watching another person who looked just like me... As everyone stared at the body, it struck me. I'm dead. I must be in the state that follows death. Now what? *And the next thing I knew, I felt a dizzying race through space and time that took a nanosecond. Well, it felt like a second, but truthfully, since the accident, I've lost all sense of time and space. Suddenly, I found myself in Grandview. I'm not sure how. But you know the saying, "All things happen for a reason"? Well, I'm sure there's a good reason why I missed the Light. Now, if you'll excuse me, I've got some unfinished business to take care of. If I could only remember what it is...*

Keep your eyes peeled because you haven't seen the last of this ghost — or any of the others featured here... 👻

www.fansofgw.com/ghostvision/

TOM GORDON

 rom the very beginning of *Ghost Whisperer*, small clues are laid into the storytelling about how Melinda's father abandoning her when she was a child had a profound impact on her life. Though his identity is kept secret through season one, he gradually comes back into Melinda's life, with dramatic consequences.

In 'Drowned Lives', viewers learn that Melinda's father came in and out of her life when she was very young, and she was clearly torn between her mother and father. Just before he stopped coming to see Melinda, he gave her a locket that was very meaningful to both of them.

His name is finally revealed in 'A Grave Matter', when Melinda confronts her anger about her dad leaving her. She almost Googles him, but then has second thoughts, not sure she wants to open that Pandora's box. But it's taken out of her hands when, in the season two finale, Tom appears to her during her near death experience. He gives her a message: there is a darkness in her and she should not fight it. Just before Melinda is brought back to life, her father also tells her that she has a brother —Gabriel.

Season three brings a myriad of revelations about Tom Gordon. The last time Melinda saw him, she was eleven years old. Because of a vision she had, Melinda believes her father is dead, and she insists to her mother, who doesn't want anything to do with him, that her father is trying to give her a message from beyond the grave.

At various times, Melinda confides in Jim that she used to have fantasies that her dad had been kidnapped by spies and they burned the letters he was trying to send to her. Then he'd finally escaped and fought his way back to her. Melinda supplies a significant insight into her feelings about her father when she says, "If he would've just come back, I would've believed anything he said to me and I could have forgiven him for anything — I wanted my dad."

In a dream about her childhood, Melinda, as a young girl, sees Tom outside her bedroom window. Before he says he has to go, she has a chance to explain how much she's missed him, and asks if he missed her too. His reply: "Every day." Melinda is comforted by her father's response but she wants to know why he left, why he won't help her now. Tom assures her she will understand someday, but she'll have to find the answer for herself. When she reminds him that he used to give her riddles as a child, Tom complies by giving her a clue.

Melinda's strange, and estranged, family begins to unravel when she discovers her mother and father once lived in Grandview. Angered by this lie by omission, she confronts her mother. When Beth can't understand how Melinda knows, she explains that her dad led her to it. Beth's animosity towards Tom is reignited when Melinda tells her mother that he has been helping her. Beth coldly responds, "I see. He gets to be the hero and I get to be the evil mother."

In 'Don't Try This at Home', Melinda makes up her mind to be more proactive in trying to find information on her father. When Gabriel unexpectedly shows up at her house, he claims Tom has been haunting his dreams as well, and they need to work

 89

together to find their father. To Melinda's surprise, Gabriel hands Melinda an envelope full of memorabilia about Tom. Gabriel assures Melinda this is the proof she needs to believe the truth of what he says. Inside the envelope there are family pictures, which include Tom Gordon, a few of her personal belongings and a small picture that fits into the locket that Tom gave Melinda as a child.

Later, when Melinda is trapped underground, Tom Gordon appears to her as a spirit and reveals that her great great great grandmother is the ghost Melinda has been trying to help. Tom tells Melinda that he led her to the underworld. It's important to him that she sees the subterranean town for herself, to discover the truth about Grandview, why she's here, the power she has, the danger she's in — every bit of it. Tom also claims that Melinda is the reason her parents split; unlike Beth, Tom wanted Melinda to embrace her gift. Tom appears to be a sweet, sensitive soul. He has to leave, but promises to find Mel soon. With that he's gone.

However, a somewhat more manipulative version of Tom is revealed when he meets with Gabriel, telling his son, "Next time I tell you to help me with your sister, try not to kill her instead." When a bicycle drives right through Tom, Gabriel reminds him that he can't keep "this" up for much longer. Tom mysteriously responds that he won't have to, "It's already in motion." He predicts that Melinda will soon be with them, "She's a smart girl, she'll make the right choice, because if she doesn't…"

In 'Deadbeat Dads', the detective Melinda hired to find information on her father uncovers a strange trail. In 1989, Tom Gordon left Melinda, and in 1991,

he cashed out his IRA, savings, everything and went back to the woman in Colorado that he had a son with. Other than that, all the detective finds is a record of Tom working as a short-order cook at a diner in Arizona — an unexpected discovery considering that Tom had been an attorney. There is no death record for Tom Gordon and the John Does can't be narrowed down without dental records. But a final clue comes out of the blue when the detective is possessed by an unidentified spirit and writes a cryptic series of numbers on the case file.

When Payne and Melinda discuss the possibility that Tom is on the run, Payne immediately recognizes the number sequence from the case folder as a 1979 court case. Melinda pulls the file and finds out that it was a case that Tom prosecuted against a man named Paul Eastman — a little boy was found dead in the woods and Paul Eastman was blamed for his death. Tom sent him to prison, where Paul escaped during a fire. Melinda is convinced that Paul is out for revenge against Tom.

Melinda has a vision flashing back to her childhood of pools of blood and bloody footprints in the hall. When she wakes up, Tom Gordon is there. She asks him about the man in the mask she's been seeing in her visions, but Tom assures her it's only a dream and warns her that she's in danger. He tells her not to trust anyone, not even him. He's pulled away before he can say anymore.

Later, Melinda finally has a flesh and blood encounter with an injured Tom in Gabriel's hotel room. Melinda is floored that he is actually alive, and she has a lot of questions, but finds him very evasive. When she warns her dad that she thinks a ghost named Paul Eastman has been possessing his body, he trades a look with Gabriel. Both men claim they don't know what Melinda is talking about. Melinda insists she's right and that Tom's displaced spirit has been visiting her. She warns that Paul Eastman is after Tom and that she thinks he wants to hurt other children as well. Suspicious of their denials, Melinda decides to try a different tack — she secretly steals a bus ticket in Tom's possession. Before she leaves, she asks why he came back now. Tom claims he heard his daughter was looking for him and decided it was time to stop hiding from his mistakes, time to start being a father again. He hopes they can have a second chance, and Melinda admits she'd like that too.

 90

But when Melinda investigates the bus ticket, she finds it was issued to a fake name. Is Tom in danger? Is that why he's lying?

Back at the hotel, Gabriel and Tom argue. Tom is unhappy that Melinda is asking about Paul Eastman.

When Gabriel leaves his father alone in the room, Tom finds a pistol hidden in his suitcase. He is immediately frightened and tells the apparently-empty room, "I won't let you do this to me."

Meanwhile, Payne tells Melinda that he doesn't trust Tom, and his suspicions are reinforced when Tom calls Melinda and cancels lunch with a lie about having tests down at the hospital, though the caller ID shows he's at his hotel. Melinda soon figures out that Paul Eastman is dead, that he was innocent, and that he wants revenge on Tom for his wrongful conviction. She races to the hotel just in time to hear the gunshot. Inside the room, Tom has been struggling against an unseen force that makes him put the gun to his head and pull the trigger.

In the hospital, as Melinda cries by her seriously-injured father's bedside, she tells him that she

doesn't know what to think of him, but she still wants to try and make their relationship work. A single tear falls from Tom's eye.

Paul Eastman's spirit leads Melinda to the discovery of his body in the basement of a Grandview house, and Jim quickly determines that it was Melinda's childhood home. But Melinda's mother is still being uncooperative, though she warns her daughter that Tom is a very bad man.

Back with Jim, Melinda says that she has a bad feeling, like when she was a kid and her dad kept disappointing her. Following this emotional admission from his distraught wife, Jim confronts the now conscious Tom at the hospital, telling him that he wishes he had never taken another breath, that he just brings Mel pain. After Jim threatens him, Tom gives his version of the events that led to the death of Paul Eastman, insisting it was self-defense. Paul escaped from prison, showed up at the house to hurt Tom, Beth and Melinda, so Tom had no choice. He didn't call the police because he didn't want to put Melinda through the media scrutiny.

Back at home, Jim relates Tom's story to his wife, prompting her to confront her father too. Melinda pleads with Tom to talk to Paul's spirit so they can have closure. Tom agrees to meet Melinda at the shop that night and tell her everything she wants to know.

When Melinda arrives home, Beth finally reveals the whole truth about her relationships with Tom *and* Paul Eastman; that she only married Tom after Paul killed another inmate in prison and she knew he'd never be released. Then Beth tells Melinda the final, most shocking secret, that Tom is not her real father — Paul Eastman is!

Angry and upset, thinking that Beth is lying, Melinda goes to Tom for answers and he takes her to her childhood home to help her remember. But Melinda's memories reveal that Tom didn't kill Paul in self-defense. It was murder. Tom gloats that he also hired someone to kill Paul in prison, in fact the inmate that Paul killed, in self-defense, guaranteeing he would never be freed. Melinda is stunned by how wrong she was about Tom Gordon. And now that Melinda has remembered the truth, Tom has to kill her. As he begins to strangle her, she calls for her real father to help her. Suddenly, Tom's body is possessed by Paul Eastman, who saves Melinda — by throwing Tom Gordon to his death.

GRANDVIEW'S GHOSTS

IDE BRIM HAT MAN & LAUGHING MAN

Laughing Man is an 'aberrant ghost', one not tied to any specific episodic story arc — so he can pop up anywhere, anytime. Laughing Man was introduced in the second episode of season one as a one-time shot. When we timed the script for 'Mended Hearts', it came in short, so we needed to add one additional scene to bring the script to time. Not wanting to disrupt the story structure that was already in place, John Gray wrote a scene that he tagged onto the tail end of the episode. The scene opened on Melinda buying tickets at the Little Broadway Theatre in Grandview's Town Square. As Melinda turns and heads back toward her antique store, a bus passes through frame. The pass-by reveals a very buttoned down-looking man in a blue suit. The man is laughing as he makes eye contact with Melinda. Then suddenly, another bus passes by and Laughing Man disappears from frame. The most significant thing about this particular ghost is, of course, the sound of his laughter. We worked with the Smart Sound team to create a unique, evil-sounding laugh that plays creepy, other-worldly, and most important, haunts you long after the episode is over.

Every Monday, following the Friday-night broadcast of *Ghost Whisperer*, we issue a report called The Monitor. We traverse the Internet,

collecting bits of buzz from *Ghost Whisperer* fans and analyze it in a report. The goal is to keep our fingers on the pulse of how 'Ghosties', as we call them, are responding to the show. (Now you know for sure that your online comments are getting traction with the creative team at *Ghost Whisperer*. So keep that buzz coming!)

After 'Mended Hearts' aired, we combed through The Monitor buzz and were stunned at how much traction Laughing Man had gotten online over the weekend. Fans were absolutely intrigued. They wanted to know if he was an omen of some kind and if he was haunting Melinda. Most important, everyone wanted to know if Laughing Man would be back. Immediately, we went online and started moving Laughing Man around, making sure that he haunted every *Ghost Whisperer*-related fan site on the web.

Laughing Man appears next in the 'Undead Comic', where he hooks up with another dark spirit — Wide Brim Hat Man (as everyone fondly refers to him, because of his silhouette). Together they warn Melinda, "We have business with you," before they are sucked into pitch black. All that's left is Laughing Man's haunting laughter, which washes over Melinda at the end of the episode.

In the following episode, 'Friendly Neighborhood Ghost', Wide Brim appears fleetingly in the second-story window of a haunted neighborhood house. He turns towards Melinda, then disappears.

All that remains is laughter, echoing around her.

The dark duo's first physical interaction with Melinda is in 'Fury'. Both ghosts appear in the teaser. They're in a crowd at the Town Square ceremony that Melinda is attending. They suck air — literally. It's a clue to what's to come with the lead ghost in this episode.

Laughing Man takes a breather in 'Melinda's First Ghost', but Wide Brim Hat Man haunts Melinda's Same As It Never Was antique shop. This is the first time one of these two has invaded Melinda's personal turf. Translation: These spirits are on a specific mission tied to her. At this point on *Ghost Whisperer*, Wide Brim is only shown in silhouette. The audience *never* sees his face — primarily because we were on an intense search to find just the right actor for the role.

At the end of 'The Vanishing' teaser, the sound of Laughing Man's laugh reverberates as Melinda drives down the road, but the ghost is nowhere in sight. Later, Laughing Man haunts Melinda's dream, laughing so loudly she wakes up in a cold sweat. At the end of the episode, the camera pans to the rooftop of Melinda and Jim's house where Wide Brim and Laughing Man are perched in the moonlight. An omen for more darkness to come from these bad boys…

By the Monday morning following the broadcast of 'The Vanishing', there was all kinds of wild online fan speculation about these two mysterious ghosts. Most importantly, everyone was ready for a deeper, more complex relationship with the two spirits from the dark side. Fortunately, the next two episodes did exactly that.

'Free Fall' brings Melinda face to face with the haunting duo when the temperature in her house drops dramatically. As she wipes frost from her window, Wide Brim is revealed pacing across the street. Then suddenly his body language becomes spasmodic, in a ghostly way. He whooshes up to the window, stunning Melinda. Then vanishes. Later in the episode, as Melinda is heading back to the store from Village Java, she sees Laughing Man standing across the street. He pulls out a pocket watch and checks the time, looks back at her, laughs, then disappears. The drop in temperature and the clock are two clues that propel viewers into the mystery of the disaster that strikes in the finale

Above:
Wide Brim Hat Man makes an appearance at Same As It Never Was in 'Melinda's First Ghost'.

of season one, 'The One'. The cold is tied to the *cause* of the disaster and the pocket-watch is tied to its *location*.

In 'The One', Wide Brim is revealed walking along the edge of the jetliner crash site on the outskirts of Grandview. Melinda is there helping the community deal with the aftermath of the crash and trying to figure out how the spirit world is tied into this horrible disaster. Wide Brim tips his hat in Melinda's direction, his image goes to negative, he smiles at her, but his face has become a frightening skull. Then, he's gone! As Melinda talks to a crash investigator, Wide Brim lays claim to the spirits of the crash victims, saying, "They're mine." Of course, she's the only one who hears him.

Later, Melinda approaches what appears to be the ghost of the airplane pilot, but when he turns towards Melinda, it's actually Laughing Man. Melinda asks where his "friend" is, and Laughing

Man responds by laughing and pointing to Wide Brim, who is walking towards the woods with the ghosts of four passengers. True to his word, he is taking possession of the first casualties of the crash.

During a debriefing of the victims' families, Wide Brim's face is revealed for the first time. He is a pale man in his forties with piercing cruel eyes (played by the very talented **John Walcutt** — we finally found our man). Wide Brim offers Melinda a deal — the souls of those who perished in the plane crash for her soul. This is an offer Melinda does not take lightly. She questions whether she is worthy to reject such a trade. But Jim reminds her that, in her lifetime, there will be many more spirits who will need her help.

The depth of Wide Brim's ruthlessness is revealed during a flashback to the jetliner crash. Wide Brim had a hand in causing the disaster. Clearly, the spirit world is getting stronger, and dark forces from the other side are starting to impact the world of the living in a profound way. It's something Melinda can't ignore.

In the final and most powerful moment of season one, Wide Brim intervenes when the spirits of the crash victims blame the pilot for their deaths. Wide Brim tells the spirits that they should stay earthbound, and reminds them they've all

Above:
Laughing Man.
Opposite:
Bleeding Man
watches Melinda in
'Love Still Won't
Die'.

94

committed very human acts of jealousy, lying, cheating… They will be judged on those acts once they go into the Light. The lost ghost thrives on the anger and hatred; it energizes him for his showdown with Melinda. But Melinda musters all her will-power and convinces most of the crash victims to defy Wide Brim Hat Man and move beyond the fear that he's planted in them, helping them to cross over into the Light. The positive energy of so many spirits crossing over diminishes Wide Brim's power. He disappears, but not without hijacking a few lost souls.

The final appearance of Wide Brim is in the premiere episode of season two, when Melinda battles for Andrea's soul. Having received a call from the now deceased Andrea, Melinda goes to meet her friend at the antique store during a horrible thunderstorm. Andrea is terrified because she is surrounded by "dark beings". Then, just as she's about to describe what it's like on the other side, the door to the store locks, and Melinda sees Wide Brim standing beside Andrea. The incident turns out to be a nightmare, but when Melinda wakes and goes downstairs into her living room, Andrea's ghost is there. Andrea says "Romano" as Wide Brim appears next to her. Finally, Melinda knows his name. And there's another, secret message from the spirit world embedded in the scene — "She belongs to me."

Romano tells Melinda that he intends to have Andrea's soul as well as hers. And he drops a clue: he was a teacher. Melinda goes to Rockland University to confer with Professor Rick Payne, and together they begin piecing together Romano's history. In the world of the dead, Wide Brim is a

Sucked Into Pitch Black
To achieve the scene in 'Undead Comic', Wide Brim and Laughing Man actually stood on an oversized skateboard that production grips yanked away. The two 'ghost' actors had to try and keep their balance on the moving skateboard while a giant Ritter fan blasted air at them. Lots of choreography and focus required for this effect!

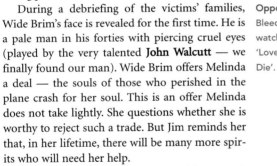

collector of souls, gathering strength from the spirits he takes. When he was alive, Romano was a powerful cult leader who convinced his congregation to commit a mass suicide along with him.

After a number of encounters with Romano in which he tries to frighten her off, Melinda succeeds in reconnecting with Andrea's ghost. Melinda tells her that everything Romano is promising is a lie. Suddenly, Wide Brim lashes out, scrawling bizarre warnings in blood all over the walls. Determined to save her best friend's soul, and not give over more energy to Romano, Melinda convinces Andrea that she will not be punished for the feelings of envy that she had toward her brother. Melinda is able to unite Andrea with her brother and heal their pain, leaving Romano too weak to come into Same As It Never Was where the three are together. As Andrea crosses over, Romano fades, getting weaker and weaker until he vanishes.

Will Romano and Laughing Man be back for a command performance? Only the spirit world knows for sure (and perhaps the *Ghost Whisperer* writing room).

www.fansofgw.com/grid/laughingman/

BLEEDING MAN

This lost spirit intersected Melinda's world in the episode 'Love Still Won't Die', mysteriously

appearing in the very last shot of the final scene. As Melinda walks down the street, Bleeding Man steps into frame, back to camera, blood dripping off his right hand.

Bleeding Man next appears in our Halloween episode, 'A Grave Matter'. Melinda is sitting at her desk and blood drips onto it. She looks up at the ceiling — there's nothing there. Then, at the end of the episode, while all the kids are trick or treating, Bleeding Man joins in on the action. As you know, ghosts get their energy from the living and there's nothing more charged up than a bunch of kids on Halloween. Bleeding Man warns, "Five signs, death will come." Only Melinda can see and hear him — Melinda and *you*, of course.

In 'A Vicious Cycle', Bleeding Man drops a clue about the five signs when a mysterious bee lands on Melinda's porch railing and is hit with drops of blood. The bloody bee flies away.

Once again blood droplets hint of Bleeding Man's presence in 'The Night We Met'. While Payne is visiting Melinda at her store, she notices blood dripping on the shop counter next to her hand. Melinda looks up to see where the blood's coming from. Payne sees nothing and looks at her like she's nuts. When Melinda looks back down at her hand, the blood is gone!

In 'Cat's Claw', Melinda spots a bee that turns in a circle five times while in a drop of blood. Anyone who delves into the spirit world knows that in ancient times, bees were considered a symbol of the soul, of death and the release of a spirit (*see* Spirit Symbolism, p77). When bees fly, a soul will rise — this bee flies.

Melinda finds herself trying to summon Bleeding Man in 'The Reckoning', in the hope that she will get a clue or two about what the writing means on Jim's back. She ponders what Bleeding Man means when he says there will be death following the five signs, and she fears the five signs mean someone close to her will die. Jim reassures her that Bleeding Man is probably just one of the many confused ghosts that pass through Melinda's life. But is he right?

Although Bleeding Man makes limited appearances in season two, much of Melinda's story arc deals with her unraveling the mystery of the five signs that Bleeding Man set up. Eventually,

Melinda discovers that the five signs are tied to five accidents, which are tied to children known as 'sensitives'. Ultimately, Bleeding Man's cryptic warning about "Death of a loved one" plays out as meaning Melinda herself.

HOMER

Melinda first meets Homer the ghost dog at the haunted inn in the episode 'Lost Boys'. The canine perished along with his three young companions during an orphanage fire on the property in 1955. But when the earthbound boys cross over into the Light, Homer doesn't follow. To Melinda's surprise, the loveable-pooch spirit attaches himself to her and settles in at the Gordon/Clancy crib. Melinda knows full well Homer needs to go into the Light, but she's not quite sure how to make it happen.

Although Jim can't see Homer, he tracks him around the house by random bouncing balls and how Melinda lights up as she plays with the adorable ghost. This is the only time Jim has encouraged Melinda to hang on to an earthbound spirit. As Jim say, "No crossing the dog over. I like him; I like the way he makes you smile." (Jim's not alone. There was a huge online buzz from fans following the introduction of Homer. Everyone wants to know how ghost rules apply to pets. It works with animals the same way it works with people, according to *Ghost Whisperer*'s technical consultant, Mary Ann Winkowski.)

Unfortunately, when Delia's dog, Bob, visits the antique store, he begins acting up, growling and barking at thin air. Or so Delia *thinks*. Melinda knows better — Homer the friendly ghost dog has attached himself to Bob the friendly living dog! Bob's poor behavior is a direct result of Homer. Like most things ghost-related, Melinda has to try and keep the unusual canine duo off Delia's radar.

Fortunately for all, world-renowned Dog Whisperer Cesar Milan is in Grandview for a book signing. Melinda, Delia and Bob — along with Homer — go to Cesar for a consultation. Cesar concludes Bob is being territorial, but is puzzled because there are no other dogs in sight. To get his advice on crossing Homer into the Light, Melinda conjures up a hypothetical situation. Cesar tells Melinda that to get a dog to go where she wants it to, she needs to "change your energy to make the dog comfortable

Above:
Homer the friendly ghost dog.
Opposite:
Scott, the unfriendly archives ghost.

96

going into the room." So the ghost whisperer acts on the Dog Whisperer's advice and…

Well, you should watch 'Children of Ghosts' to find out what happens, so if you find you're being haunted by the spirit of a pet, you'll know what to do.

SCOTT

Scott, the archives ghost, is introduced in the 'The Underneath'. When Melinda goes into the dusty archives located in the basement of City Hall to dig up information on a ghost-related incident, she encounters Scott, who's a much livelier presence than the guy who actually works there.

At first Scott seems like a friendly, helpful ghost who knows where all bodies are buried, shall we say. But without warning, he turns on Melinda. Scott is linked to the spirits on the dark side. He tells Melinda to leave and never come back. Later that night, when Melinda does return, Scott and his ghostly pals rock out — the lights go out and spirit arms reach through the walls, trying to pull Melinda in. While one angry spirit lurking behind the wall has Melinda in a choke-hold, Scott tells her, "He is angry with you. He wants to take you down with him." Defiantly, Melinda tells Scott that she doesn't take orders from ghosts. Scott threatens, "You know, there are a lot of very angry people down here. I think it's time I let you meet them." Melinda comes back at him with all the power she can muster — "I'm not afraid of you!" Scott leans in close and whispers in her ear, "You will be." Suddenly, the arms release Melinda, and the lights flicker on. Scott is gone.

Melinda bumps into Scott down in the archives once again in 'Don't Try This At Home'. Though he warns Melinda that she had better leave the dead to rest, she pushes Scott until finally he tells her what he knows about the real Bloody Mary, who happened to live in Grandview (*see* Ghostly Urban Legends, p104). Melinda leaves the archives and, perhaps surprisingly, Scott's information turns out to be invaluable in solving the Bloody Mary ghost mystery.

In 'Weight of What Was', Scott intercepts Melinda and Professor Payne in the archives and tells Melinda that it is his job to make sure what's buried stays that way. Literally. So when Melinda finds a passage into the underground tunnels beneath Grandview, Scott immediately manifests himself to Melinda's evil brother Gabriel, summoning him to the archives. Together, Scott and Gabriel watch Melinda pass through a secret door into the tunnels. The door slams shut, trapping Melinda. Scott and Gabriel then remove all traces of Melinda having been in the archives that night so that Jim, Payne and Delia won't know what's happened to her. In the tunnels, there is

a cave-in — you better believe Scott had something to do with this hellish action.

As far as we know, Scott is still lurking in the creaky basement looking forward to more visits from Melinda. This lost spirit does get lonely down there. So if you find yourself in a basement, and a presence brushes against your body, it could be Scott and he may have brought along some of his pals, "the others". BEWARE!
www.fansofgw.com/flashlight/

G-MAN

Interestingly, we launched the lost ghost dubbed "G-Man" on the Internet and then introduced him into the TV series. The G-Man, a.k.a. Robert Hall, born on February 5, 1928, in Norfolk, Virginia, was the only child of John and Ellen Hall. Hall senior was a mechanic working at the port of Norfolk in post World War I peacetime. Shortly after Hall senior died in an undisclosed accident in 1939, Ellen moved herself and her young son back to her hometown of White Oak, Maryland. Having excelled in his classes and graduated with honors from the local high school, Hall was admitted to Georgetown University, where he continued his education. After graduation in 1950, not much is known about Hall until he resurfaced as a member of the Secret Service team assigned to protect President John F. Kennedy. One can only assume that those 'lost years' can be attributed to his training for this phase of his career. On November 22, 1963, Hall was sighted along the Kennedy motorcade route, at the corner of Main and Houston in Dallas, Texas, at the moment President Kennedy was assassinated. According to several eyewitness accounts, Hall was shot and killed in the melee. There is no record of an official autopsy. Hall was buried in a closed-casket ceremony in December 1963. Forty-two years later, Hall was sighted again — this time on the set of *Ghost Whisperer* episode 'On the Wings of a Dove'. (Take a look at this episode — G-Man is haunting three different scenes. Can you find him? Clue: This spirit is drawn to dangerous situations.) Clearly, G-Man has a story to tell about what went down in Dallas on that fateful day, but he needs someone who can talk to the dead.
www.fansofgw.com/grid/gman/

MELINDA'S
SPIRIT GUIDE

GHOSTLY SIGHTS & SOUNDS

Spirit Photography

Spirits make themselves known in many ways. They move things, slam doors, and even ring doorbells. They also make lots of sounds like walking, howling and breathing. Next time you experience one or more of these, grab a camera, snap some pictures, and see if you're able to capture ghost energy. This is called 'spirit photography'. It is the capturing of unexplained supernatural images using a camera. What takes place between the photographer and the spirit is 'electronic spirit communication'. The link between electromagnetic energies and machines is made when someone is looking to communicate with the spirit world. These spirit-related images are not visible to the naked eye without the aid of a camera. That is unless you have specific abilities to communicate with the other side.

Sometimes ghost energy appears in photographs in the form of spirit orbs (*see* Recognizing Ghosts, p25). Another way that spirit energy appears in photographs is as a foggy-looking mass known as ectoplasmic mists. If you look carefully at the mist-like image captured on camera, you may detect a human shape that could represent the image of the ghost that is present.

Find examples of both types of spirit photography here: www.fansofgw.com/ghostgallery/

When doing spirit photography, you need to be focused (not just the camera, but you as well). To create a welcoming environment for your subject — the ghost — you may want to hold a very detailed, deliberate visualization of what you see, and then keep your mind fixed on it. Then get ready to shoot.

The technical requirements for spirit photography are very simple. You can use a film camera or a digital camera, it doesn't matter. No special lenses or shutter speeds are necessary.

Experience and intuition are a major part of spirit photography. As James Van Praagh says, "Everyone has intuition" — so you're equipped! You will not only begin to recognize what you have captured on film as spiritual in nature, but you will sense the presence of spirits around you as you snap the photos.

One final suggestion: Save the negatives or digital film cartridges of your spirit photography. If you capture some amazingly incredible shots, you may someday need to produce the originals for authentication. Better safe than sorry.

Ghost Whisperer has had its share of spirit photography. At various times throughout production and post production, we have discovered a number of ghostly images in our dailies.

When we shot a car accident on the Universal backlot in the dead (no pun intended) of night in 'On the Wings of a Dove', we were both there as our stunt coordinator, Alex Daniels, flipped the vehicle that Jim Clancy was riding in. We personally knew every single crew member and actor on set that night and saw every second of the action. The next day when we looked at dailies, we discovered an unidentified one-legged man walking toward the wreck and away from camera. One-Legged Man Ghost (as we affectionately dubbed him) appeared in two frames of the film. Then he vanished!

Another time, we were shooting late at night at the Chicken Ranch, a dilapidated-looking house on the backlot which was originally built for the movie *The Best Little Whorehouse in Texas*. John 'Ziggy' Ziegler, our special effects supervisor, created a fire for a scene where three little boys are trapped in a burning orphanage. As Ziggy ignited the sweeping staircase, we watched the monitor as the actors did their work. When we looked at dailies the next day, we were astounded to discover an old woman walking down that staircase, headed directly into the fire.

The old woman was not one of our actors or crew — we had never seen her before.

Jennifer Love Hewitt took both film segments with her when she made an appearance on *The Tyra Banks Show*. Everyone was fascinated by Love's show-and-tell.

www.ugo.com/channels/filmTv/features/ghostwhisper erchronicles/hauntings-4.asp

Electronic Voice Phenomenon

In 'Voices', the ghost of a desperate mother reaches out from beyond the grave through 'white noise' on radios, telephones, televisions and computers to summon Melinda's help. What's fascinating about this occurrence is the spirit voices are heard by the living as well. It's known as electronic voice phenomena (EVP).

EVP is static noise that transmits from electronic equipment and has snatches of voices. These voices (which anyone can hear if they listen closely) are interpreted by paranormal investigators as words or short phrases uttered by ghosts.

Recording EVP has become a technique mastered by those who contact the souls of dead loved ones or during ghost hunting activities. Portable digital voice recorders are the technology used by EVP investigators to do this. Since the recording devices used to hear EVP are very susceptible to radio frequency (RF) contamination, it is a challenge to record pure

Above:
A camera can pick up the spirits surrounding Melinda.

EVP. There can be no noise in the audio circuits of the device used to produce the EVP. One method of recording is to use two recorders, one to produce EVP and one to record it; the device producing the voices from the dead should have a different quality audio circuitry than the device recording the voices, since the person recording the spirit voices relies on noise heard from the poorer-quality instrument to generate the EVP.

In the complex arena of EVP, *Ghost Whisperer* has received great guidance from the American Association of Electronic Voice Phenomena (AA-EVP; www.aaevp.com). This nonprofit organization, whose mission it is to increase awareness of EVP and to teach standardized methods for capturing it, has shared some of their actual EVP recordings with us. We feature them in the 'Voices' opening teaser. Since 1976, AA-EVP has made hundreds of recordings of messages from deceased friends, relatives, and other individuals. To hear, go to:
www.fansofgw.com/grid/evp/
to sample 'authentic' ghost voices the AA-EVP downloaded from white noise mixed with voices we created. Can you figure out which are authentic voices of the dead?

One more thing — the next time you're annoyed because your radio or cell phone spouts white noise, listen closely. Ahh... Closer yet... Are those spirit voices you're hearing?

HAUNTED OBJECTS & PEOPLE

he Underworld

In mythologies, cultures and religions around the world, the 'underworld' refers to any place in which dead souls go. It is known as that realm of the afterlife that is anything but heavenly.

In *Ghost Whisperer*, Melinda Gordon discovers that the underworld is literally beneath her feet; her beloved town of Grandview was built on top of a secret subterranean town that has trapped many of the lost sprits she is trying to help.

Actually there are a number of underground cities and tunnels throughout the world which have been covered up by new cities and towns built over them, including London, England; Edinburgh, Scotland; New York, NY; Atlanta, GA; Ventura, CA; Seattle, WA, and Donora, PA, hometown of Kim Moses.

www.fansofgw.com/flashlight/

Dream Visits From the Spirit Realm

As you may know, Melinda has had many 'dream visits' from the other side, particularly from her grandmother who, even though she's passed, has maintained a very strong connection to Melinda. In dreams, Grandma visits, giving Melinda advice and cryptic clues to help her solve ghost-related mysteries or deal with what's going on in her personal life. One of the best examples of how Grandma advises Melinda in a dream visit is in 'The Gathering'. She tells Melinda how to deal with forces from the dark side. And an example of Grandma giving Melinda clues in family matters plays prominently in 'Melinda's First Ghost', when Melinda gains insight into her relationship with her mom through a dream visit with Grandma.

According to our technical consultant, Mary Ann Winkowski, "Once people cross over into the Light they can come back and visit the living, but it is usually through dreams. These dreams can be interactive experiences that give us an opportunity to have a conversation with the people who've passed." Mary Ann assures us, "It is even possible to bring our loved ones to us in our dreams." To do this, she suggests, "Create a mantra that you say when you lay down to go to sleep, calling to the loved one, saying that you will dream about them tonight. Repeat this over and over again until you fall asleep."

What if they don't visit the night you do your mantra? Mary Ann recommends that you continue the practice the next night, and keep repeating it until you are visited. She says usually spirits that have crossed over don't visit you for at least the first six months after they've gone into the Light. And people who have not crossed over do not come to us in our dreams. Mary Ann says a good indication that someone has not crossed over is if no one is dreaming of them.

Visions

A spirit-related vision is something seen in, or as if in a dream or trance. Visions generally have more clarity than dreams, but traditionally fewer psychological connotations. In 'The Ghost Within', Melinda envisions the ghost's house assembling around her. Comparatively speaking, in 'The Vanishing', Melinda is taunted in her dream by the metaphor of a tiger leaping at her. The house vision gives Melinda specific details of the ghost story she is investigating. The tiger dream implies her personal life is under siege in some way and gives her a clue to the mystery she is solving.

There are three types of visions: corporeal, imaginative, intellectual. A corporeal vision is a supernatural manifestation of an object to the eyes of the human body, or it can be a sensation that is

so powerful, the person having the vision experiences it as if they are truly seeing it. An imaginative vision is experiencing the vision without the aid of a physical organ; the vision is experienced in the mind and not through the eyes. An intellectual vision is perceiving the object without a sensible image — the object known exceeds the range of the understanding. A good example of this is perceiving the essence of the soul, where the intellectual vision takes place in the pure understanding, and not in the reasoning faculty.

If you're experiencing visions, the spirit world may be trying to tell you something. Pay attention!

www.fansofgw.com/darkmelinda/scariestmoments.mov

Spirit Possession

This is when a spirit takes control of a human body, resulting in noticeable changes in behavior and attitude. It is believed that people with physical illnesses or weak minds are more likely to be possessed by ghosts. Some people even believe that up to thirty percent of the world's population may suffer from spirit possession!

Most victims of spirit possession don't remember anything that happens to them while being possessed. In other cases the possessed individual can stop breathing while they are in this state. It is sometimes called 'black energy'. Spirits use black energy to possess the individual (as in 'Fury'). When this occurs, there is no control by the ghosts over the mind and intellect of the targeted person — the ghost is controlling the physicality of the person but has not succeeded in merging with the person's consciousness.

There have been possessions in which the host has even spoken languages they had no knowledge of previously, including ancient obsolete tongues, or expertly played musical instruments with no prior training. Once the person is disconnected from the possessing spirit, the host has no recollection of the language or musical instruments.

Season four on *Ghost Whisperer* promises a major storyline on possession.

www.fansofgw.com/grid/fridaythe13th/

Walk-In

A type of possession. A walk-in occurs when the

Above:
Melinda has a
vision in 'The
Ghost Within'.

soul departs the body and immediately a new soul steps in to replace it. A typical walk-in is similar to a near death experience, involving a person who is gravely injured, ill, incapacitated (i.e. in a coma), has experienced suicide or deep emotional trauma, or seems to have died but then recovers.

After recovering, the behavior of the walk-in individual may be extremely different from previously established patterns of behavior (e.g. identifying oneself by a different name, speaking in an unfamiliar language). Ordinarily, the walk-in individual has no memory of events prior to this, including the walk-in event itself.

'The Walk-In' episode is a good example of how this unusual spirit-related event works. (Stand by, because there's more to come on walk-ins in the *Ghost Whisperer* world.)

www.livingnightmare-gw.blogspot.com/

Reincarnation

The literal translation of 'reincarnation' is 'to be made flesh again'. It is believed by religions and mythologies of many cultures throughout the world that some essential part of a living being survives death to be reborn in a new body. When reincarnation occurs, a new personality is developed during each life in the physical world, but some part of the self remains constant throughout the successive lives. A powerful example of this is in 'Deja Boo', when a spirit struggles with the possibility that he might have to endure another lifetime of torment, but this time it could be as the child of Melinda and Jim.

GHOSTLY URBAN LEGENDS

host Handprints

There is an urban legend about a school bus filled with children that stalled on train tracks in southwestern Pennsylvania. According to local lore, everyone on the bus was killed by an oncoming freight train. The ghosts of the children from that accident are reported to haunt train tracks throughout the United States, protecting others from their horrible fate.

When a vehicle stalls on train tracks at exactly the time of the school bus accident, the wind picks up and the stalled vehicle miraculously rolls off the rails, saving the frightened passengers in the vehicle from being crushed by an oncoming train. When the shaken passengers examine the exterior of their vehicle, child-size handprints can be seen on the back bumper. As the wind dies down, the handprints disappear.

Check out *Ghost Whisperer*'s 'The Crossing' for connections to this urban legend.

Bloody Mary

According to the *Ghost Whisperer* interpretation of this ghostly urban legend, in 'Don't Try This At Home', Mary was a real girl who lived in Grandview. Accidentally buried alive by her parents, when Mary awoke in the coffin underground, she rang a bell outside (its rope was tied to her finger) to summon help. But her father had sedated her grieving mother and fallen asleep himself. The next morning, when he found the bell overturned, he frantically dug up the grave and found his daughter — dead, with eyes fixed in terror, hands covered in blood. Bloody Mary had tried to claw her way out of the coffin.

Bloody Mary is a ghost who appears in the mirror if you chant "Bloody Mary" three times in the dark while standing alone in front of a mirror. If you successfully summon Bloody Mary, she will either scare you to death or pull you through the mirror into the dark side. Don't try this alone!
www.rubloodymary.com

Vanishing Hitchhiker

The vanishing hitchhiker reveals herself as a beautiful girl to truckers driving solo cross-country late at night. The hitchhiker usually hints at the driver's imminent misfortune. When the driver looks over at his beautiful passenger and discovers to his horror that she has transformed into the Grim Reaper, the

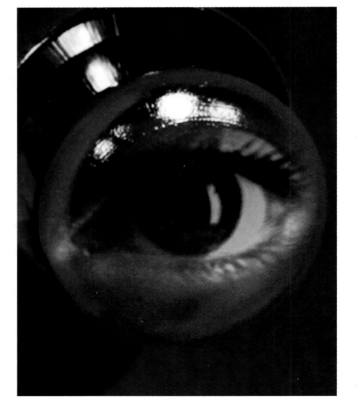

driver is so shocked he crashes his truck. Stephen King, in his short story *Riding the Bullet*, did a variation of this urban legend where a man picks up a young hitchhiker who tells the driver of his mother's upcoming death and subsequently disappears. *Ghost Whisperer*'s version of the vanishing hitchhiker is played out in 'Speed Demon'.

Biker's Bell

A motorcyclists' urban legend. As the legend goes, evil road spirits haunt motorcyclists, causing mechanical problems with their bikes. A special bell, known as a 'Biker's Bell', is used as a spirit 'trap' (they are drawn into the bell's hollow center), then the constant ringing of the bell drives the spirits mad. Insane, they drop to the ground, creating a pothole where they land on the road. The bell's potency is doubled when given to a biker by a friend or loved one.

Ghost on the Line

This is truly an unforgettable urban legend, told at slumber parties everywhere. As the tale goes, a teenage girl is hired by a young couple to babysit their two small children while they go out for dinner. After she puts the children to bed and sits down to watch late-night TV, her cell phone rings,

Above:

Melinda calls Bloody Mary in a mirror.

Opposite:

In *Ghost Whisperer*, Bloody Mary can appear in any reflective surface.

startling the half-asleep teen. When she answers it, she hears heavy breathing and a ghostly male voice telling her that he's "coming to get her." Unnerved, the girl slams the phone down and dismisses it as a prank call.

Fifteen minutes later, the phone rings again. When she answers it, the voice tells her he's closer. Frightened, the babysitter calls the police. The police say it's probably just a prank call but they're happy to trace the next call if she can keep him on the phone as long as possible.

When the phone rings again and the babysitter answers it, the voice tells her he has come to get her. Unnerved, she starts upstairs to check on the children, but before she can, the phone rings again and caller I.D. indicates it's the police. They tell her to get out of the house *now*. The man is calling from an upstairs phone.

The babysitter runs from the house as the police arrive. The windows are sealed and the doors are locked, but the children are found upstairs murdered with an axe.

This scene has been played out in movies numerous times. The 1979 movie *When a Stranger Calls* and its 1993 sequel, *When a Stranger Calls Back*, gives more than a nod to this haunting urban legend.

THE DEPARTED

THE DEPARTED

et's face it, once you're born into this world, the only absolute in life is that someday you will die. Everything else is up for grabs.

Most people's biggest fear is that once they die, *it's over*. They will never be with their loved ones again, never get another chance to speak with them. What if that's not the case? What if death is just one of the many stops along the way? And what if the white light that Melinda Gordon helps earthbound spirits cross into truly is a portal into the spiritual dimension of the everlasting? And what if, once you've crossed over to the other side, you realize it's not the end of the trail, but instead the journey continues on? That's a much better scenario, don't you think?

Once you die, according to *Ghost Whisperer*'s paranormal investigator Mary Ann Winkowski, you are at a crossroads. You can choose either to go into the Light or stay earthbound until you've tied up all your loose ends. This choice, according to Mary Ann, is of free will. If you decide to remain earthbound, you're on your own to figure out what's keeping you here and how to deal with it. If you're lucky, you'll hook up with a ghost whisperer to help you handle your business. And if you choose to go into the Light immediately after death, what awaits you? According to medium James Van Praagh, "The spirit world is made up of thousands of levels, and spirits gravitate to particular levels depending on their soul's evolution."

Translation — the journey continues.

But what about the 'departed' part of this scenario? What exactly happens when you die? It's one of the greatest questions of life. Finding out is easy, reporting back is the challenge. One thing is certain, once you're dead, there's nobody 'home' — your body is vacated. Van Praagh explains the separation of body and spirit as being "like moving, only without all the bother of packing. You move into a new neighborhood; it takes getting used to, but you're the same when you arrive."

Until you make the proverbial "move", we suggest you enjoy life without worrying about the 'after' bit, because in good time, bad luck or genetics will hand you the answer to "What is it like to die?" That's what has happened to some of *Ghost Whisperer*'s most beloved characters. Their departure from the world of the living kicked off their journey as spirits, each with a unique story. Andrea Moreno, Melinda's best friend in the world of the living, ran into some very bad luck. A case of 'wrong place, wrong time' when she died in a jetliner crash, suddenly, Andrea found herself operating from the other side, lost and confused. Conversely, Rockland University blogger Justin Yates had become more and more confused due to illness toward the end of his young life. Death gave Justin clarity.

For more about *Ghost Whisperer*'s departed, read on and move forward into the unknown. ☺
www.fansofgw.com/grid/cemeterygame/

ANDREA MORENO

hen we were casting for the character of Andrea Moreno, we knew as soon as we looked at **Aisha Tyler**'s reel that it was a perfect match of material to actor. Aisha had TV series experience in drama and comedy (remember her run in *Friends*?), *and* she had that 'pop' that we were looking for. The bonus was that Aisha does stand-up, so we knew she would be fun to have on set. We were right — she's a blast! Andrea (and Aisha) got the opportunity to show her comedic chops in 'Undead Comic', when she takes to the stage for open mic night at a comedy club. Aisha approached this scene like a Vegas club date, of which she's done many. She was hysterical.

Aisha says she took the role of Andrea because the character is "observant, smart, snarky, loyal, and loving. Best of all, Love and I hit it off great on set and developed a real-life friendship!"

When we started the series, Andrea was slated to be Melinda's best friend in life and confidant on the ghost front. Therefore, the relationship between these two characters needed to play as real and connected. In the first year, the on-camera chemistry between Aisha and Love happened so quickly and naturally that the storytelling was able to advance the relationship almost immediately. As a result, in 'Mended Hearts', Melinda and Andrea become business partners in the beloved Same As It Never Was antique store.

Prior to moving to Grandview, Andrea gave up her job as an assistant DA in New York City to start a new life. Her brother, Mitch, a high-powered real

estate investor/developer in the city is married to a beautiful model named Maya. Both of Andrea's parents are deceased, which comes into play at the end of season one.

At the start of the series, Andrea and Mitch try to overcome their differences and re-establish a relationship that is strained by the past. Mitch even buys a second house in Grandview so he can expand his business and spend more time with his sister. Although tempted, Andrea turns down his offer to move into his Grandview house and instead keeps the apartment in Town Square. Truth is, she's crazy about her cozy place just steps from her favorite haunts: Lento's, the antique shop and Village Java.

Several hauntings occur in Andrea's building, one of which takes place in the apartment above her, when the introverted tenant loses the love of her life in a triathlon accident. Even closer to home is the haunting Andrea experiences when she's tormented by a colleague from her past. And in the season two premiere, a spirit vandal scrawls bloody messages all over the walls of her living room, leaving Melinda and Mitch to decipher what it all means.

As season one moves forward, Andrea and Melinda grow so close they consider themselves sisters. Melinda never hesitates to share her ghost dealings with Andrea, and Andrea finds the parallel universe of the dead and all its ghost rules absolutely fascinating. Fact is, the first time Melinda tells Andrea about her gift, Andrea doesn't doubt it for a second. She thinks it's the coolest

courage when a spirit attaches itself to her and, with Melinda's support, she helps save the life of the spirit's brother. This is as personal as it gets between friends — until a new development kick's Andrea and Melinda's friendship into high gear. In a strange twist of fate, Andrea gets a hint of impending doom when she and Melinda visit a psychic in a traveling carnival. The psychic foresees Andrea's brother Mitch surrounded by tears and pain. Andrea believes this premonition is the fore-telling of doom for her sibling.

In the season one finale, the psychic's prediction serves as the catalyst for Andrea to drive to Mitch's apartment when she believes he's a passenger on a doomed jetliner. It seems that Mitch has died when he appears alongside Andrea after the crash, but then Mitch *walks right through* Andrea's spirit essense. Mitch didn't catch the flight and was out of harm's way, but the crashing jet crushed Andrea as she was driving to her brother's place.

Melinda is devastated and feels partially respon-sible for Andrea's death. She wonders if she hadn't involved Andrea in the spirit world, would this still have been her fate? But there's work to be done for the ghost whisperer. Melinda must get to the bot-tom of Andrea and Mitch's unfinished business so that she can help Andrea cross over.

Two years earlier, when their father died, Mitch was angry at Andrea because she wasn't there for him. As retribution, he withheld a message for her

thing she's ever heard. For Andrea, the ghost world is a bonus to working in the antique shop. Given how Melinda's been ostracized throughout her life because of her abilities, Andrea's acceptance and support makes her feel *safe*.

Regardless of how menacing the spirits may be, Andrea always maintains her sense of humor and support. In 'Hope and Mercy', when a spiteful spir-it causes upheaval in the shop, Andrea tells Melinda, "What's a malevolent spirit or two between friends." And when Melinda's ex-best friend Lexie surfaces unexpectedly, in 'Wings of a Dove', Andrea is fiercely protective of Melinda.

In 'Dead Man's Ridge', we see Andrea's true

Opposite top: Andrea and her BFF in 'Ghost Bride'.

Opposite bottom: Andrea gets to show her comedic chops in 'Undead Comic'.

that their father had relayed on his deathbed. With Melinda's help, Mitch discloses that their father was proud of her and he wasn't angry that she wasn't there when he died. He loved Andrea very much.

In turn, Andrea needs Mitch's forgiveness. When she realized it was *she* who was killed in the crash and not Mitch, for one split-second Andrea wished their fates had been reversed. The guilt from this single thought cracked open the door for Romano to enter into Andrea's presence. The dark spirit plays on Andrea's shame to keep her from crossing into the Light. Romano convinces Andrea what waits for her on the other side is judgment. By bringing Andrea and Mitch together to forgive each other, Melinda is able to guide Andrea peacefully into the Light.

In the last stage of post production on series television, there is a sound mix session where music, loop-lines and sound effects are finalized. At the end of the mix session on this episode, we looked around the room, and everybody — from the technicians to the executive producers — was weeping. Saying goodbye to Andrea was very heartfelt for all of us. ✍

LOVED ONES

MARY ANN

Melinda's relationship with her Grandma (**June Squibb**) is probably the single most important relationship of her life — other than that with her husband Jim, of course. It's so important that for every episode of the first two seasons, *Ghost Whisperer* starts out with Melinda explaining who she is and how she communicates with earthbound spirits. The first images of this powerful sequence (in production,

they call this a 'saga sell') are of Melinda as a frightened child at a funeral home, being encouraged by Grandma to not be afraid of the dead.

Grandma and Melinda are kindred spirits — they have the same gift. Both can see and talk to earthbound spirits. Through acts of love and patience, Grandma taught Melinda from a very young age to cherish and develop her abilities. This is in direct contradiction to Melinda's mother, Beth, who has the same gift as her mother and daughter, but tries to push it away every chance she gets.

Melinda's Grandma died in a nursing home when Melinda was a teenager. It was a devastating loss to Melinda, because ever since she was a child, Grandma had mentored and supported her. Melinda's encounters with Grandma are always during visions, in which her spirit reaches out to guide Melinda, or in flashbacks, when Melinda recalls an important memory. The fun of the flashbacks is that the audience gets to go back in time and watch Melinda hone her skills as a young ghost whisperer under Grandma's guidance. In 'All Roads Lead to Grandview', Melinda has a memory flashback of how Grandma taught her to filter out the cacophony of spirit voices so she can focus on the one voice she really needs to hear.

One of the most striking situations involving Grandma's spirit occurs in 'The Vanishing' after Melinda injures her head and slips into a coma. In a dramatic out of body experience, Grandma tries to help Melinda into the Light, but Melinda suddenly has a revelation that she's not ready to leave

Jim. (To make it appear as though Melinda is in limbo, Jennifer Love Hewitt, in a gorgeous billowing red dress, was perched on a giant rotating turntable with a Ritter fan aimed at her.)

Several times through the series, Grandma gives Melinda a warning or slips her an unexpected clue. In 'The Gathering', Grandma does both: she warns Melinda "they" are going to come for her, and advises her why she shouldn't be afraid — "You must protect the balance."

The most valuable advice grandma gives Melinda is also the most universal, "Just listen with your heart."

TESSA LUCAS

In 'Weight of What Was', more of Melinda's family lineage is revealed when a confused and fearful ghost leads Melinda to the secrets buried beneath Grandview. She tells Melinda that "they" told her she was crazy and took her baby. Before Melinda can find out more, voices bellow up from the underworld and Tessa (**Amy Acker**), the lost ghost, is sucked into the wall.

As Melinda continues to encounter Tessa's spirit over and over, it becomes obvious the ghost is guilt-ridden and must find her child. The next revelation is that Tessa could see spirits when she was one of the living. As it turns out, Tessa died along with many other citizens of Grandview in 1848, when a disease caused people to go insane. Melinda shares this information with Tessa, and together they unravel the rest of the mystery. Old Grandview was buried to cover up that horrible tragedy — and a new Grandview was built over the original town.

When Melinda is encouraged to open the locket she is wearing (www.cbsstore.com), Tessa immediately recognizes the picture inside. It's of her baby, the one that was taken from her just before she died. Tessa thought her child had died beneath Grandview. Melinda is stunned when she hears the child's name: Julia Lee Lucas. It's the name of Melinda's great great grandmother. This, of course, means Tessa is Melinda's great great great grandmother. On Melinda's mother's side of the family, at least one woman in every generation (going back to at least Tessa) has inherited the ability to communicate with earthbound spirits.

Knowing that her baby had survived and that

Above:
Melinda meets her great great great grandmother, Tessa, in 'Weight of What Was'.
Opposite:
Melinda's Grandma, Mary Ann.

the gift of ghost whispering was passed down through the family bloodline, Tessa crosses over into the Light.

PAUL EASTMAN

Though there is no indication of who he is at the time, Melinda's biological father, Paul Eastman (**Corin Nemec**), is introduced in 'Horror Show'. When Melinda dreams of a man with a scary face peering at her from behind a bizarre face-mask it is Paul. Melinda wakes with a start and knows this was no ordinary dream; it's a memory from childhood

When Tom Gordon realizes Melinda knows the truth about his shady past, he tries to kill her. But the spirit of her father, Paul, comes to her rescue when she calls for help, and kills Tom.

Paul had been stuck beneath Grandview since his death, along with all the other lost, trapped souls, but when Melinda entered the tunnels, her presence awakened him. When Paul saw the ideal that Melinda had created about Tom Gordon, he became determined to reveal the truth about Tom to his daughter. Although it was difficult for Melinda to see at first, Paul truly loves his daughter. When she finally calls him "Dad", Paul is able to let his rage go and move forward into the Light.

DAN CLANCY

In the pilot, when Jim's brother Dan (**Rodney Scott**) approaches Melinda at their wedding reception, it seems like a perfectly natural thing — the beautiful bride talks to her brother-in-law about her new husband. Wrong! Dan Clancy is an earthbound spirit, but as he says, he wasn't going to let that stop him from attending his brother and Melinda's wedding. How Dan died remains unexplained, but one clue is what he's wearing…

When Jim is having a crisis of confidence in his career, Melinda shares details of her encounter with Dan. Jim is deeply touched by his brother's visit and promises to carry Dan's vote of confidence with him always.

The last sign from Dan is when Jim's mom visits during 'The Crossing', and Melinda and Jim notice that a photo featuring Dan has a spirit orb in it.

CLANCY SENIOR

Although Jim's dad never makes an appearance in Ghost Whisperer, his influence on his family is made clear when his wife visits Melinda and Jim.

While Jim and his brother Dan were growing up, their dad was a stockbroker. He was disappointed when Jim chose not to follow in his footsteps, but to become a paramedic instead. Jim reveals the conflict in their relationship in 'The Curse of the Ninth', when he talks to Ned about keeping Melinda's gift a secret.

All his life, Jim's dad was a big Yankees fan. When Jim was a kid, he and his dad had season ticket seats behind the Bronx Bombers' home-plate. One game

— a memory that propels Melinda down a road that rocks her world.

Hoping to figure out who the man in the mask is, Melinda hires a detective to help her investigate her past. But the lead she's been hoping for takes a surprising form — Melinda watches as the detective, in a trance-like state, writes a number on the outside of a file folder before he hands it to her. However, he can't explain what the numbers mean because he doesn't remember writing them down seconds before. Later, Melinda discovers that the numbers refer to a court case that Tom Gordon — the man Melinda believes to be her father — prosecuted in 1979. The defendant was Paul Eastman, who was eventually convicted of strangling a young boy in the woods near his home.

Upon further digging, Melinda discovers that Paul escaped from prison during a fire and has never been found. When Melinda describes the face-mask the man was wearing in her dream to Jim, he concludes the man is a burn victim, because that's what those masks are used for. Through twists and turns, Melinda discovers that Tom Gordon married her mother after framing Paul, who was wrongly convicted and incarcerated. Paul Eastman is her real father. And Tom Gordon murdered him after he escaped from prison and came looking for the Gordons. Since his murder, Paul's spirit has been possessing Tom's body as an act of revenge.

Above:
Paul Eastman moves forward into the Light in 'Pater Familias'.

Opposite:
Despite childhood camping trips with his father, Jim's camping skills aren't *always* top-notch.

Reggie Jackson hit four home-runs. That was the last game Jim and his dad went to together.

In 'Giving Up the Ghost', Jim and Melinda get a kick out of seeing Jim's dad's amateur videographer skills as they watch a home video he shot of Jim's only home-run in Little League baseball — right over the centerfield fence.

Jim's dad used to take Jim and his brother Dan camping when they were young. As a result, Jim's camping skills are top-notch, as he demonstrates in 'A Vicious Cycle'. The love of camping, instilled by his father, leads Jim into the woods whenever his schedule allows. Unfortunately, Melinda — not a natural outdoorswoman — finds herself in tow much of the time!

CHARLIE BANKS

In a jewelry store heist, Delia almost loses a custom-made emerald ring. This is her most treasured connection to her husband Charlie (**Fredric Lehne**). Thanks to Melinda, the thief is caught and the ring is returned safely to Delia's finger. Even though Charlie is deceased, Delia confides in Melinda that she still feels married to him.

Charlie passed away before Delia met Melinda, but he takes full credit, in 'Delia's First Ghost', for introducing the two women. Charlie is very protective of his wife and son, Ned, so when he becomes an earthbound spirit, he tries to give his wife and son lots of unexpected help.

Charlie's actions are misinterpreted by Ned as spooky hauntings and by Delia as signs that she's losing her mind. 'Every Breathe You Take, by The Police was Delia and Charlie's song when they dated, so he uses it to reach out to Delia from the grave. The song blares from Jim's ambulance radio, from random cars and from the clock-radio in Delia's bedroom. But, because Delia is a skeptic when it comes to the spirit world, Charlie's efforts don't work the way he intended.

In order to help Ned and Delia sort out the strange happenings in their lives, Melinda researches Charlie's history. His business burned down in a fire when Ned was seven years old. After Charlie was rescued from the blazing building, the only thing that survived was the blueprint of Ned's model airplane. Though struck by the realization that all the architectural drawings and plans that he had worked on day

and night were gone, Charlie didn't care. What mattered was that he had missed the first seven years of his son's life by being a workaholic. And he wasn't going to miss another minute. Charlie changed his lifestyle, making more time for Delia and Ned. Life was joyful for the three of them. Unfortunately, two years later, Charlie's life was cut short when he was shot during a random robbery at an ATM machine.

Charlie had a great deal that he wanted to tell Delia and Ned when he died, but he wasn't able to do it. As an earthbound spirit, Charlie needs Melinda's help. Once Melinda reconnects Charlie to Delia and Ned, Charlie finally lets go of his beloved family and crosses over into the Light.

KATE PAYNE

Professor Rick Payne's wife, Kate (**Rachel Shelley**), is introduced to us through a note that he finds stuck to the door of his kitchen refrigerator, "Back

in one hour." As the camera pans through the house in 'Cat's Claw', there is a great deal of evidence that their marriage is in play. There's even a glimpse of Kate as she peers out of the bedroom window when Payne heads to Melinda's house. (When we shot this scene, we hadn't yet cast Rachel — that's an extra peering out the window.)

The next time Kate pops up, she's roaming the halls of Rockland University. Melinda encounters her on her way into Payne's office. Kate is terse with Melinda. Perhaps she's jealous of her husband's budding friendship with such a beautiful woman. Who could blame her?

In 'The Collector', the mystery of Payne's complicated wife is finally revealed: Kate is a ghost. And of course, she needs Melinda's help to break through to her husband. But when Melinda directs Payne to read a hidden journal that Kate left behind, he's floored. The journal chronicles Kate's affair while she and Payne were married. Kate tells Melinda she would never have hurt her husband by letting him in on the affair, but Gabriel manipulated her into doing so. Gabriel, she claims, wants to hurt the people Melinda cares about because he believes it will weaken Melinda.

Kate confides in Melinda how lonely she is, how

Above:
Melinda helps Kate Payne resolve things with her husband in 'Deadbeat Dads'.

much she loves her husband, and how she misses him at least as much as when they were married. Desperate to get the professor to pay attention — something she believes she was unable to do while she was alive — Kate haunts him. And when an ex-girlfriend of Payne's surfaces in Grandview with the intention of hooking up with him, a jealous Kate ratchets up the hauntings. Payne tells Melinda to stay out of it, until Kate drops a piano on him. Finally he admits, "The scientist in me is very intrigued, but the human being in me has hair standing up in places I didn't even know I had."

Now on the case, Melinda discovers that the circumstances surrounding Kate's death were random and tragic — a construction crane at a renovation site plummeted eight stories and crashed onto the street where Kate happened to be making a u-turn in her car. She died moments before her body was freed from her vehicle.

Eventually, Kate confides in Melinda that she wanted to have a baby, but her husband said he wasn't ready yet, that they had lots of time. Three weeks later, Kate was dead. Now she's angry with Payne because they can never have that child.

When Melinda makes Payne aware of the problems in his marriage, Payne apologizes to Kate for

 116

being so selfish. He just wanted her to himself. And he misses her terribly. This final admission brings Kate peace, and she crosses over into the Light. But not before she releases the wedding ring that's been stuck on her husband's finger since her death.

JUSTIN YATES

Justin Yates (**Omid Abtahi**) was an Emerging Technologies graduate student at Rockland University who suspected that Melinda has some strange relationship with the dead. Initially unable to prove it, Justin was not above stealing research, hacking computers and shadowing Melinda to get what he needed. Justin used his blog, And Shame the Devil (www.andshamethedevil.net), to slam his college professors and 'out' the Grandview community, creating mayhem and mischief. (This character was inspired by *Ghost Whisperer*'s own digital media guy, Justin Fisher — but the real Justin never swiped a byte in his life!)

Although tempted to expose Melinda, Justin decided to stockpile his investigative research on her strange behavior until he needed a favor. When Justin's behavior turned threatening, Melinda confronted him, only to learn that he had a brain aneurism that could kill him at any time.

Driving himself crazy with guilt over an accident that killed his girlfriend three years earlier,

Right:
Justin's website, And Shame the Devil, turned upsidedown by his dead girlfriend.
Below:
Justin realizes he is dead in 'The Gravesitter'.

Justin tried to shut Melinda out. Melinda dug anyway, and learned it was the ghost of Justin's girlfriend that was driving him crazy. She wanted him to join her on the dark side.

After Justin died of a brain aneurism, Melinda helped him understand he was not responsible for his girlfriend's death. This released him from guilt so he could cross into the Light (and out of the clutches of his deadly former babe). But before Justin crossed over, he was able to say a final goodbye to his brother and sister.

At the last moment, Justin promised Melinda he would find a way to come back and report to her what's on the other side…

www.andshamethedevil.net/

117

MELINDA'S SPIRIT GUIDE

COMMUNICATING
WITH THE DEAD

People ask us all the time, "Do you really believe in ghosts?" Of course, we're the executive producers of *Ghost Whisperer*! The question that always follows is, "How do you really *know*?" There is an old saying: "To those who believe, no proof is necessary. To those who don't, none is enough." And we know because we have two people attached to the show who are experts in the spirit world — Mary Ann Winkowski is a consultant and James Van Praagh is a co-executive producer.

Mary Ann Winkowski is a real life 'ghost buster' who can see and talk to earthbound spirits. They're the ones that have not crossed over into the Light because they have unfinished business. Mary Ann helps these spirits find closure and then crosses them over. Some of what Melinda Gordon experiences in front of the camera is inspired by what happens to Mary Ann in her everyday life.

World-renown medium James Van Praagh is the flip-side of this unusual coin. He communicates with spirits that have already crossed into the Light. These are known as 'enlightened spirits'; they've moved on from their issues here on Earth.

James uses a very interesting analogy to explain the intersection of the spirit world with the world of the living and why everyone cannot see and talk to the dead. "We live in a multi-dimensional universe — the spirit world exists in the fourth dimension, which penetrates the other dimensions. A good example is television. We transmit images of a TV show into the air. No one actually sees those images in the air but the images are received thousands of miles away on your TV because it is tuned into a specific frequency. In the same way, the fourth dimension is a higher frequency band that most people are not tuned into, so they don't see spirits. Mediums attune themselves to that higher frequency band and

are able to see and talk to the dead."

Still not sure about the spirit world? Think about this. Today it's established that the Earth is a sphere (yes, yes, the equator bulges out a bit because of the Earth's rotation, but nonetheless the Earth is considered *round*). Back when Christopher Columbus proposed reaching India by sailing west from Spain, the consensus was that the Earth was *flat*. And if you sailed too far, you would fall right off the edge into the unknown. Why flat? Because if you stood on the seashore and watched a ship sail away, it gradually disappeared from view. Seeing was believing. But Christopher Columbus was able to convince Queen Isabella to overrule the experts. And the rest is history. Just because you can't see and hear spirits today, doesn't mean they don't exist. Who knows what tomorrow will bring in terms of discovery?

If you have witnessed one of James' online séances, or watched Mary Ann ghost bust a hospital crawling with spirits (spirits are attracted to hospitals because spirits need energy and hospitals are chock-full), which she does on a regular basis, we're sure you'll agree these two emissaries of the spirit world are quite amazing.

Séances

A séance is an attempt to communicate with spirits. The word séance comes from the Old French word *seoir*, which means 'to sit'. In English, 'séance' refers to a meeting of people who are gathered to receive messages from spirits, or to listen to a spirit medium relay those messages. In truth, participants do not need to be seated while engaging in a séance.

Medium James Van Praagh is a master at séances. During his sessions, he brings people together to open up their hearts and minds while they use him as a medium to communicate with the spirits.

During *Ghost Whisperer*'s online séances, James performs readings *live* for the general public via streaming video on CBS.com. During these séances, the public is able to call Van Praagh and speak with him personally as he connects them to the dead while others simultaneously converse in designated chat rooms.

Be sure you join-in on the next online *Ghost Whisperer* séance with James Van Praagh.

www.fansofgw.com/seance/halloween1.mov
www.fansofgw.com/seance/holiday
www.fansofgw.com/seance/halloween2
www.fansofgw.com/seance/valentine.mov

Tarot Cards

The tarot is a set of cards featuring twenty-one 'trump cards', The Fool, and an extra face card (The Page) per suit, in addition to the usual fifty-two cards found in an ordinary playing card deck. The four tarot suits are swords, batons (also known as wands, rods or staves), coins (a.k.a. pentacles or disks), and cups. The non-suit tarot cards make up the most important group (or 'major arcana'). These are the 'trumps' — in order, The Magician, The High Priestess, The Empress, The Emperor, The Hierophant/Pope, The Lovers, The Chariot,

Above:
A psychic reads Melinda's tarot cards in 'Miss Fortune'.

Strength, The Hermit, Wheel of Fortune, Justice, The Hanged Man, Death, Temperance, The Devil, The Tower, The Star, The Moon, The Sun, Judgement, The World — and The Fool. The remaining fifty-six suit cards are known as the 'minor arcana'.

In English-speaking countries, tarot cards are used primarily by psychics and mediums as a tool for divinatory purposes. The 'reader' uses the tarot cards to gain insight into the current and possible future situations of the subject, known as the 'querent'. The insights may include the subject's known and unknown thoughts and desires, as well as past, present and future events. Some of these readings are guided by spiritual forces, while others are used to help tap into a collective unconscious.

Each card has a variety of symbolic meanings that have evolved over the years. The minor arcana cards have astrological connotations that can be used as general indicators of time of year, based on the Octavian (western) calendar. The court cards (King, Queen, Knight, Page) can signify different people in relation to the subject of the reading, with each suit having its own 'nature' that indicates certain physical and emotional characteristics in the person signified.

To perform a reading, the tarot deck is shuffled by either the reader or (if they are a separate

121

individual) the querent, and laid out in one of a variety of 'spreads' or patterns. The reader then interprets the spread. Each position in the spread is assigned a number, and the cards are turned over in sequence, with each being interpreted before moving on to the next. Each card position is associated with an aspect of the question. Sometimes the 'first' card in the spread, rather than being selected randomly in the shuffle, is specifically chosen and placed as the representation of either the question or the querent. This card is called the 'significator'.

In the episode 'Miss Fortune', a tarot card reader does a reading for Melinda and foretells a hanged man and a death curse, which plays out in the 'Last Execution'. As foretold by the reader, Melinda's life is put in great jeopardy.

If you're interested in owning *Ghost Whisperer* Collector's Edition Tarot Cards, check out the season two DVD set (www.cbsstore.com).

www.fansofgw.com/grid/tarotcards/

Apport

An apport is the transference of an object from an unknown source to you or to another place by unknown means. It happens instantaneously without traveling through space. The inverse can also occur when an apport is transferred from a known location to an unknown location (Kim swears this happens to her car in mall parking lots...). Medium James Van Praagh says, "In my world, an apport is where the molecular structure of an object is broken down from one location and

Below:
An apport spooks
Professor Payne in
'Cat's Claw'.
Opposite:
The *Ghost
Whisperer* Online
Crystal Ball.

122

rematerializes fully in a different location."

Apports are usually associated with ghost energies, and the out of place items can be found somewhere in the house or, on rare occasions, someone will witness the object (usually small items like jewelry and car keys) falling to the floor or dropping from the ceiling. Sometimes, an apport (flowers, water or perfume) will manifest at séances.

The mystery of the apport is one of the most fascinating aspects of spiritualism. The objects vary in size, are both inanimate and animate, and seem to be unaffected by the strange way that they're transported. A great example of apports is in 'The Ghost Within', when Melinda discovers the beautiful ornaments she bought at a flea market are being manipulated by a ghost.

www.fansofgw.com/saturnawards/saturn.mov

Ouija Boards

'Ouija' is derived from the French word *oui* for 'yes' and *ja*, the German word for 'yes'. A ouija board — originally called a 'talking board' — is a tool used for communicating with the spirit world and can also function as a spiritual gateway. These boards are usually rectangular flat surfaces, printed with the letters of the alphabet, the numbers 0 to 9 and symbols. There is also a moveable indicator or 'planchette'. The participants place fingers on the indicator, and after the question is asked, the indicator moves from letter to letter, spelling out the answer.

A note of warning: Mary Ann Winkowski suggests staying away from talking boards unless you absolutely know what you're doing. "They cannot be controlled. It's a tool that can be used by a *very* select group of people who know how to handle it. I believe James [Van Praagh] likes the ouija board, but he knows how to protect himself."

Medium James Van Praagh confirms that he does work with ouija boards, but also cautions that "It's not a game *at all*. Protect yourself. Say a prayer, bring in energy of pure love and raise your vibration. Then ask for protection and open yourself up to whatever happens. If you're getting negative messages, start all over, because you've opened up to lower levels."

Mary Ann believes most people who use talking boards are teenage girls who use it to ask, "Who am I going to marry? Who am I going to go to the

Protection

When clearing a building of earthbound spirits, ghost buster Mary Ann Winkowski gives the owners special quince seeds, sent to her from Italy, to protect dwellings. Quince seeds traditionally signify protection, love and happiness — in Ancient Greece and Rome newlyweds would share a quince to ensure the success of their union. "An earthbound spirit does not like quince seeds," Mary Ann explains. "It's not the seed, it's the energy that the seed produces or that it has around it." Once these seeds are in place, an earthbound spirit will not come back into that house or building.

Carrying them is thought to protect against evil, physical harm and accidents. According to Mary Ann, quince seeds work on some curses as well. "If somebody has a curse on him and I take it off, and they carry a seed on them, nobody can ever reinstate that curse."

---

prom with? How many children am I going to have?…" She says, "I've run across women in their thirties who've had a ghost attached to them since their teens from playing with a ouija board."

Mary Ann suggests that calling a spirit for help with information is dangerous. In her opinion, anytime you are calling a ghost, an earthbound spirit will arrive, and it is not guaranteed that it will be a good spirit. "Even boards with pictures of angels all over them still have the same concept. Changing the symbolism on the board does not change the dynamic of the interaction."

www.fansofgw.com/grid/halloweenflash/

Palm Reading

Palm reading (also known as chiromacy, hand analysis or palmistry) is the foretelling of a person's future through the study of their palm. Palm reading is a worldwide practice, though often with cultural variations. True palm readers have some level of psychic ability that can connect to the spirit world.

'Reading' the palm of a person's hand usually begins with the reader looking at the person's dominant hand (the hand the subject uses the most). In some traditions, the other hand is believed to carry karmic or past-life and hereditary traits information. Various lines and mounts (or bumps) and their relative sizes, qualities and intersections are suggestive of certain interpretations. In some traditions, readers will examine the characteristics of the whole hand, including the overall shape (usually classified as Earth, Air, Fire or Water), fingers, fingerprints, the palm's skin patterns and shape, skin texture and color, and flexibility of the hand.

In 'Miss Fortune', a palm reader foretells of the death of someone in Andrea's family due to the jetliner crash that takes place in 'The One'.

Crystal Ball

A crystal ball (or 'shew stone') is a tool used to aid clairvoyance. Large ones can be expensive and small ones can strain the eyes and make gazing (reading, in layman's terms) difficult. Experienced readers prefer four to five inch sizes, since they are easiest on the eyes.

When using a crystal ball, make sure you are in a state of calm and in a quiet environment. Stare deep into the center of the crystal. Try clearing your mind of everything as you continue to gaze into it. This is a passive/receptive state. Maintain this state looking into the crystal for a few minutes at a time. Picture yourself and the crystal ball as an empty bowl waiting for water to pour in.

www.fansofgw.com/grid/crystalball/

MARY ANN WINKOWSKI
ON COMMUNICATING WITH THE DEAD

Talk about your gift, and what it means.
I cannot see spirits that have already crossed over. I would love to see an angel — I *can't*. I would love to see my father who has crossed over — I *can't*. Unlike James Van Praagh, the spirits that I see are most definitely earthbound, and these are the ones that cause problems or issues for people.

What's the difference between you and James?
James is a medium and I am a paranormal investigator. We both see spirits, but James can't see mine and I can't see his. As a medium, James is an instrument, if you will, in communicating with the dead. Mediums are able to communicate with a higher dimension of reality, and in James's case, it's spirits that have already passed into the Light. I, on the other hand, can only see spirits that made the choice not to go into the White Light when they died. My specialty is helping those spirits figure out what unfinished business is holding them here. Once we do that, I help them to resolve it and they move on.

Can you give some examples of the unfinished business that you deal with?
It runs the gamut from a funeral that didn't adhere to the person's specifications; knowing the where-abouts of a safety deposit box key that's missing; an unsolved murder… By the way, almost every spirit attends their own funeral, so I suggest you try to stick to their requests as best you can.

How do you feel about ghost busting?
I'm a people person. I like positive feedback: Kid sleeps through the night, business picks up 100 percent, no more talk of divorce. Ghost gone — mission accomplished. *Next!*

Debunk an urban legend about haunting, will you?
I actually met a man who was one of the producers of *The Amityville Horror* and I told him, "One of my dreams has come true. I wanted to meet you so I could just go over and strangle you." He said, "What? *What?*" I asked, "Why did you stick flies in the attic in that house?" He said they had seventeen seconds to fill in the movie, so they did the fly gag. I said, "Do you know how many times I've gotten phone calls over the years from people who think they have a ghost in the house because they have flies in the attic?!"

Got another?
Yeah. I have never, ever, ever, ever, *ever* found a ghost hanging around an Indian burial ground. What would keep them there? Burial grounds aren't exactly pulsing with human energy. Same with cemeteries.

Once a ghost takes up residence in someone's house, how do you get them to move on?
I give 'em two options: I create the Light for them and they can move on to a place where they'll see all their loved ones who've already crossed, or I'll trap the spirit forever. Given these options, spirits almost always choose to cross over because they don't like to be confined. And, for some of them, once they're caught, it's like the fun has gone out of it for them.

Most spirit encounters go really well, but every once in a while I'll have a run-in with a problem spirit, like the one who threw the axe. The other thing that's a handful, is trying to cross over groups of spirits all together. I once cleared a movie theatre of sixty earthbound spirits. About half of them went into the Light, the others moved on to different theatres in town. I ran into one at anoth-er theater. *(Big chuckle)* He asked if I was going to kick him out of this theatre too.

The most spirits I've ever crossed over at one time was at a county morgue in Cleveland. In the

1930s the Kingsbury Run Butcher decapitated people and dumped them all over the city. The spirit of one of the victims was still at County Morgue along with about 200 other spirits. He and I got to spend a little time together before I crossed them all over. He was fascinating! [Melinda faced the challenge of crossing over 200 spirits at once during the season one finale in 'The One'.]

The Cleveland county hospitals I do every six months, and there can be from 100 to 300 spirits depending on how bad things are in Cleveland at the time. Unfortunately, I can't keep the Light open indefinitely — I let spirits through in batches.

How does the Light work?

The White Light is what people who have had near death experiences talk about — seeing it, going into it, actually seeing people who they've lost waiting for them in the Light — but then that person comes back into their body and doesn't die. The White Light is there for every one of us the very second after we take our last breath. When you die, it's your choice whether you go into the Light

Above:

Mary Ann Winkowski with Jennifer Love Hewitt on set.

or not. If you choose not to, that Light will only stay with you for about three days after the funeral. Or if you're cremated, it'll stay with you seventy-two to eighty hours after the last memorial service. You can go into the Light anytime during that period. The spirits of those who have crossed before you beckon you, "come, come." They can't talk to you, but you can see them.

This is all about free will; if you don't want to go, you don't have to. If you choose not to go into the Light during the timeframe that I mentioned, the Light disappears. Those are the spirits that I see, they're the ones that cause problems because they don't eat or sleep for energy — they need human energy to keep going. Earthbound spirits are a drain on any person they are close to or the residents of the house they land in.

Got any parting advice?

Don't wait until you're dead to take care of business. ◉

www.askmaryann.blogspot.com/
www.maryannwinkowski.com

BEHIND THE SCENES

BEHIND THE SCENES

Every new television series that's launched has to make particular choices. For example, if it's a cop show, you have to decide to what degree you're going to explore the characters' personal lives versus portraying police procedures. Each decision impacts the tone, look and sound of a show, and once they are made, the shows tend to be formulaic. Launching *Ghost Whisperer* was different. We started off exploring a new world. A paranormal world. A world not overly exposed to the television audience. While the show is fiction ("*feasible* fiction"), from the beginning it was important that we ground it by establishing rules, and then being consistent with those rules. But the rules must evolve — as the show grows so grow the rules.

We knew that unless the show felt authentic, it would quickly 'cross over'. Having James Van Praagh and Mary Ann Winkowski on board from the beginning, guiding us on how the spirit world works, and what the rules are when the living intersect with the dead, has been enormously valuable. They spent time with the producers, the writers and actors, taking us on 'ghost bustings'. They shared their personal experiences in the spirit world, suggesting stories that might work for the show, and answering tons of questions.

Once this initial research was complete — it's never really finished; the education is continuous — we had to figure out how to translate the spirit world into film and soundtracks. In doing so, we've developed a style and tone for the show that is unique. Unlike most TV series, *Ghost Whisperer* changes from week to week. One week we're making a horror show, the next week we're taking the audience on a heartfelt journey about a child who's parents split up over her death, and sometimes we're doing a dark comedy where the spirit world gets the last laugh.

In breaking down the elements of each episode, it is one part procedural, one part character-based on the domestic front, one part the exploration of the world as we know it, and one part the paranormal world of ghosts. But always, it is a mystery that ends with a cathartic, often tearful, climax. This complex mix impacts every single aspect of the show. Therefore, we have to have the best and the brightest in series television to bring *Ghost Whisperer* alive for the viewer.

Our costume designer is not just doing wardrobe, she's creating Melinda's Closet. The look must be different from any other character in any other show because there is no one like Melinda Gordon on the television landscape. Our two directors of photography shoot 'ghost vision'. And because other TV shows don't travel to the underworld, that world does not readily exist anywhere in the world. Therefore, our production designer and location manager must get really creative — but quick, because every eight days, we finish shooting one episode and begin shooting another. Our line producer Barbara Black and department heads do it all beautifully, with lightning speed and nothing less than passion and enthusiasm.

Once a show is shot, it has to go through a complex post production process. This involves editing, scoring, visual effects, color correcting, sound dubbing and more. At any one time there are three episodes in post production going through one or more of these phases. It is often said that post production is where the movie is really made. Production provides the raw material, post is where the puzzle is assembled. This is especially true on *Ghost Whisperer*. Many shows have fifteen or twenty minutes of music; *Ghost Whisperer* will always have thirty-five to forty minutes. As the show has evolved and grown, our budget for visual effects — designed to help viewers comprehend how the spirit world works — has quadrupled.

In addition to the department heads featured in this section, there are hundreds of crew members and staff; a wealth of talent behind the scenes who work collaboratively to produce *Ghost Whisperer*.

GHOST STORIES

Ghost Whisperer is not a normal TV show. Or at least, it's not like any single normal TV show. The reason I and the rest of the writers have so much fun with this show is probably the same reason the fans do: *Ghost Whisperer* is really four or five different shows. First and foremost it's a show about human emotions. But it's also a genre fantasy show about ghosts and the paranormal, a procedural drama with mystery elements, and last but not least, a romantic comedy about a joyfully married young couple, balancing a pretty typical home life with some pretty atypical work.

I came onto the show as a big fan, having watched all the episodes, but still, like any writer, with a few new ideas of my own. My first instinct was to refocus the show on what it did best: telling scary but personal stories on a human scale. And the more personal they could be to Melinda, the better. The season before I got here, *Ghost Whisperer* explored a 'mythology' that was more global in scale. I think those shows are terrific, but it sometimes felt like a canvas that took us away from what we knew and loved best: Melinda, her loved ones, and her home town. So John Gray and I talked about how to break new ground without looking further outward, but inward instead. We wondered if we could dig deeper into our characters and our world by doing literally that: digging down, underground. What if Grandview turned out to be a place with a history, a dark complex history, which not only accounted for why so much ghost activity seemed to take place here, but also accounted for why Melinda was drawn here in the first place. What if she didn't come here by accident? What if her family's history was woven into the town's history? And what if those two histories weren't as pretty as charming, bucolic Grandview appeared on the surface? This became the arc, or mythology, of season three, and gave us lots of wonderful, scary and moving stories to tell throughout the year.

People often ask how we come up with stories and scripts for the show. Ask any writer on the staff and they'll tell you: It's a lot harder than it looks. Writers on our staff come from all different backgrounds. We've written on shows as varied as *CSI*, *Heroes*, *Lost*, *Party of Five*, *The Wonder Years*, *Doogie Howser, M.D.*, *Law & Order*, and *Beverly Hills 90210*.

Right:
Melinda hears voices.

The truth is we use muscles developed on all of those shows every time we 'break' a story. It starts with the germ of an idea: What about a haunted house episode? Something that features all-new ghost powers? What if Santa Claus turned out to be a ghost? Then we begin to discuss who the characters are. Who's the ghost? What do they want? What do they have to learn? How can we make them as creepy and scary as possible? Then we look for good twists. Interesting clues to guide Melinda through complex mysteries. But what makes our job hardest is what we call "the cross over". This is the scene where Melinda helps earthbound spirits finally see and go into the Light. And it's why we don't have the luxury most other mystery shows do — the luxury of having a bad guy. Our "bad guys" have to find redemption; they have to move on into the better world waiting for all redeemed spirits.

And we have to do all that while finding smart unexpected ways to be scary, and funny, and sad, and true.

After we've put the whole story beat by beat (or scene by scene) up on a white board, a writer (or writing team) goes off and grinds out an outline. This gets revised a few times, with help from the network and studios, and then turned by the writer into a script. More revisions right up to the last minute, then casting, more "prep", and finally we're on the set, bugging everyone to make sure what we're filming conforms to our "vision". Well, that, and hanging with the real heroes of our production, the cast and crew. Oh, and eating free food.

Meanwhile, back in the writers' room, we're breaking the next episode and the one after that and rewriting ones in between. Not to mention reviewing 'cuts' of already filmed episodes. It's a hectic job, with writer-producers like me simultaneously managing anywhere up to eight episodes at a time.

But it's worth it. When you sit on the 'dub stage' — the last stop for an episode, where the sound elements get mixed together, sometimes just hours before it airs — you see the finished product together with all of your partners. And on this show, which some of us rate on a "hankie scale" (five hankies meaning a major tearjerker), screening an episode often has grown men and women jumping out of their seats during ghost scenes, and then ends with all of us wiping our eyes and complaining of "allergies". That's when we know we've done our job right.

P.K. Simonds

MELINDA'S CLOSET

In the *Ghost Whisperer* pilot, Melinda Gordon was a girl in transition — running an antique shop, newly married, and trying to find her way with the spirit world. Her wardrobe reflected the youthful romanticism of her adventurous spirit. By season three, Melinda had grown up, evolving into a confident young woman with a successful business, making exciting strides on the ghost front, and taking her marriage to the next level. Her updated closet reflects this journey beautifully.

Costume designer Joseph Porro embraced an "antique vintage look with a twist" for the first two seasons. Typical casual-wear for Melinda was the pairing of authentic period pieces like a vintage French corset with jeans and sexy, contemporary heels. Instead of bracelets, Melinda wore several

Above:
The costume design sketch, with fabric swatches, for Melinda's red dress in 'Holiday Spirit'.
Opposite:
Melinda in the final creation.

vintage watches clustered around her wrist. A typical evening look for Melinda was a one of a kind 50s black cocktail dress with the back cut down low to show skin — very Audrey Hepburn inspired but with a twist.

"It's the kind of clothes young girls across the country can find by raiding antiques stores," Jennifer Love Hewitt explains of Melinda's early look. "There are so many time periods you can revisit. And it was fun to wonder who wore it before... and to where."

When costume designer Dorothy Amos came aboard in season three, she made changes to Melinda's Closet that complimented the growth of the show's leading lady and made her more 'fashion forward'.

"When I first looked at film from the previous two seasons, I decided it was time to bring more movement in through Melinda's clothes," Dorothy explains. "Melinda is always on the go. She's the ghost whisperer — all these things are happening to her constantly. And with each season, more and more action is taking place. It's very important to keep that in mind when designing a look.

"Love and I talked about it and decided to shut down the prints, except when we're moving into summer. We decided to make Melinda's wardrobe a little darker, more serious, and more sculpted for each episode. Silhouettes are very important in filmmaking and I'm extremely lucky to be working with Love. She has such an incredible figure — the perfect silhouette, really.

"I love working with Jennifer Love Hewitt — she's incredibly collaborative and very focused on what works for her character. Love receives many awards for her on-camera work and walks dozens of red carpets, so it's fun to see Melinda's wardrobe transcend the world of *Ghost Whisperer* when Love crosses one of our outfits over to a Hollywood event."

Love says, "Looking hip is not necessarily about looking like everyone else in the magazines. It's about finding your own thing."

Q&A With Dorothy Amos

How did you approach recreating Melinda's Closet?

I often like Melinda in outfits that are basic, casual, because it's really appropriate for the storytelling. And dresses are a really important part of her look — fans tune in to check out what Melinda's wearing. Love does dresses like nobody else, and on her, each one is perfection.

Everything I do is inspired by the script. When the storytelling calls for an action sequence, Melinda's outfit must enable her to move. It needs to be made of fabrics that look and feel fluid.

I like to use colors to depict tone and mood. Love wore a fawn-colored dress in 'Pater Familias' to symbolize that Melinda is being hunted by the underworld, like a deer. In that episode, every piece was very soft, very organic — light, buttery tones to keep the subliminal visual theme alive. By contrast, in 'Horror Show' we did a lot of black on her to add darkness to the show's tone.

Weather is another consideration. We shoot in LA, so when you have a day like today — 104°F — it's very difficult to have Love in a coat. If the script places us in the middle of winter, then I use wardrobe sleight-of-hand to make sure that Love is dressed appropriately for the season and yet the fabric is light enough to breathe. We do use a lot of coats on Melinda for several reasons: layering, weather, night scenes and locale. Grandview is supposed to be located on the East Coast, just outside Manhattan.

What's the process in designing a Melinda outfit?

First I read the script to determine how many changes Melinda will have in the episode. Standard is six to nine. There's usually a scene that calls for a nightgown (we get tons of fan emails on Melinda's special nightgowns), and almost always a scene that calls for a coat. I consider the action of the change, if we need to double her or provide multiple matching outfits for her stunt person, if we need to protect her from the elements, whether or not she's going to be running, and, of course, the insight Love has about what's going on with her character in the story, and what time of day the director of photography is going to shoot the scene. All these things help dictate how I'm going to put Melinda's outfit together.

Next is fabrics. There is this stockpile of fabrics, and sometimes, depending on what we have and

what's coming up in the episodes, we'll get an idea and 'build' it. We're one of the only TV series in Hollywood that still builds costumes for its leading lady. You won't see something Melinda's wearing anywhere else.

I'll look at a fabric and it'll inspire me, then we have to turn it around quickly because we only have eight days to prep an episode before we begin shooting it. When we build an outfit, it's usually a combination of something that's 'fashion', and something 'vintage'. I'll do a quick little sketch for our dynamite seamstresses, Margaret Jegalian and Esther Hamboyan. Then I drape the fabric on a Melinda form. We tweak and adjust, then fit it on Love, rework it — she always has input — then fit it again. And before you know it, it's up on the screen.

How about those glorious Melinda shoes?
Love loves to wear high, high heels, and she looks fabulous in them. Also she functions in them like nobody you've ever seen! On the character side, there's a part of Melinda that is still classic, so I always want to keep her stylish in the shoe department, but not too trendy. She also wears lots of boots — they're very practical for the show and very good with a lot of Melinda's changes.

What's it like to dress Jennifer Love Hewitt?
She's incredibly gracious and creatively gifted. Often Love will show me pictures of things she likes or we'll talk about ideas. She has such a busy schedule, and we do fittings within seconds, but Love is always a very important part of the creative process and her ideas are invaluable. I won't usually make anything until I know she loves the fabric. When I show her the fabric, I'll also show her a thumbnail sketch. If we agree it's a "yes", then my team and I go to town on it.

How are you making Melinda's Closet accessible to fans?
We did a CBS online auction for one of Melinda's outfits in 'Horror Show'. It was extremely versatile. It accommodated the storytelling, the night shooting, the running, and had a great deal of movement. It made the online auction a homerun.

You're responsible for the looks of all the other characters in the series, too. What about Delia Banks?
In this series, every character is in constant evolution. That's what makes my work so exciting. Delia started off conservative. Once she took the job at Melinda's shop, we began shifting her to a more Sheryl Crow look — jeans with tops that really rock and great boots. Camryn has graceful movement with her hands when she talks, so I like adding interesting details to her sleeves. And it's why bracelets play especially well on her. Camryn wears jewelry really well. She can carry off big earrings with lots of style because of her lovely long hair.

And Jim Clancy?
David wears clothes beautifully because he's got the perfect frame, so we're able to embrace simplicity with Jim's wardrobe. As a paramedic, Jim is an everyday hero. There's a very quiet style to him. This guy's not a label groupie but he knows what he likes. Lucky me, I get to dress him!

What about Professor Rick Payne?
It's not hard finding inspiration for Professor Payne. All you have to do is spend six minutes watching Jay zip around the set, doing stand-up in between delivering his scripted lines. We actually opened up Payne's look, making him a bit more relaxed, a tad more youthful, but still maintaining the 'professor look'. Payne's thing is striped shirts, animal ties, and soft, not-too-structured coats — it's a nice genuine everyday look. Then when we dress him up he looks really special because Jay Mohr wears suits beautifully.

During a fitting recently, Jay accosted me: "What happened to the animals? I was really into it!" The animals are on his ties, one favorite being the 'turtle tie'. I had picked up some ties that look witty — psycho bunnies, horses, dogs, and yes, the turtle. We'd even started doing custom ties because I was running out of what's on the market. So I decided to take a brief break from the ties. Needless to say, after Jay's

132

prompting, we're back with the ties.

How do you keep the costumes from clashing with the sets?

I work closely with the production designer, Mayling Cheng. We have a nice long history, and she's so extraordinarily talented, organic and exciting. When a new set comes up I'll go talk to her about color, ideas. If you don't plan correctly, an actor can either turn into a floating head or disappear altogether, say, if he's wearing the same color green as the sofa he's sitting on. That's no good, unless, of course, he's a ghost!

We're dying to hear about the ghosts.

The cardinal ghost rule is the spirit wears what they died in. Period. However, the condition of the ghost's clothes, now that's a different story. I distress the clothing based on each ghost's backstory. We talk through the ghost's timeline with the executive producers and the writer — how and when the ghost died, the activity of the ghost, specificity of the character [before death]. Then we put together four to six sets of the same outfit. We buy and modify — lots of times we over-dye the clothing because it's a quick way to make something look like it didn't just come out of a store. Also, this puts my creative stamp on it. It's the small details that make things look special — I like to change buttons. Next, we age the clothes down — wash them and wash them. Then we fit the actor. After, we go through our distressing process to varying degrees

Below: Dorothy Amos (right) and "dynamite seamstress" Esther Hamboyan at work.

Opposite: Melinda in the auctioned outfit from 'Horror Show', complete with Black Widow spider pendant.

to match whatever catastrophic situation the ghost encountered in the world of the living. The whole process is jammed into our eight-day prep schedule.

What's your favorite ghost look?

So far, my favorite was Tessa in 'Weight of What Was' — a period ghost with a terrific history. I love to do period, especially on this show, because the contrast with the contemporary is really exciting.

Do you believe in ghosts?

I believe in lots of esoteric things and metaphysical things, but I don't believe in ghosts specifically. I believe that there's a presence and energy that, at different times, is in a person's life. Example: When I gave birth to my son, I felt my mother's energy; I didn't see her, but I felt her presence.

www.ghostwwhispereroncbs.wetpaint.com/page/Jay+Mohr's+Ghost+Whisperer+Tie+Challenge
www.youtube.com/watch?v=_WWT5AU4f6E
www.fansofgw.com/grid/melindas_closet/
www.seenon.com/television/cbs/ghost-whisperer/

GHOST WORLD

Before *Ghost Whisperer* was launched, the creative team collaboratively decided on an overall visual sense for the show, including color palette, lighting, photographic framing, shapes and transitional styles. Once those decisions were made, the production designer — with the assistance of the department heads — became responsible for the overall 'look' of all elements that go in front of the camera. From set construction, to choosing locations, dressing sets, selecting costumes and wardrobe, and props, they must be sure that *everything* is consistent with the creative team's vision.

John Gray lives in Nyack, New York, and although the exact location of the fictitious town of Grandview is never really identified, Nyack was always the model. When we began prepping the pilot of *Ghost Whisperer*, we knew it would be impractical to shoot a series in Nyack for financial reasons and because most of our cast was rooted in Los Angeles. And the pilot had not yet been ordered to series, so we couldn't invest loads of money into building full sets. So the challenge for production designer Roy Forge Smith (*Monty Python and the Holy Grail, Bill and Ted's Excellent Adventure, Teenage Mutant Ninja Turtles, The Hunley* and *Martin and Lewis* — the last

133

two directed by John Gray) was to find locations in and around LA that would give the pilot the look of a small yet sophisticated Northeast town.

Roy and the location manager scouted for days and ultimately brought us to the town of Orange, California. Orange had a great town square, and, just as important, it did not have many *palm trees*, which, if seen in a shot, would instantly give away that we were not on the East Coast.

In the center of Orange's town square was a fountain. One of the story points in our pilot involved a war memorial in the center of town (inspired by a real memorial in the coal-mining town of Donora, Pennsylvania), so Roy and his team designed the memorial, which covered the fountain. Little did we know that it would become an iconic Grandview landmark. We also found a store, which we redressed to be Melinda's antique shop, Same As It Never Was.

For Jim and Melinda's first home we moved to Altadena, California, where we found a lovely house which Roy and his team redressed and altered to our specifications. We also shot the cemetery there.

A few months later, when *Ghost Whisperer* was ordered to series, we needed to approximate the look of the pilot by building sets on soundstages in the LA area. The moment we were shown the Universal Studios soundstages and the *Back to the Future* town square, we knew we had found Grandview — with modifications and adjustments,

Above:
The interior set for the Grandview underworld church.
Opposite:
A miniature model of the basement of Same As It Never Was.

134

of course. Jim and Melinda's house was also on Universal's backlot, on Elm Street, once Atticus Finch's house in *To Kill a Mockingbird* (which our cast and crew are convinced is haunted!).

Once we found the exterior locations, we built matching key interiors on the Universal soundstages: Melinda and Jim's house, Same As It Never Was, and a giant greenscreen stage for visual effects shots. We also needed enough space to build 'swing sets', different sets that come up episodically.

Production designer Mayling Cheng (*Tour of Duty, Lois & Clark, Someone She Knows*, produced by Ian Sander, *The Rosa Parks Story, Invasion, The Nine*) took up the reigns for season three. As the season was being mapped out, we decided this would be the year to really explore the secrets and mythology of Melinda's world. The very talented P.K. Simonds also joined us as an executive producer and brought with him a fabulous idea — let's deconstruct what's buried in Melinda's family history and parallel that with what lies beneath Grandview. So in addition to revamping and sprucing up our existing sets, Mayling was faced with the challenge of designing and building sets that were to exist below our traditional locations: the Same As It Never Was basement, City Hall's records archive, and a maze of tunnels leading to the ancestral town of Grandview. This underground town (inspired by Kim Moses's hometown of Donora, Pennsylvania) also had to play like it had been buried for 150 years, with cobblestone streets, storefronts and a church, all jutting out of the dirt.

'Weight of What Was', written by P.K. Simonds, reveals Grandview's underworld for the first time. Inspired by that script, Mayling designed and built most of the underground sets from scratch. Building out town streets that have been buried for decades is a mammoth undertaking. So instead we headed over to European Street on Universal's backlot, where Mayling brought in tons of dirt to cover portions of the cobblestone. She revamped and aged-down the storefronts and trucked in nineteenth century statuary, gas streetlamps, carriages and other period dressing. And she built the façade of a half-burned church layered in cobwebs. Mayling and her team attached tree roots to the buildings to show how far under the Earth's surface the town was. Then her paint team got to work aging everything down to sell the passage of time. Mayling also worked with the visual effects team, using CGI to create the enhancements needed to sell the underground world.

Q&A With Mayling Cheng

What's your creative approach to *Ghost Whisperer*?
It always centers on the idea of mythologies. All societies have their own mythologies told to generations through elders. Our show uncovers its mythology through the point of view of our heroine, Melinda — through her communication with spirits that she enables to cross over into the Light. At its core, *Ghost Whisperer* is a story about the human psyche. It's universal. Melinda (and the viewer) never knows what to expect from one episode to the next. I try to incorporate the essence of all this into the look of the show.

Orson Wells was a mentor. [Mayling worked with Wells on *Cradle Will Rock*, his unmade autobiographical feature film.] He taught me a very aggressive approach — use every means I can to tell the story and do not get hung up on logic or practicality. My other mentor, the wonderful costume designer Nino Navaris, taught me the importance of color and how to effectively use it to convey emotion and tone.

Your process?
I always sketch the sets. I think of everything in spatial terms, not flat. Then I think in colors. And lighting is so important. It affects everything — space, color, shape. Daytime sun is completely different than

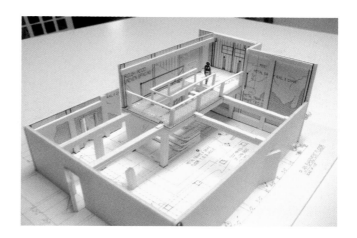

Same As It Ever Was?
Melinda's shop was originally named Same As It *Always* Was, but it didn't clear through legal, because a shop actually existed somewhere in the US with that exact name. So we swapped 'Never' for 'Always' — which also suits Melinda's unique sensibility better.

night lighting. In practical terms, spatial thinking is critical to designing a set because I'm not just designing a space for the actors and ghosts to play their scene, I must create enough room for the camera and the behind-the-scenes crew shooting the scene. As a general rule, anything smaller than fifteen feet, with a camera and an actor in, all you'll see is a talking head. *Ghost Whisperer* is hardly a talking heads show!

What are your challenges week to week?
With episodic TV, there are two major obstacles: the time limit and the cost. While being creative, you always have to take those into consideration. When I have a vision, by the time it enters production, I'm only happy with fifteen percent of the original concept that is captured in the set. *(Wide smile)* Did I mention I'm a perfectionist?

How do you take an idea from the page to the screen?
The first priority when reading a script is to determine where our actors and ghosts are entering the set, where they're playing the scene, and where

Our goal has been the same since the very first day we started on *Ghost Whisperer* — enable viewers to 'experience' the ghosts. Helping us figure it out on a daily basis are two extremely talented but very different directors of photography. James Chressanthis was a solo act in season one and Crescenzo Giacomo Notarile came aboard in season two. Ever since, they've been leap-frogging episodes and creating ghost magic.

To 'manifest' a ghost into and out of a scene, each scene is shot twice: once with the ghost and once without (a.k.a. "MOG" — "*mit* out ghost"). It's expensive, complicated and time-consuming, but necessary. When filming ghost scenes, the set almost looks like the director and actors are engaged in child's play. Midway through the scene, the director shouts "Freeze!" The actors stop mid-

they're exiting. Once I've determined that, I start adding color, dimension, features, etc. Another critical consideration is the lighting positions (the purview of the director of photography). I work closely with both our DPs. The script itself, the way the scene is described, often dictates what my design will be. I always use models in addition to sketches because they are three dimensional — idea, sketch, and then mock up a model. Then I know exactly what trouble I can get into.

Which is your favorite set?
The most creative set was also the most challenging. We designed a partially burned and buried underworld church. One of the biggest obstacles was creating a set that exists in darkness. Remember, something that is underground has no organic lightsources, but the DP still needs to light the set so you can see the action. Approaching the creation of a set must be done as a team — construction, art director, set decorator... I come up with a concept and then I have my art director, Bruce Buehner, find materials. Texture is very important. It has depth and spatial elements and does subliminal work.

http://www.youtube.com/watch?v=xoxypapNwoU

CAPTURING THE SPIRITS
Pop Quiz: Have you ever actually *seen* a ghost? In *real* life? Well, we haven't. And that's the challenge. How do you visualize and photograph something that almost no one in the world has ever seen?

Above:
An underworld street
Right and Opposite:
Storyboards by Ricky Lewis depicting the ghost "attack" from under the lawn at the end of 'The Underneath' Act 1.

"GHOST WHISPERER" EP. #301

CLOSEUP - A VINE COVERED FACE EMERGES FROM THE GROUND !!! "YOU... IT WAS YOU!"

MED CLOSE. GHOST HANDS CLAWING & MELINDA'S HANDS PULLING.

TIGHT ON MEL FREAKING OUT.

motion, the camera locks off, and the ghost runs to the next position in the scene. The director shouts "Go!" and the action picks up exactly where the ghost and the actors left off. When we edit it all together, the ghost magically disappears from one place and reappears somewhere else on the set.

For actors and directors new to the show, this unusual shooting process takes a bit of getting used to. Our blooper reel is full of mishaps, like a ghost running to the wrong place, or actors trying to remember where they left off, or losing their balance mid-freeze and falling over!

James and Crescenzo On Shooting Ghosts

James: Let me say up front, I'm agnostic on the subject of ghosts. However, because of my documentary background, even with what I view as an 'unreal' subject, I try to make the photography believable.

Crescenzo: Since we're doing 'true confessions' here, I'll admit, before joining *Ghost Whisperer*, I never entertained the concept of believing in ghosts. Honestly, being part of this show has made me embrace the concept. There have been some strange moments on set where someone in the cast or crew felt a spirit touching them or even grabbing them. My mind has been opened up.

In our series, ghosts appear and disappear, cross over into the spirit world, act loving, behave angry — it all provides for visual stimulation and interpretation that's different from other shows. When I read our scripts, I close my eyes and allow my mind to take an exciting journey.

James: We approach lighting each episode like you would a feature film. Melinda's daylight Grandview is a golden, lush and beautiful world full of colors and tones. Her 'ghost world' is another matter entirely; it's the dark side of her gift and the spirits she interacts with are reflected in our 'cool' lighting choices and things dropping off to shadow.

Crescenzo: Because we believe ghosts have a unique point of view of the world, we use an extreme range of camera lenses, from fish-eye to long telephoto, to let viewers *experience* those POVs.

James: As the ghosts delve into the mysteries of their unfinished business, we use alternate frame rates, ramping of frame rates, slow-motion photography and a hand-cranked camera to help the audience see the puzzle pieces as they come together. Believe it or not, we sometimes use consumer format [industry-speak for home video cameras] to deliver a special sensibility that a ghost has.

Crescenzo: My favorite way to reveal a ghost is by using silhouettes or having a spirit appear from a shadow into a ray of light.

James: But during cross overs we never, ever shoot what's *in* the Light — we leave it to the viewer's imagination.

Crescenzo: Can I say there's only one Jennifer Love Hewitt?

James: If you don't, I will!

www.fansofgw.com/grid/valentine/

MANIFESTING GHOSTS

In 'The Gravesitter', the story centers around Justin Yates, the Rockland University web blogger who is being haunted by his dead girlfriend, Julie. She died in a boating accident and has returned from the ominous underworld to haunt Justin. This episode is packed with special effects — many of them digital. Here, visual effects supervisor/associate producer Armen Kevorkian and visual effects supervisor Art Codron share their 'battle plan' for executing the visual effects. (Keep in mind, some of the more complex shots have over 100 elements.)

Sequence 1: The ghost of Julie involved water-type effects, as she drowned in a boat accident. So when Justin first encounters her ghost, a flow of water was to gush out of her mouth as she was revealed. On the day of production, the special effects appliance that was supposed to spray the water did not work properly. There was no time for the special effects department to fix the rig, so the effect fell on our plate unexpectedly.

We shot a production plate over Justin's shoulder onto the pavement. We then shot a corresponding plate of the "spirits", matching lens size and angle. Because this was shot late in the day with no time left, they were shot without a greenscreen. In post, a matte painting looking down on the underworld was made and the spirits were composited into it. That was then composited into the over-the-shoulder shot, as Justin reaches down and the ripple reveals what lies beneath. For the reverse angles looking up at Justin, the sky was enhanced with stars and clouds as it was a stark pitch-black night sky behind him in the production shots. For the overhead shot where he is sucked into the ground, Justin fell into a pad on the ground and was rotoscoped and put into a clean plate of the pavement. A ripple effects was added in Fusion as he vanishes.

Sequence 4 (opposite top): While Justin is underground, he is overwhelmed by the centuries-old town that exists beneath Grandview.

For his POV, a production plate was stitched and enhanced to add numerous details to the ghostly locale.

Sequence 5 (opposite bottom): The bittersweet conclusion. Justin has crossed over to the afterlife. But this time it is different… As we pull back from Melinda and Justin's family, the tone changes…

 138

Julie the ghost was tracked by our animator and a flow of water was added using Realflow. The water element was then composited into the shot using Fusion.

Sequence 2 (above): Justin flees to the bathroom. As he looks in the mirror above the sink, he sees the full-length mirror on the other side of the bathroom become a "window" to the church in our underworld. Julie is in front of the church calling for him. She then walks closer to the mirror and walks right out of it, into the bathroom with Justin.

For this effect, we shot the bathroom with a greenscreen in place for the full-length mirror which Julie was standing in front of. A matte painting of the church was tracked and composited into the mirror behind Julie. She then walks forward into the bathroom with the greenscreen still behind her. We again tracked and composited the matte painting of the church into the mirror. We then did a transition effect in Fusion for Julie's transition from the church underworld to the bathroom interior. The lighting was very precise on set when we shot Julie, to make the transition from the cool-toned underworld into the tungsten-lit bathroom as real as possible. When she disappears at the end of the sequence, in the profile shot of her and Justin, there was no clean plate. A clean plate was made and tracked into the moving shot in Fusion.

Sequence 3 (right): We are over Justin's shoulder and he touches the pavement, revealing many haunted spirits. One of the spirits is Julie. As they call out to him, he is sucked underground to join them.

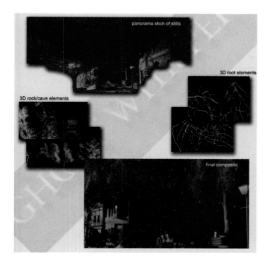

Ominous music begins as we crane away, skimming the pavement... As we come upon an area of the pavement, ghost spirits are pushing up from the street.

For this effect, we shot the production plate on the Universal backlot and added all visual effects elements in post. First, the street was digitally tracked and replaced. Then "ghosts" were animated in Lightwave and composited in Fusion to make them

look like they were pushing from the ground below. Cloth simulations were made to enhance the effect of the pavement being pushed up.

www.youtube.com/watch?v=hc42gRK-TWk

Art and Armen On Manifesting Ghosts

Art: *Ghost Whisperer* is not considered a visual effects show... but it really is! It's a drama with ghostly spiritual overtones achieved through visual and physical effects. For that reason, it's important that the show stay 'real', which makes it all the more challenging for us. It's much easier to go crazy with visual effects than to walk the fine line between 'grounded reality' and the 'what if?' While the producers have created these guidelines, they have also given us immense freedom to come up with new concepts and looks. *Creativity* is strongly encouraged! It's what makes the show so rewarding to work on.

Armen: Most ghosts in our show look different from one another. Some are apparition-like, some look as real as you and I do. It all depends on the story. Our job is to serve the story. If we're creating an angry ghost, the disappearance will usually be fast and aggressive. If it is a pleasant ghost who's lost, it will be slower."

Art: In cross overs, a ghost's unfinished earthbound business is resolved so the spirit is usually at peace, relieved of all anxiety. We make the cross overs soft and beautiful and try to impart a lyrical delicateness. Conversely, if a spirit is sucked under to you-know-where, it can be whiplash-fast and violent. We try and make it look painful.

Armen: That's how we imagine it to be!

CHANNELING THE SPIRITS

Casting director Donna Rosenstein and her team work with the executive producers on casting the main stars, as well as the many, many guest stars and supporting characters. In season two, when Andrea's character was killed off, Donna worked many a late night to find the perfect fit for Melinda's new friend, Delia Banks, and then cast the hysterically funny Jay Mohr as Professor Rick Payne, Melinda's go-to guy on all things strange and paranormal.

In most TV series, guest stars are ancillary characters who service the stories of the show's

main cast. The advantage *Ghost Whisperer* has is that the guest stars, who play ghosts and other lead characters, get to be *true stars* of the show on a week to week basis. The show has featured a raft of very high-profile actors — Mary J. Blige, Anne Archer, Orlando Jones, Christine Baranski, David Paymer and Abigail Breslin, to name just a few.

Q&A With Donna Rosenstein
How did you cast Melinda Gordon?
We auditioned and tested a lot of women for the crucial role. I knew Love from working on another project prior to *Ghost Whisperer*. Executive producers Ian Sander and Kim Moses knew her as well — their development office was next door to her office at Touchstone Studios and they had been talking about developing a show together. We all thought Love was hugely talented, very beautiful, and if we could get her to come back to television

Below:
David Conrad prepares for his next scene during a break in shooting on 'Haunted Hero'.

— remember *Party of Five?* — it would create lots of excitement. When she suddenly became available, we focused on how to bring her aboard.

And how was the casting process for Melinda's husband Jim?
We auditioned lots of guys and tested a number of actors for the part. David Conrad was one of the first people we read for Jim and was always the best.

And Delia?
Finding the perfect friend for Melinda was difficult after Andrea. Most people know Camryn Manheim from her TV series work, but I knew her from her one-woman show in New York (which hinted at shades of Delia). Camryn's body of work, and fan base, made it so that she was offered the role of Delia.

Jay Mohr's entry into the show as Professor Rick Payne was more gradual.
That's right. Jay started out in season two as a recurring guest star and evolved into a series regular by season three. Jay brings a kinetic energy to his scene work and the writers write great material for him. The on-screen chemistry between Professor Payne and Melinda is undeniable.

When reading a script, do you immediately have a sense of who each character should be?
I do. *Ghost Whisperer* is close to me, and with my knowledge of actors, often the image of an actor I know will come to me for a specific role while I'm reading. Often times, the person I am envisioning actually books the role.

How do you translate the character from script to a flesh and blood person on screen?
It all starts with releasing a 'breakdown' of character descriptions to the entertainment community of agents and managers. After they submit their clients for specifics roles, we go through the submissions and pick people to come in and audition. Either they will audition live in person, or they will be hired off their impressive body of work, which entails looking at their film. And each and every actor who walks into our casting room brings their own personality and magic to the role they are auditioning for.

How much input does an episodic director have?
In our *Ghost Whisperer* sessions, the directors always have a lot of input into the decision-making process. And then, of course, it is processed with the executive producers' and the writer's input.

What is your particular approach to casting an episode?

I think about every episode as its own mini-movie. With so few series regulars, and a revolving guest cast, every episode we showcase a mixture of fresh faces and recognizable actors that our audience will know. That is the recipe of our success.

What happens behind 'closed doors' in your casting sessions?

First, we activate a red 'police bubble' that flashes in the hallway outside the casting offices to alert everyone, "Quiet please, actors are auditioning." The casting session starts with bringing in actors who have prepared for the role. We ask them if they have any questions about the part or any circumstances regarding the role. The writer, director or executive producer will help them with backstory, motivation, etc. Then the actor reads the 'sides' (the section of the script we have provided for them to memorize). If we want to see an adjustment, we'll give the note and have the actor do it. We repeat the process until we've seen everyone up for the role. When the audition process is over, we discuss who's right for each role.

How do you feel about the evolution of *Ghost Whisperer* over the three seasons?

As time has gone on, we've gotten more recognizable actors wanting to be on our show because it gives them the opportunity to play emotional and meaningful characters that they don't always get to play on, say, your typical cop drama. Over the seasons we have kept the family and friends of Melinda and Jim close and we have more recurring roles and storylines.

Do you believe in ghosts?

I don't necessarily believe in ghosts but I do believe in spirits. I believe they are around us and they send us signs. I believe that my father, who passed away eighteen years ago, watches over me from Heaven and is with me a lot.

www.fansofgw.com/clips/bloopers.mov

HAUNTING MELODIES

World-renowned, award-winning composer Mark Snow created *Ghost Whisperer*'s main theme, and composes the original score in each episode. Other famous themes Mark has created include *The X-Files* (remember the whistle?), *Millennium, Starsky &*

Gordon Fordyce On Song Selection

"The show always comes first. The band or artist has to fit our show. A great example is in 'Holiday Spirit', which was our untraditional Christmas story — we needed untraditional Christmas songs. Reliant K, a punk-pop band, did a holiday cover of 'Have Yourself a Merry Little Christmas' with a contemporary edge. It was such a perfect match tonally to the episode, that the editor cut the picture to the tracks and the song stayed in the episode all the way through to broadcast. Fans loved it!"

Hutch, Hart to Hart, and, of course, *T.J. Hooker.*

Q&A With Mark Snow

How did you make your way to *Ghost Whisperer*?

I came out of Julliard School, my first composing gig was Aaron Spelling's *The Rookies*, and now here I am at *Ghost Whisperer*. There were plenty of twists and turns along the way! I actually scored a television movie, *When He's Not a Stranger*, which John Gray directed and Ian Sander produced too many years ago, and we've maintained a relationship since.

Start with creating the opening theme, since that's the gateway to the show each week.

I must have written twelve or more [versions] before everyone agreed on it. It was challenging, because the visual title sequence is so unique for a TV drama series. The theme had to be exciting and haunting but it couldn't overpower the visuals. I think I got it right.

What's your creative approach with the score?

It includes three main musical elements: emotional heartfelt melodies, creepy ambient sounds, and pulse/rhythm. Put them all together, and it spells *Ghost Whisperer*.

How has your creative approach evolved?

The first year, the music was really in your face, making a meal out of every moment. As the storytelling has dimensionalized, I've toned it down.

How are you inspired on a weekly basis?

It's the visuals that get me going — I need that for

my ideas to take shape. *Ghost Whisperer* is an extremely visual show.

This series is known for its creative use of songs. What's the approach?

My music team, Gordon Fordyce, Grant Conway and Lindsey Wolfington, do a great job interfacing with major labels like Interscope and CBS Records as well as the small indie labels to ferret out the right music to help tell the story.

By way of pieces that you've composed, what's your favorite in ghost land?

It's hard to say, I have so many, especially in the cross over moments. One piece that stands out is a cue from 'Haunted Hero', the Iraq War episode. I wrote this piece for trumpet and strings that was very anthemic and moving, almost hymnal, when one of the characters remembers his friend.

Do you believe in ghosts?

Not until I started doing the *Ghost Whisperer* music. Then one night, as I was writing one of the scores, I felt a tap on my shoulder, turned around, and saw Stravinsky giving me a 'thumbs up'! So, yes, I'm a believer now!

www.sandermoses.com/SMInteractive/MJB.html

www.youtube.com/watch?v=0Qp84cW27Tw

THINGS THAT GO BUMP...

Ghost Whisperer takes place in the normal world but employs elements of the paranormal world.

Above:
One *Ghost Whisperer* answer to "What does the world of the living look like to a ghost?" Bloody Mary watches Melinda and Jim in 'Don't Try This at Home'.

Opposite:
The Santa ghost disappears to the sound of jingling bells in 'Holiday Spirit'.

This presents the challenge of creating a unique style for sound design as well as editorial. Do all ghosts sound alike? Do all ghosts look alike? Absolutely not. And on the flip-side, what does the world of the living look and sound like to a ghost? These are just some of the questions which get answered in our post production department, headed up by Juanita Diana Feeney. She says the phrase 'total immersion' comes to mind when asked about the approach of her and her team.

Q&A With Juanita Diana Feeney

Can you give an overview of the sound design process?

Our sound team, sound supervisor Tim Terusa and Mark Friedgen at Smart Post Sound, deliver sounds for us to audition early on in the process. We play with them in Neal Mandelberg, Anthony Miller, and Michael Knue's fabulous editorial cuts, so by the time we get to the mix stage we have a pretty good idea of where we want to be sonically. Once we are on the stage, we shape and mold the sound to support our audience's emotional journey.

How have the ghost audio tones evolved?

We have gone from a big bang and boom every time you see a ghost to a much more suspenseful approach to the sound design.

How do you create ghost sounds from thin air?

I read the script and make notes of all the areas that

will need to be developed. For example, in our episode 'Don't Try This At Home', we knew that the sound of a bell was heard every time our Bloody Mary ghost appeared in the mirror. We began to immediately pull in every type of bell and sample them for the executive producers, writer and director Ian Sander. We probably listened to fifty variations on the bell and tried many of them in the various cuts. By the time we got to the final mixing of the episode we had clearly defined the sound we needed to tell the story. With a droning bell, there is just so much of it a viewer can handle before going mad and ultimately turning off the show, so getting the right bell sound at the right volume became a challenge.

How does the post production process incorporate special effects, sound, and music?

We use visual effects to tell the viewer, "Hey, there's a ghost over here and look what they're doing!" Many of our visual effects lean toward the organic — fire, water, wind — as opposed to a more sci-fi approach — creatures, laser beam fights, flying. Then comes the sound. On a specific level, it brings the visual effects to life. On a technical level, it allows viewers to clearly hear the dialog, and in some cases that means re-recording the voices because of noise in the original production tracks. On an emotional level, it can take the viewer to the scare, it can make you cry, or it can make you laugh. We had an episode where we had a ghost who always appeared naked. The director, Kim Moses, strategically placed various items to cover up his 'not for prime-time' parts and we created sound effects to accompany the visuals. In one scene, the ghost appears suddenly behind a parking meter and just as he does the meter *Pings*! *(Grins)*

What's your favorite episode?

'Holiday Spirit'. I'm a connoisseur of Christmas episodes. That is one of the best I've ever seen. The story lends itself to all those classic Christmas images, plus you have a Santa ghost… Brilliant! Santa would touch his nose before disappearing. We put the sound of a tinkling bell on the touch and then jingling bells as he disappeared. Very slight, but every time — magical!

Do you believe in ghosts?

I had an encounter about ten years ago. I'd made plans for a night out with an old high school friend who was having lots of personal problems. I had been waiting hours for her and was worried. When I went to my car to get a sweater, I was suddenly surrounded by a whirling gray cloud. In the middle of the cloud I saw a dark haired woman screaming as if she was going down a drain, and she was moving away from me. I was sure something had happened to my friend, and I went to find her. Fortunately, she called the next day and was fine. So yes, I believe in ghosts.

Has any strange phenomenon happened on set?

Every once in a while one of our editors or assistant editors finds ghosts in the film. It's pretty freaky stuff.

What are your beliefs about the paranormal in general — mediums, séances, tarot cards?

I believe in all of it, but I think it's very dangerous to get readings from people who are frivolous with the information. Once, I was having lunch with a humpbacked dwarf psychic… no really… and she decided to give me a reading in front of a table full of woman I didn't know that well, and it was all very, very personal info. She was right on, but I didn't want it shared with a table full of strangers!

Any other thoughts?

Everyone here gives more than is required, and I really love watching them work. We also manage to laugh each and every day. Having worked on commercials, trailers, HBO movies, directed and produced shorts and features, I am very grateful to have a job like mine. ☺

www.fansofgw.com/halloween/

143))

EPISODES
& BEYOND

GHOST WHISPERER'S PARALLEL UNIVERSE

hen *Ghost Whisperer* was originally ordered, we knew it would be an uphill battle to turn it into a hit. Of all the network shows that have premiered on a Friday night in the last ten years, only *eighteen percent* went on to a second season. Couple that with *Ghost Whisperer* being a paranormal show in the CBS landscape — at that time — of primarily police procedurals, and with a single female lead in her twenties — well below the age demographic that CBS traditionally had been servicing — and you had a real long-shot.

So we took it upon ourselves to not only produce *Ghost Whisperer* the TV series, but to deliver its audience as well. Having produced content, both original and promotional, for the Internet over the previous three years, we knew the web was where we'd find our core audience. As soon as the show was ordered, we began creating original content and posting it online to let browsers know that *Ghost Whisperer* was coming to CBS. Consequently, there was awareness and anticipation of the show — and a grassroots following — well before the pilot premiered in the fall of 2005.

Today, *Ghost Whisperer* has the most diverse and advanced presence on the Internet of any drama on television. And we create and execute everything right here where the heart of the show beats. First and foremost, we're storytellers, so everything we do, from *The Other Side* webisodes to the interactive journey in Payne's Brain, tells a story relative to *Ghost Whisperer*. The fans are getting involved online too. A perfect example is *Ghost Whisperer's* Scariest Story Ever Told (www.youtube.com/watch?

v=DkODQNk0ifw), featuring our stars and fans telling a unique story that everyone created together. The week it was posted, it was the number one most responded YouTube video of the week and the number twenty-four most responded YouTube video of all time.

With the advent of TiVo and DVR and the growth of various forms of available entertainment, the television business is being revolutionized, and

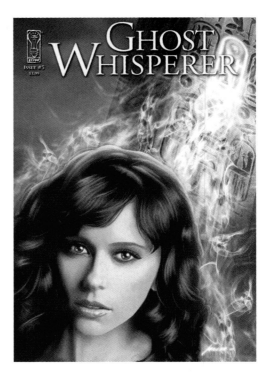

we're determined to stay at the forefront. We test assets we've created online, and as they get traction, we team with department heads at the studios and networks and roll them out onto various platforms that service our fan base. The aim is to make *Ghost Whisperer* a multi-dimensional experience which the viewer can interact with in their own way, on their own schedule.

Go beyond what Melinda Gordon is experiencing in the spirit world of an episode by interacting online with all sorts of viral initiatives that we've created; post how you're feeling about the show at www.cbs.com/primetime/ghost_whisperer/community/ (we look forward to hearing from you!); use your TV remote to interactively explore a haunted house in the Special Features section of the season three DVD boxed set; own merchandise like Beth Colt purses and jewelry, sold *exclusively* at Melinda's Same As It Never Was shop (www.cbsstore.com).

To continue your *Ghost Whisperer* experience between the broadcast of each episode, you can read graphic novels and original novels (store.idw-publishing.com/) while you're listening to *Ghost Whisperer* music from major and indie record labels (www.sandermoses.com/SMInteractive/

Right:
The Melinda's Closet website.
Below:
The haunted house Special Feature on the season three DVD boxed set.
Opposite:
The striking Brian Miller cover of the fifth issue of the *Ghost Whisperer* comic

MidnightVid.html).

We've created this book for you to use as your map to navigate the *Ghost Whisperer* world. And to stay up to the minute on what's happening behind the scenes, check out our *Ghost Whisperer* tumbler at www.ghostwhisperer.tumblr.com.

www.sandermoses.com/spirit

Ghost Whisperer: The Other Side
This is an original online web series that runs as a companion to the TV series. We created it in direct response to the thousands and thousands of emails

we were receiving from around the world asking, "What's it like to be a ghost?"

The Other Side invites fans to see the world through the eyes of a ghost, exploring the world of earthbound spirit Zach as he tries to solve the mystery of his death. Zach learns to navigate the spirit world as he meets an array of ghosts who teach him how to use his ghost powers to intersect with the world of the living.

When *The Other Side* was launched, it created a multi-platform connection between TV and the Internet, with Zach appearing in the season two finale, 'The Profit', hard on the heels of streaming the final webisode. In 'Deadbeat Dads', Zach is back from the dark side and trying once again to get Melinda's attention. This time it's in a hospital maternity ward — definitely an awkward place for a bike courier to drop in! Unfortunately, Melinda is tied up with another ghost. Zach finally gets his opportunity to interact with Melinda while she's having coffee at Village Java. The spirit confesses he's fearful of going into the Light because before he understood his ghost powers, he scared a friend to death. Now he's worried about consequences from a higher authority. Melinda reassures him with a ghost rule specific to his experience: "Your time earthbound has been your redemption — you've made that sacrifice." Check out how it all plays out by watching the web series.

We are proud to say that *The Other Side* won the TVGUIDE.com award for Best TV Drama Webisodes. And it was so successful that Zach's journey is continued in *Ghost Whisperer: The Other Side 2* (www.cbs.com/primetime/ghost_whisperer/the_other_side2). This round of webisodes covers

new territory as it explores the underworld as seen through the eyes of this earthbound spirit. It picks up at the end of the *Ghost Whisperer* TV series' season two finale, in which Zach tries to connect with Melinda Gordon, but before she can help him, he gets sucked into the dark side. Zach struggles to find his way out after wrongly avenging his death.

Because a web series is viewed on the Internet, we approach the filmmaking in an unconventional way. Webisodes need to be more visual than verbal. The director, Claudio Faeh (*Hollow Man II*, *Coronado*, *Starship Troopers: Marauder*), did a great job of helping us tell the story while treating browsers to wild visual goodies, and the powerful score was composed by gaming rock star Inon Zur

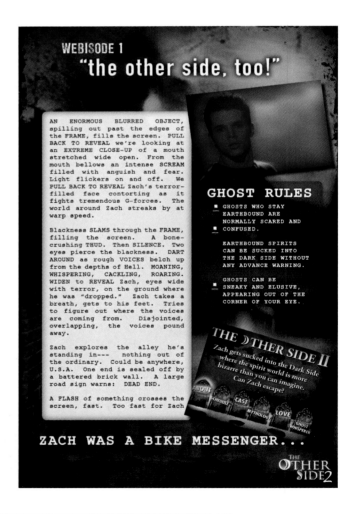

WEBISODE 1
"the other side, too!"

AN ENORMOUS BLURRED OBJECT, spilling out past the edges of the FRAME, fills the screen. PULL BACK TO REVEAL we're looking at an EXTREME CLOSE-UP of a mouth stretched wide open. From the mouth bellows an intense SCREAM filled with anguish and fear. Light flickers on and off. We PULL BACK TO REVEAL Zach's terror-filled face contorting as it fights tremendous G-forces. The world around Zach streaks by at warp speed.

Blackness SLAMS through the FRAME, filling the screen. A bone-crushing THUD. Then SILENCE. Two eyes pierce the blackness. DART AROUND as rough VOICES belch up from the depths of Hell. MOANING, WHISPERING, CACKLING, ROARING. WIDEN to REVEAL Zach, eyes wide with terror, on the ground where he was "dropped." Zach takes a breath, gets to his feet. Tries to figure out where the voices are coming from. Disjointed, overlapping, the voices pound away.

Zach explores the alley he's standing in--- nothing out of the ordinary. Could be anywhere, U.S.A. One end is sealed off by a battered brick wall. A large road sign warns: DEAD END.

A FLASH of something crosses the screen, fast. Too fast for Zach

GHOST RULES

- GHOSTS WHO STAY EARTHBOUND ARE NORMALLY SCARED AND CONFUSED.

- EARTHBOUND SPIRITS CAN BE SUCKED INTO THE DARK SIDE WITHOUT ANY ADVANCE WARNING.

- GHOSTS CAN BE SNEAKY AND ELUSIVE, APPEARING OUT OF THE CORNER OF YOUR EYE.

THE OTHER SIDE II
Zach gets sucked into the Dark Side where the spirit world is more bizarre than you can imagine. Can Zach escape?

ZACH WAS A BIKE MESSENGER...

THE OTHER SIDE 2

(www.inonzur.com).

Happily, General Motors/Saturn, the sponsor of *Ghost Whisperer: The Other Side 1* and *2*, has come aboard for another go around and *The Other Side 3* is in the works. You won't believe what happens next!

As you can see on the microsite that hosts *The Other Side*, ghost rules, mythology and Melinda Gordon components surround the web series. Unlike TV, all the character and storytelling information does not have to be packed into the webisodes in a linear fashion. To shoot them, we don't use traditional scripts like we use to make the TV series. We create concept boards that represent the unique sensibilities needed to tell all aspects of the story and nail down the visual tone, as you can see from the concept boards for one of the webisodes (opposite bottom and above). ☺

www.cbs.com/primetime/ghost_whisperer/the_other_side

149

The Other Side Credits
Zach (Mark Hapka), a young earthbound spirit seeking answers regarding his death; Danny (Matthew Alan), a friend of Zach's who Zach holds responsible for his death; Sarah (Robin Hines), Zach's temptress and teacher in the spirit world; Sam (rapper DNA), a spirit who entertains and enlightens Zach; the Shadow Spirit (Graham McTavish), a ghost from the dark side; and Katie (fashion model Taylor), Zach's girlfriend. Director: Claudio Faeh.

The Other Side 2 Credits
Zach (Mark Hapka) is joined by; BJ (Lucas Alifano), an urban skateboarder stuck in the dark side for nearly twenty years; Luke (Peter Douglas), a dark, mysterious spirit collector who is fixated on Zach; Haley (Marie Westbrook), a spirit seductress who makes disingenuous attempts to befriend Zach; a Lost Spirit (Braden Lynch); and Girlfriend (Tara Hunnewell) and Boyfriend (Gabriel Praddo), both haunted by the spirit world. Director: Claudio Faeh.

SEASON ONE

Melinda Gordon is a young newly-wed with the unique gift to communicate with the spirits of people who have died. The dead seek out Melinda's ability to help them relay significant messages and information to the living. Despite her fear, compassion compels Melinda to help these earthbound spirits cross over by completing their unfinished business with the living.

Here, show creator John Gray shares his insight on season one…

Season one was designed to consist of strictly standalone episodes, i.e. no continuing mythology, nothing a viewer would have to keep track of in order to follow the stories. This was at a time where many serialized shows were faltering, and the sense at the network was that the audience

wanted to be able to miss an episode or two of their favorite shows and still be able to pick up right where they left off.

We were also experimenting with doing some episodes that were purely emotional, some that were totally scary, others that were comic. But each episode pretty much wrapped itself up and if you missed it you'd have no trouble following next week's episode.

Then a funny thing happened... an episode I had written and directed came out short by a couple of minutes. CBS asked us to come up with some kind of coda that was creepy and fun that would fill out the minute or two that had to be made up. I remembered once, as a kid in Brooklyn, seeing a drunk on a street corner laughing hysterically — at what I didn't know. But he felt me watching him, and he turned towards me, and laughed even harder, with his eyes penetrating right through me. It scared the hell out of me... It was as if he knew some secret about me that even I didn't know. So I wrote a page where Melinda is seeing Jim off to work, and as she crosses the square on the way to her store, she notices a guy sitting in a café across the street, staring at her. She stares back, and the guy gets up, locks eyes with her, and starts to laugh, really hard, without ever taking his eyes off of her. Melinda is creeped out, and when the guy disappears, we realize he's a ghost.

We thought maybe we'd follow up on that ghost in some other episode, maybe not; we were really just trying to get the show to time and on the air. However, Laughing Man became a mini-phenomenon, stirring up a tremendous response from our audience, especially online. We started using him more, and he led us to the extremely evil spirit Romano, whose face was always hidden in darkness. Little by little we started developing a mythology that played in the background, but if you were paying attention you could track where it was going, and that paid off in the big season finale. I think this helped pave the way for the network to encourage us to follow a more visible mythology in the second season.

And the funny thing is, the drunk guy from Brooklyn is now asking for royalties — Just kidding! ☺

Melinda: "If there's one thing I know, it's that what happens to people in those last moments really matters."

EP. 1.01 9/23/05
PILOT
Writer: John Gray
Director: John Gray

During Melinda and Jim's wedding reception, Melinda notices an uninvited guest — *a ghost.* Later that night, the ghost does something no other ghost has done before — he comes into Melinda's home. The invasion of privacy disrupts the romantic bliss of Melinda and her new husband. Despite being afraid of the scary-looking spirit, who turns out to be a lost soldier, Melinda must help him unravel the mystery of his unfinished business so he can reunite with his son and cross over into the Light.

Music: 'Loneliness', Annie Lennox
www.fansofgw.com/grid/
cemeterygame/

Ghost Rule: Initially, a spirit's appearance can be distorted, even scary. Once they start to interact with the living, they begin to look more like they did when alive.

151

EP. 1.02 9/30/05
THE CROSSING
Writer: Catherine Butterfield
Director: Ron Lagomarsino

When a train collides with a broken-down car on the railroad tracks, a young boy is accidentally killed inside the vehicle. Melinda helps the boy convince his mother that his death was not her fault. Meanwhile, Melinda and Jim stop the boy's father from exacting revenge on the guy who sold him the car.

Music: 'Blah, Blah, Blah', Patty Medina
www.facebook.com/profile.php?id=1152894437&ref=ts

Melinda: "Kids can almost always see spirits. Where do you think imaginary friends come from?"

Ghost Rule: Children under ten can sometimes see ghosts, but usually grow out of it.

Mary Ann: "Do you have any idea how many people I've helped cross over? I'm beginning to feel like a travel agent who's never been on a plane."

EP. 1.03 10/7/05
GHOST, INTERRUPTED
Writer: Jed Seidel
Director: Ian Sander

A teenage girl is sent to a psychiatric clinic after her parents observe her odd behavior on the heels of the death of her identical twin sister. The girl slips away and hides in Melinda's antique store, where the ghost of her twin appears and blames Melinda for notifying the authorities. Convinced the girl's odd behavior is because she's being haunted by her twin, Melinda must help the deceased twin figure out her past betrayal so she can move on and her sister can be freed from the clinic.

Music: 'Until We Meet Again', 'Paying Out the Hard Way', Lori Denae
www.fansofgw.com/ghostgallery/

EP. 1.04 10/14/05
MENDED HEARTS
Writer: John Gray
Director: John Gray

After a man is killed in a triathlon accident, his devastated fiancée tries to take her life. In an effort to save her, Melinda helps the grieving young woman reconnect with the love of her life. But there's one last piece of business — Melinda must track down the man who received the fiancé's heart and turn his life around. Also, the Laughing Man spirit reveals himself to Melinda for the first time.

Music: 'Monochrome', 'Wellingtons', Phontaine
www.fansofgw.com/grid/laughingman/

Ghost Rule: Ghosts do not always retain memories from their experiences in the world of the living.

Melinda: "Sorry we woke you. This one is having boundary issues."
Jim: "Don't they all."

EP. 1.06 10/28/05
HOMECOMING
Writer: Lois Johnson
Director: James Frawley

The spirit of a teenage boy, Jason, approaches Melinda about finding his birth mother. Unsure of where to begin, Melinda reaches out to the boy's adoptive mother for more information and learns that his birth mother does not want to know him. Melinda must figure out how to secure an affirmation of the birth mother's love for her son so he can cross over. This episode marks Melinda's first encounter with a 'Guardian' spirit.

Jason: "What if she doesn't remember me?"
Melinda: "I've never given birth, but from what I've heard, it's not something you forget."

Music: 'In Your Head', Patty Medina
www.ghostwhispereroncbs.wetpaint.com/

Ghost Rule: 'Guardians' are spirits responsible for bringing babies to the Light when they do not have someone to meet them.

Hope: "Nobody can see me except for you."
Melinda: "It's a gift I have. Can I tell you, you're a little pushy."
Hope: "If you were in my position you would be too."

EP. 1.07 11/4/05
HOPE AND MERCY
Writer: John Wirth
Director: Bill L. Norton

Jim is involved in a car accident, and when Melinda visits him in the hospital she finds herself being haunted by a young woman, Hope, who died of complications during a routine surgery. Melinda helps the ghost investigate why she died, only to discover a devastating cover-up.

Music: 'Pleasure and Business', Phontaine
www.fansofgw.com/grid/mythology/

Ghost Rule: Ghosts often stay earthbound in order to help a grieving loved one to heal and move on with their life.

EP. 1.05 10/21/05
LOST BOYS
Writer: David Fallon
Director: Peter O'Fallon

Melinda and Andrea are hired to auction off furniture from a dilapidated inn before the structure is torn down by the new owner. Upon rummaging around in the basement, Melinda discovers the inn used to be an orphanage and is being haunted by the spirits of three young boys and their dog Homer. They all died in a fire years ago. Melinda must help the mischievous spirits cross over before the structure is destroyed or they will be destined to drift as earthbound spirits forever.

Music: 'Stars Shine in the Sky Tonight', Eels

Melinda: "Well, they [ghosts] build up so much energy over the years, and then they break things."
Andrea: "Great. Another fun fact from Melinda."

Ghost Rule: When a child's ghost gets attached to a place, it is hard to cross them over.

EP. 1.08 11/11/05
ON THE WINGS OF A DOVE

Writer: Catherine Butterfield
Director: Peter O'Fallon

After Jim starts to suffer from anxiety and depression, Melinda determines that he is experiencing the spirit of an ex-con — the victim of a motorcycle accident who Jim could not save. Melinda learns that the spirit attached to Jim needs her help in making amends to the family of the man he killed several years ago. When Melinda's attempt fails, she must figure out another way to help the ghost make amends so he can detach himself from Jim and cross over. Also, G-Man ghost is embedded in this episode.

Andrea (to Melinda): "What's a malevolent spirit or two between friends?"

Music: 'Helen Reddy', Trembling Blue Stars
www.fansofgw.com/seance/halloween1.mov

Ghost Rule: Ghosts feed off our emotions and can in turn influence us.

Jim (re. his mother): "She likes to think she's low maintenance."
Melinda: "Don't we all."

EP. 1.09 11/18/05
VOICES

Writer: John Belluso
Director: Kevin Hooks

When Melinda and Jim hear voices in the static of their car radio, Melinda determines it's EVP. Soon after, Melinda finds herself under siege from EVP embedded in white noise. Spirit voices blare from Melinda's computer, TV, and every other electronic device in her house. Realizing that one of the spirit voices is from the mother of a troubled teenage boy, Melinda must figure out a way to piece together the messages from the mother and effectively communicate them to the son so he can straighten out his chaotic life.

Music: 'Jenny', Aidan Hawken
www.ugo.com/channels/filmtv/features/ghostwhisperer chronicles/hauntings-4.asp

EP. 1.10 11/25/05
GHOST BRIDE

Writer: Jed Seidel
Director: Joanna Kerns

The ghost of a deceased bride is back with a vengeance, haunting her husband's new fiancée because she cannot bear the thought of him loving anyone but her. The haunting causes the bride-to-be to assume that her fiancé is still in love with his dead wife, who was killed in a car crash on the eve of their wedding. Melinda must straighten out any doubts that the young living bride has, while giving closure to the angry spirit bride so that the pending nuptials can take place.

Andrea: "I gotta tell you — I didn't realize that spirits were this, I dunno, like interactive, I guess."

Music: 'Until the End', Fonda; 'Do I Love You', Ella Fitzgerald
www.fansofgw.com/grid/evp/

Ghost Rule: Because of the resentment an earthbound spirit feels about his/her tragic death, the spirit can wreak havoc on the living.

EP. 1.12 12/16/05
UNDEAD COMIC

Writer: Doug Prochilo
Director: Eric Laneuville

As Andrea prepares to do stand-up at a local comedy club, Melinda encounters a crowd of dead comedians engaging in their own comedy acts. One dead comic, Marty, stands out because he's stuck between worlds. By communicating with 'funny' spirits and the comic's living girl-friend, Melinda helps the ghost discover what lead to his mysterious death, and he finds laughter on the other side. Also, Melinda sees that Laughing Man and Wide Brim Hat Man are kindred spirits.

> Marty: "Dying is easy. It's the comedy that's hard."

Music: 'We All Dance', Paul Trudeau
www.fansofgw.com/grid/haunted america/

Ghost Rule: When a person commits suicide, his/her spirit can be stuck between the worlds of the living and the dead.

EP. 1.11 12/9/05
SHADOW BOXER

Writer: Emily Fox
Director: Joanna Kerns

The aggressive spirit of the mother of an amateur boxer pops up in Melinda's life because she needs help in reuniting her husband and son. The son is angry with his father for forcing him to compete against his will. Melinda must broker peace between them so that the son can achieve his dreams. Only then can the mother cross over and leave Melinda alone.

Music: 'Until You Are Here', Tyrone Wells; 'Paper Tigers', Caesers
www.melindasdiary.com

> Andrea: "Just once I wish one of these ghosts follow-ing you around would buy something."

Ghost Rule: Some earthbound spirits only stay behind to help protect the people they love.

> Jim: "Now don't go making me the bad guy just because I care about you."
> Melinda: "Don't get all noble. There's a difference between caring and controlling."

EP. 1.13 1/6/06
FRIENDLY NEIGHBOR-HOOD GHOST

Writer: Lois Johnson
Director: David Hugh Jones

Strange behavior, like boarding up his windows, causes Melinda and Jim to question the sanity of their new neighbor. It isn't until Melinda sees a ghost attached to him that she realizes the ghost is trying to kill the poor guy. Under further investigation, Melinda discovers the ghost is seeking revenge, but she's convinced her neighbor is innocent. Jim is not so sure. Melinda must keep the neighbor out of harm's way until she can persuade the ghost, the neighbor and her husband that things are not as they seem. Also, Melinda and Jim take in a unique stray — Homer the ghost dog.

Music: 'Sometimes', Damon & Naomi

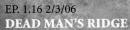

EPISODE GUIDE

EP. 1.14 1/13/06
LAST EXECUTION

Writer: David Fallon
Director: James Frawley

Upon attending a local art exhibit, Melinda is stalked by the ghost of an executed prisoner whose work is on display. In an effort to get Melinda's help to uncover a scam involving the artwork and his daughter, the ghost puts Melinda's life in jeopardy. Melinda must help this ghost set things right in order to save her own life.

Jim: "The shower's broke."
Melinda: "Again?"
Jim: "You can use the kitchen sink. I do all the time."
Melinda: "I really wish you hadn't told me that."

Music: 'Edge of the World', Deathray; 'Soon Enough', Silverjet; 'Walk Into the Sun', Dirty Vegas
www.fansofgw.com/seance/holiday

Ghost Rule: Ghosts can force visions of their death onto the living. If those memories are extremely violent, the person's life can be jeopardized

Melinda: "I didn't always want this gift, and sometimes I absolutely hate it, but I do good with it, mom."

EP. 1.15 1/27/06
MELINDA'S FIRST GHOST

Writer: Catherine Butterfield
Director: Peter Werner

When Melinda gets a surprise visit from her first ghost, it triggers memories of how she first discovered her unique gift and the strain it put on her relationship with her mother. Now that Melinda is older and has embraced her gift, she wants to help the ghost find her parents so she can have closure. This can't happen until Melinda is able to reach out to her own mother and convince her to share important information about the ghost's family.

Music: 'I Could Fly', Mojophonic
www.fansofgw.com/grid/melindas _closet/

Ghost Rule: Ghosts have no sense of time.

EP. 1.16 2/3/06
DEAD MAN'S RIDGE

Writer: John Gray
Director: James Frawley

The spirit of Andrea's friend begins haunting her while his body is in an unconscious state. Every time he flatlines, his spirit gives another clue to the location of where his brother is trapped. In order to find the trapped brother, Melinda must convince doctors to let Andrea's friend flatline longer so she can piece together his clues.

Music: 'Here by the Window', Miranda Lee Richards
www.fansofgw.com/iyhh/

Andrea (re. the ghost): "If he's after my last pint of Cherry Garcia, he can pry it out of my cold dead fingers."

Ghost Rule: Out of body experiences occur when a person flatlines and is resuscitated.

EP. 1.18 3/10/06

MISS FORTUNE

Writer: Emily Fox

Director: James Chressanthis

When a traveling carnival comes to town, Melinda encounters the spirit of a vengeful magician who believes his death during a dangerous underwater stunt was no accident. As Melinda puts the pieces together leading up to the magician's death, she learns of an unlikely suspect in this strange carni world.

Music: 'Mystery of Joy', MRDC
www.fansofgw.com/grid/gman/

Ghost Rule: A spirit can use its energy to cause a physiological response in people, even making it difficult to breath — this is particularly dangerous for 'sensitives' and the gifted (like Melinda).

Lilia: "So you're here to have your fortunes told."
Andrea: "Wow, you are psychic."

EP. 1.17 3/3/06

DEMON CHILD

Writer: Jed Seidel

Director: Eric Laneuville

Melinda encounters the spirit of an angry young boy who is attached to items she bought from a local homeowner. It turns out the spirit is the homeowner's dead son and he's terrorizing his mother and baby sister. Melinda realizes that the young ghost needs help releasing his anger toward his mother, and decides to take on the challenge of helping him figure out why he's so angry. Also, G-Man ghost is embedded in this episode.

Music: 'Maybe', The Tao of Groove
www.fansofgw.com/grid/tarotcards/

Jim (to Melinda): "I'll be happy to have a whole brood of baby ghost busters with you."

Ghost Rule: Ghosts can use the negative energy they have pent up to move objects.

EP 1.19 3/31/06

FURY

Writer: Rama Stagner

Director: Peter Werner

The ghost of an African-American man, who was killed during a fight with a white co-worker in the 1970s, haunts the former prosecutor-turned-judge who refused to file charges against the perpetrator even though there was plenty of evidence. Melinda must help the wronged ghost find justice at a higher level in order to erase his own son's racist views.

 157

Andrea: "Ever notice how people will shop in pouring rain, but one hint of thunder and they scurry like roaches?"
Melinda: "Hmmm. Nice visual."

Music: No featured music
www.fansofgw.com/grid/askmelinda/

Ghost Rule: Spirits can group together for a common purpose and use the strength of their numbers to interact more powerfully with the world of the living.

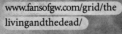

EP. 1.20 4/7/06
THE VANISHING
Writer: Catherine Butterfield
Director: Ian Sander

A head injury puts Melinda's abilities at risk. She discovers that she can no longer communicate with earthbound spirits and fears that she has lost her gift forever. While Melinda is dealing with this new development, she is asked to help comfort a teenage girl who is devastated by the recent death of her boyfriend. Now, Melinda faces the challenge of helping the devastated teen cope with her loss as she questions whether her gift will ever return.

Melinda (to Jim): "I haven't seen a ghost since my accident. Not even in the hospital… What if the problem is that I just can't see them anymore?"

Music: 'The Voice Within', Christina Aguilera; 'You Are What You Love', Jenny Lewis and the Watson Twins; 'What Would You Do', Deathray
www.fansofgw.com/grid/the livingandthedead/

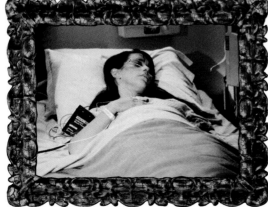

Jim (to Melinda): "That is the $64,000 question. How do they [spirits] ever know to come to you?"

EP. 1.21 4/28/06
FREE FALL
Writer: John Gray
Director: John Gray

When the heat repeatedly goes out in Melinda's house and antique shop, she starts getting strange visits from the ghosts of an airline pilot and flight attendant who complain of being cold. Initially, Melinda has trouble understanding the messages they are trying to communicate, but eventually she figures out that they are trying to warn her about a jetliner that is going to crash just outside of Grandview. Despite Melinda's efforts to warn transportation officials and her community, the jet crashes, killing hundreds on board, and leading up to what will be Melinda's biggest challenge yet.

Music: 'Shine', Stewart Lewis
www.sandermoses.com/SMInteractive/Campus.html

EP. 1.22 5/5/06
THE ONE
Writer: John Gray
Director: John Gray

After a jetliner crashes outside of Grandview, Melinda faces the overwhelming challenge of helping hundreds of the jet's passengers cross over. During this crisis, Melinda encounters the evil spirit Wide Brim Hat Man, who is working against her to keep the spirits earthbound. Melinda must earn the trust of confused passenger ghosts, including her best friend Andrea, as well as cynical investigators, while facing off with Wide Brim.

Melinda (re. Wide Brim's offer to release the souls of the plane passengers in exchange for hers): It was 250 people, Jim. Do I really have the right to ignore that? Jim: "What about the thousands of people you could help the rest of your life? Do you really have the right to ignore them?"

Ghost Rule: When an extremely large group of souls crosses over together it is possible for the living to see the Light.

SEASON TWO

n season two, Melinda Gordon continues to develop her ability to communicate with earthbound spirits as she uses her gift to provide closure for them and their loved ones. Melinda and her husband, Jim Clancy, are joined by a new friend, Delia Banks, and quirky professor of the paranormal Rick Payne, as Melinda battles a dark force threatening to take over her beloved town of Grandview.

Here, show creator John Gray gives the lowdown on developments in season two…

Obviously one of the hardest decisions we made at the end of season one was to kill off Andrea… An idea that excited and scared us. We loved the character, and we loved Aisha Tyler, who played her, and we didn't want to lose what she brought to the show. We were also worried about angering an audience that loved the character and the actress. However, we wanted to keep the audience off-balance and let them know that in this show anything could happen. I think it's fair to say that we kept our audience wondering all summer about whether or not Andrea was "really" dead… and it allowed us to do a really nice send-off episode where Andrea got to reconcile with her brother and turn her back on the dark power of Romano. Bittersweet, to be sure, but they were fun episodes to do!

The departure of Melinda's best friend left us with a void to fill, and led to one of two big changes

we made in season two. We batted around a lot of ideas for a new friend for Melinda — a male apprentice at the store, maybe a ghost companion — but we kept coming back to a living, breathing person who clicks with Melinda. And wouldn't it be fun to finally get to have a character who doesn't know what Melinda can do? What if that character were a pragmatic, real world adult, raising a son on her own? I personally had been dying to get Melinda into situations where she has to hide what she's doing from a close friend, and although we knew we didn't want Delia to be in the dark for the whole season, we would have a lot of fun for at least half the season before Delia was presented with the truth about Melinda. One very interesting aspect of Delia's character that Camryn Manheim herself suggested was that she would not become a true believer. Unlike Andrea, who believed without hesitation, Delia is not so quick to embrace the supernatural. She concedes that Melinda certainly believes, but she herself takes it all with a grain of salt. This allowed us to keep a certain tension between them, while still involving Delia and her son, Ned, in helping Melinda from time to time.

The other character addition was Professor Rick Payne. In him we felt we wanted to have a character who knew a lot about the supernatural, yet wasn't necessarily a believer; someone Melinda could go to for help and who could also team up with her from time to time. And last but not least, we also wanted a character who could inject more humor into the show, which is why we were thrilled when Jay Mohr expressed interest in playing Payne. The professor, who is secretly (or not so secretly) in love with Melinda, is a perfect foil for her; a fountain of information and sarcasm, with moments of unexpected emotional honesty.

This season we also introduced a more tangible and present mythology, which paid off in a pretty big way (we hope) at the end of the season. This was great fun for us, planting seeds here and there, while still keeping the episodes accessible to an audience who may not be watching every single week. The audience responded really well, and the network encouraged us to go even further with a more complex but more personal mythology for Melinda in season three. 🌀

160

EP. 2.01 9/22/06
LOVE NEVER DIES
Writer: John Gray
Director: John Gray

This episodes picks up where season one left off — Melinda's best friend, Andrea, was killed in the jetliner crash just outside Grandview. When Melinda reconnects with Andrea's spirit, she discovers Andrea is being influenced by Wide Brim Hat Man. Melinda turns to Professor Rick Payne for help in winning the battle for Andrea's fate. Professor Payne, an expert in the paranormal at Rockland University, is a new acquaintance to Melinda. Meanwhile, an unidentifiable guy, seemingly obsessed with Melinda, plots to get closer.

Melinda: "Professor Payne."
(Shakes his hand) "Melinda Gordon."
Professor Payne: "Good for you."

Ghost Rule: Light spirits protect souls and help them cross over. Dark spirits are evil and collect souls to keep them earthbound. If a dark spirit takes the soul of a light spirit, the dark spirit becomes invincible.

EP. 2.03 10/6/06

DROWNED LIVES

Writer: Jed Seidel

Director: Ian Sander

When Melinda and Jim visit a married couple who are having problems with their new house, Melinda discovers the ghost of a six year old girl who drowned in the swimming pool. While uncovering why the child's spirit is wreaking havoc in the house, Melinda meets the ghost's older brother, who blames himself for his sister's death. Meanwhile, Delia, who sold the couple the house, is desperate to stop them from moving out.

www.askmaryann.blogspot.com/

Melinda (after three changes): "Well, what do you think?"
Jim: "I think you look beautiful. But for the record, you looked beautiful in the first two dresses."

Ghost Rule: A child ghost will often remain earthbound waiting or searching for their parents.

EP. 2.02 9/29/06

LOVE STILL WON'T DIE

Writer: John Gray

Director: John Gray

The spirit of a guy wants Melinda to visit his wife and help him make amends. But Melinda discovers the guy's "wife" divorced him because he was obsessed with his ex-girlfriend. As she delves further into the story, there are two revelations: the ghost's ex-wife resembles Melinda a great deal, and the ghost is intentionally concealing his identity from Melinda. Meanwhile, Melinda meets Delia Banks, the mother of a boy who stole valuable memorabilia from the antique store. Melinda is surprised to find out what motivated the theft.

Melinda: "I never thought that I was gonna be able to trust anyone after Kyle… and then there was Jim."
Jim: "You're not gonna break into song right now are you?"
Melinda: "I might."

Music: 'Not Gonna Wait', Miranda Lee Richards
www.fansofgw.com/saturnawards/
saturn.mov

Jim: "I'd offer to mind the store, but…"
Melinda: "I know, you're off saving lives while I'm saving the dead."

EP. 2.04 10/13/06

THE GHOST WITHIN

Writer: Lois Johnson

Director: Frederick E.O. Toye

Melinda senses the beautiful ornaments that she and Delia purchased at a flea market are haunted. When Melinda touches the ornaments, she experiences the wild visions that are in the ghost's mind. And yet, the ghost refuses to communicate with Melinda. Melinda brings Professor Payne into the picture to see if he can help with this phenomenon.

Music: 'Believe Me', Tim K. Cullen
www.ugo.com/channels/filmtv/
features/ghostwhispererchronicles/

Ghost Rule: When a soul crosses over into the Light, the handicaps it had in life are gone. Every soul is perfect.

161

EP. 2.05 10/20/06
A GRAVE MATTER
Writer: Catherine Butterfield
Director: Eric Laneuville

When Melinda visits Andrea's gravesite, she meets a confused ghost who's convinced he's buried in the wrong grave. At first, the ghost is unable to identify himself, but he believes the widow weeping at the graveside every day is not his wife. Slowly, the ghost is able to remember bits and pieces of his life and confesses to Melinda that he abandoned his wife and young daughter. The ghost's story mirrors Melinda's own history with her father. Melinda struggles to put aside her personal feelings as she tries to get to the bottom of who is really buried in the grave.

Melinda: "You know what? It's fun brainstorming this stuff with you."
Jim: "They say ghost busting is a great way to keep a marriage alive."

Music: 'The Only Thing', Salme Dahlstrom
www.fansofgw.com/grid/halloweenflash/

Jim (re. his haunting): "I don't know how you do this every day."
Melinda: "Women are better multi-taskers."

EP. 2.06 11/27/06
THE WOMAN OF HIS DREAMS
Writer: Catherine Butterfield
Director: John Showalter

While Melinda is out of town, Jim is under siege from strange occurrences around the house. First beetles invade a poker game with the boys. Then there are the bizarre dreams about a gorgeous woman with an exotic cat — the same cat he and Melinda saw days earlier. Melinda suggests Jim check in with Professor Payne because she believes these incidents are tied to a ghost. When Melinda finally returns home, she discovers that Jim is being haunted by a beauty from his past.

Music: 'Nitty Gritty', Primal Scream; 'The Look', Roxxett; 'Eternal Flame', The Bangles
www.fansofgw.com/grid/fridaythe13th/

EP. 2.07 11/3/06
A VICIOUS CYCLE
Writer: Jeannine Renshaw
Director: Eric Laneuville

While camping, Melinda gets hooked into a ghost story in which she must uncover the truth about a mother's death in order to save her daughter from the same fate. Claiming her daughter needs help, the ghost convinces Melinda to track the young woman down. While Melinda is engaging with the daughter, the ghost attacks the daughter's fiancé. To stop the cycle of violence, Melinda must help mother and daughter acknowledge their darkest secrets.

Music: 'Fall to Pieces', The Shore; 'Don't You Forget About Me', Simple Minds
www.sandermoses.com/spirit/

Delia (to Melinda): "Alone time? Hmm. Okay, fess up — do I detect a biological alarm clock going off?"

Ghost Rule: A ghost can lash out when it feels threatened.

EP. 2.09 11/17/06
THE CURSE OF THE NINTH
Writer: Breen Frazier
Director: Peter Werner

It seems the ghost of a young musician's father is terrorizing his son, until Melinda discovers the ghost has a ghost of its own. Jealous that he's no longer in the band, a deceased band mate is after the young musician as well as his father's ghost. Melinda must find a way to end the jealous ghost's rampage so that the talented musician in the world of the living can return to his music and his father's ghost can cross over into the Light.

Delia: "Serendipity, thy name is Melinda."

Music: 'Pain', 3 Days Grace; 'Nothing Lasts Forever', 'Running Away', 'Different', Midnight Hour; 'Until Yesterday', J.S. Chasez; 'Wasted', Miranda Lee Richards www.sandermoses.com/ SMInteractive/MidnightVid.html

Ghost Rule: Ghosts can use infrasound, a frequency that's so low we can't hear it, to make their presence felt.

EP. 2.08 11/10/06
THE NIGHT WE MET
Writer: David Fallon
Director: Peter O'Fallon

Even though a ghost combusts before her very eyes, Melinda is convinced he is not guilty of the arson that he is accused of. As she works at clearing the ghost's name, Melinda flashes back to the night that fire erupted in the building next door to where she lived. It was the night Jim swept Melinda off her feet.

Music: 'Somersault', Decoder Ring www.sandermoses.com/SMInteractive /ComC.html

Ghost Rule: A ghost who experienced a violent death may relive this experience while trapped as an earthbound spirit.

Jim: "Hey… remember me?"
Melinda: "Yes. You threw my slipper at me."
Jim: "Tossed. I tossed it at you. There's a difference."

EP. 2.10 11/24/06
GIVING UP THE GHOST
Writer: Jim Kouf
Director: Peter O'Fallon

While attending a baseball game with Jim, Melinda encounters the wildly angry ghost of a pro baseball player. Melinda discovers that the pro player was killed in a car crash and his ghost is trying to get back in the game by taking over the body of a talented high school pitcher. In order to save his life, Melinda must help the scared and confused high school pitcher turn his back on the powerful spirit.

Jim: "It's frustrating when the dead can do more than I can."

Music: 'What Do You Want', OK Go www.fansofgw.com/seance/ halloween2

Ghost Rule: Ghosts are often confused about the way they died, blaming the wrong people for their death.

EP. 2.11 12/15/06
THE CAT'S CLAW
Writer: Jim Kouf
Director: Victoria Hochberg

Melinda's strange encounters with a mud-covered ghost transport her from her bedroom closet to a dangerous tropical jungle. Unfortunately, the ghost is plagued by a horrible condition that limits his speech and makes it difficult for Melinda to understand his needs. After a visit to Professor Payne links him to the ghost, Payne suspects Melinda is tied into the spirit world way more than he could ever have imagined.

Melinda: "Do you have to be this crass or can't you help it?"
Payne: "I can help it. I usually do it as a defense mechanism so I don't get too emotionally attached to humanity."

Music: 'Before I Met You', Miranda Lee Richards; 'Love If You're Real', Senor Happy
www.ugo.com/channels/filmtv/features/ghostwhispererchronicles/catsclaw.asp#

Payne (to Melinda): "Okay, there is actual hair standing up on the back of my neck. Do you want to feel it?"

EP. 2.12 1/5/07
DEAD TO RIGHTS
Writer: Wendy Mericle
Director: Peter Werner

While making volunteer hospital rounds with Delia and her therapy dog, Melinda encounters a desperate spirit trapped in an out-of-body experience while his body is on life support. Stuck between life and death, the spirit bitterly watches his parents and wife argue about his fate as Melinda tries to intervene. Also, a bizarre haunting brings Melinda and Professor Payne closer together.

Music: 'I'm There Too', Michelle Featherstone; 'Darkest Things', Submarines
www.youtube.com/watch?v=tjcTis-tz-4

Ghost Rule: When a person is brain-dead, and on life support, their soul is outside the body but still tethered to it.

EP. 2.13 1/12/07
DEJA BOO
Writer: Elle Johnson
Director: Gloria Muzio

With a close friend's pregnancy in danger, Melinda must prevent a seemingly dark spirit from harming the unborn child. Professor Payne tries to guide Melinda in dealing with the ghost and his multiple personalities. While sorting through the desperate fears the ghost has about reincarnation and reliving a terrible past, Melinda must come to terms with her own complex feelings about giving birth.

Music: 'Regular Time', Buddy; 'Look After You', The Fray
www.ghostwhispereroncbs.wetpaint.com/page/Jay+Mohr%27s+Ghost+Whisperer+Tie+Challenge

Payne: "You know what, I'm getting a little tired of you just using me for my brain."
Melinda: "Uh, if only that were possible, but so much of your mouth comes with it."

Ghost Rule: Souls are assigned new bodies when they are reincarnated.

EP. 2.14 2/2/07
SPEED DEMON

Writer: Alan DiFiore
Director: Jim Frawley

When Melinda's car mysteriously breaks down on a remote road, she finds herself face to face with a skeletal ghost that gives a frightening prophecy of death. This sets Melinda off on a journey to crack the mysterious code that is linked to a secret drag racing society. When she discovers that Delia's son, Ned, may be involved with the underground racing group, Melinda follows him to a hidden location to uncover the truth about a race of revenge.

Jim (to Melinda): "Why can't we just go home at night and watch DVDs like normal couples?"

Music: 'Begin', The Shore; 'When Your Heart Stops Beating', Plus 44; 'Congratulations', Blue October featuring Imogen Heap
www.fansofgw.com/seance/valentine.mov

Ghost Rule: Ghosts like to go back to the beginning, where they died.

EP. 2.15 2/9/07
MEAN GHOST

Writer: Jeannine Renshaw
Director: Ian Sander

With a cheerleading championship competition just days away, Melinda scrambles to determine why the spirit of a high school cheerleader is maliciously attacking her former squad mates. When Melinda notices a connection between the angry teen ghost, the new cheerleader captain and a withdrawn goth student, she reaches out to the squad's skeptical coach for help.

Music: 'We Ride', 'You Know', 'Show Love', Mary J. Blige
www.sandermoses.com/SMInteractive/MJB.html

Melinda (to Delia): "In my high school you were either a cheerleader or valedictorian. Anything in between, you may as well have been dead."

Ghost Rule: An earthbound spirit about to cross into the Light can convey messages to the living from spirits already in the Light through dreams.

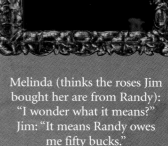

Melinda (thinks the roses Jim bought her are from Randy): "I wonder what it means?"
Jim: "It means Randy owes me fifty bucks."

EP. 2.16 2/16/07
THE CRADLE WILL ROCK

Writer: Jed Seidel
Director: Jim Cressanthis

When a jewelry store is robbed, Melinda and Delia are among the victims. Safe but shaken from the incident, Melinda is confronted by a ghost, Randy, who wants her to contact his widow. Melinda tries to deliver the message to the widow but is held hostage by the criminal who committed the robbery. Trapped and fearing for her life, Melinda must save herself even when it seems there's no way out.

Music: 'Boston', Augustana; 'Suddenly I See', Katie Tunstall
www.fansofgw.com/grid/valentine/

Ghost Rule: Ghosts exhaust their powers when they act aggressively.

EP. 2.17 2/23/07
THE WALK-IN
Writer: Breen Frazier
Director: Eric Laneuville

After a corpse disappears from the local morgue, Melinda, Jim and Professor Payne try to piece together what went down in the body snatching. Melinda discovers that the missing corpse has been possessed by an earthbound spirit. Now she has to uncover the identities of two earthbound spirits: the one that hijacked the body and the other which was displaced.

Payne: "Uh, we've been talking for like three minutes. You might want to give me eight to nine minutes before I unravel the entire mystery, okay?"

Music: 'See the Sunrise', The Poems; 'Ohh La La', Goldfrapp; 'Human', Jon McLaughlin
www.livingnightmare-gw.blogspot.com/

Ghost Rule: A walk-in can only occur to a corpse if the spirit originally inhabiting the body abandons it.

Jim: "You can't fix two broken hearts by trying to stitch them together."
Melinda: "That is the sappiest thing I've ever heard."

EP. 2.18 3/30/07
CHILDREN OF GHOSTS
Writer: Teddy Tennenbaum
Director: Fred Toye

Melinda and Jim's family grows when they become foster-parents to a teenage girl who's mother is missing and Homer the ghost dog comes back for some TLC. Melinda discovers the teen is haunted by unexplained poltergeist activity. With Professor Payne's help, the mother manifests to confess a secret that allows Melinda and Jim to help the teen find her true home.

www.youtube.com/watch?v=xoxypapNwoU

Ghost Rule: Spirits choose to manifest, you can't make them do it.

EP. 2.19 3/30/07
DELIA'S FIRST GHOST
Writer: Jeannine Renshaw
Director: Kim Moses

Melinda helps Ned with a basement-lurking ghost who is scaring the daylights out of him. Meanwhile, this same ghost is sabotaging Delia's dating life. Melinda and Delia's friendship is put to the test when Melinda has to tell Delia, who's a skeptic, that she and Ned are being haunted by Delia's dead husband. In the meantime Melinda is being hounded by a naked ghost.

Music: 'Every Breath You Take', The Police; 'Begin', The Shore
www.fansofgw.com/grid/crystalball/

Ghost Rule: Ghosts are able to manipulate electricity to cause havoc.

Melinda (to Jim): "So maybe we could move, somewhere no one would ever come and visit, like the Antarctic… or Queens."

EP. 2.20 4/27/07
THE COLLECTOR
Writers: Melissa Peltier & Jim Kouf
Director: Ian Sander

Melinda is intrigued when she meets Gabriel, another ghost whisperer. Eventually Melinda's fascination turns to fear when she realizes Gabriel is operating on a different parallel — he's collecting souls, including the ghost of Professor Payne's wife, to *keep* them earthbound. Then Melinda discovers a room in Gabriel's house that is covered in photos of her and her loved ones. Gabriel has been stalking Melinda for a very long time and she needs to figure out why.

Melinda (re. ghost cross over): "Okay, crossed her over going sixty and never took my foot off the gas. How's that for your grandmother's ghost, Gabriel?"

Music: 'Bare Naked', Jennifer Love Hewitt; 'All Good Things Come to an End', Nelly Furtado

Ghost Rule: The recently-departed can be manipulated by dark spirits to stay earthbound through their negative emotions.

EP. 2.21 5/4/07
THE PROPHET
Writer: John Gray
Director: John Gray

A 'prophet ghost' shows Melinda visions of a deadly future which causes her to fear for the safety of her loved ones. Those visions allude to five accidents but only four signs, meaning something else is going to happen. According to the ghost's prophecy, the fifth accident will be "Death of a loved one", and four children, known as 'sensitives', will be involved. Meanwhile, Gabriel, the ghost whisperer Melinda does not trust, is lurking in Grandview, collecting souls.

Music: 'Everyday', Dope Sixx; 'Beast', 'Paint This Town', The Hangmen; 'Shine', The Wilshires
www.fansofgw.com/comicteaser/

Payne (to Melinda): "You drink the champagne — I only get the hangover."

Ghost Rule: Ghosts can manifest real objects in the world of the living.

Melinda (to the sensitives): "I know what it's like to be different and have people make you feel like you're not quite right."

EP. 2.22 5/11/07
THE GATHERING
Writer: John Gray
Director: John Gray

Before the fifth disaster strikes, Melinda and Professor Payne search for meaning behind the prophet ghost's mythological clues. They discover the location of the fifth impending disaster is in the heart of Grandview, the disaster will take place on the one year anniversary of the jetliner crash that killed Andrea, and the four sensitives will be involved. Melinda must rescue the children before it's too late.

Music: 'Keep Holding On', Avril Levigne; 'Only Fooling Myself', Kate Voegele
www.fansofgw.com/tos/

Ghost Rule: People who die, even for a short time, and see the Light, always come back changed.

SEASON THREE

oing into season three, *Ghost Whisperer* was the number one show in the US on Friday nights. We were at the tipping point. Now we needed to take it to the next level. In the lead up to the new season, we made adjustments to the character of Delia Banks, made Professor Payne a regular, and upped Ned Banks' age to sixteen so we could cover the teen front. We pushed forward on the Internet with an even more aggressive strategy for fans and we produced a second round of webisodes. We used untraditional methods — merging user-generated content with our professional content — to draw more eyeballs to the show. We pushed out on all digital fronts. And we refined the brand. Our mandate for the season was to change the storytelling formula to scary + emotion + lots of mystery.

Here, executive producer P.K. Simonds gives you the inside scoop on season three…

In season three, *Ghost Whisperer* plunges into new territory, literally rocking the foundations of the series. At the end of season two, Melinda met the ghost of her estranged father, who tells her she has a brother. Melinda's search for the truth about her family history grows more and more complex and dangerous when she learns that her roots are bound to the roots of Grandview itself. And the roots of Grandview run deeper and darker than anyone could have imagined. Melinda and Jim begin to wonder whether this small town they chose for its peace and tranquility might have actually chosen them. With the help of Professor Payne and loyal but skeptical friend Delia, Melinda literally digs for answers. She discovers that in the town's desperation to bury its own dark past, a whole other world was left festering, literally beneath their feet.

EP. 3.02 10/05/07
DON'T TRY THIS AT HOME

Writers: Laurie McCarthy & Teddy Tennenbaum
Director: Ian Sander

When a student at Rockland University falls into a coma under suspicious circumstances, a rumor quickly spreads that she was a victim of the Bloody Mary urban legend. Melinda is skeptical that the incident is related to the supernatural. However, when a second student ends up in a coma, Melinda isn't ruling anything out. Melinda discovers it is definitely not the ghost from the myth doing the damage, but rather a *real* ghost who has come back for revenge on those she thinks are responsible for her death.

Music: 'I Don't Want to Let You Go', Ross Copperman
www.rubloodymary.com

Melinda: "The quote is 'Truth is the first casualty of war.'"
Payne: "You're right, you're right! It's amazing, we're like two heads — one brain."

EP. 3.03 10/12/07
HAUNTED HERO

Writers: Karl Schaeffer & Breen Frazier
Director: Eric Laneuville

When Jim and Melinda's army friend Matt returns from Iraq as a wounded soldier, it becomes obvious that he's got spirits attached to him. Melinda discovers the spirits are men in Matt's squad who were killed in an ambush. Matt's memory of the incident is vague but he fears he may have deserted his men in the heat of battle. A video of the ambush surfaces and confirms Matt's worst fears. However, Melinda learns from the soldier spirits that they've attached themselves to Matt to ensure that the real story comes out — Matt is a true war hero.

Music: 'Makes Me Wonder', Maroon Five; 'Heavenly Day', Patty Griffin; 'Two Ways to Say Goodbye', Pat Monahan
www.twitter.com/ghostwhisperer

EP. 3.01 9/28/07
THE UNDERNEATH

Writer: John Gray
Director: John Gray

After a near-death experience during which she encounters her father, Melinda is determined to learn the truth about Tom Gordon and her half-brother Gabriel. Meanwhile, she is haunted by a ghost, killed in a gas explosion in Grandview's Town Square, who blames Melinda for the death of his wife twenty-five years ago. Checking out the accident records, she discovers her mother was present when the man's wife died — his accusation is a case of mistaken identity. The ghost thinks Melinda is her *mother*. When Melinda confronts Beth, she admits she was involved in the woman's death. Also, Scott warns Melinda to beware — dark forces are working against her.

Melinda: "There was a face behind mine in the x-ray."
Payne: "Even your x-rays are haunted — that's hardcore."

Music: 'I Said', Michelle Featherstone

Payne (to Melinda): "I've offered a little extra credit for anyone who does the Bloody Mary ritual. The first kid that dies I'm giving an automatic 'A'."

EP. 3.04 10/19/07
NO SAFE PLACE
Writer: Jeannine Renshaw
Director: Peter O'Fallon

Melinda encounters an attorney, Shane, who is being haunted by the ghost of a woman, Colleen, who apparently stalked him while she was alive. Melinda quickly discovers that the stalker was in fact the attorney, not Colleen, and he made her life a living hell. As payback, she has attached herself to Shane so he will experience the misery he caused her before she died. As Melinda sorts this out, Shane becomes obsessed with *her*. Hampered by vague stalking laws, Melinda is helpless until she and the ghost hatch a plan in which they turn the tables on the deranged stalker.

Music: 'You Give Me Something', James Morrison
www.fansofgw.com/sset/scarieststory_instructional.mov

Melinda: "Oh, I know you are not about to take that peanut butter up into *my* bed."
Jim: "Uh, no. I was about to take this peanut butter up into *my* bed."

Jim (re. Gabriel): "Now you want to save him? After what he did?"
Melinda: "This is what I do. I help people fix their worst mistakes."

EP. 3.05 10/26/07
WEIGHT OF WHAT WAS
Writer: P.K. Simonds
Director: Gloria Muzio

Gabriel makes contact, claiming he needs Melinda's help in finding their father. After inspecting a keepsake Gabriel leaves with her, Melinda is visited by the ghost to whom it belongs. While helping the ghost search for answers about her strange past, Melinda discovers an entire underworld buried beneath Grandview — a secret world that could entomb Melinda forever. Meanwhile Jim, Delia and Professor Payne frantically search for Melinda before the tunnel she's trapped in runs out of air.

Music: 'Umbrella', Rihanna

Ghost Rule: Dark spirits feed on negative emotions (anger, hate, jealousy).

EP. 3.06 11/02/07
DOUBLE EXPOSURE
Writer: Laurie McCarthy
Director: Eric Laneuville

Melinda tries to figure out the identity of a ghost haunting a photography professor friend of Payne. During her investigation, Melinda discovers a twisted love triangle between the professor, a student and the student's girlfriend. But Melinda has trouble understanding who is dead and who is still alive. Once she's sorted that out, Melinda takes on the otherworldly photography that the angry spirit is using to frighten the beautiful professor.

Music: 'Last Request', Paolo Nutini; 'Ashes & Wine', A Fine Frenzy; '11.22', Buddy
www.fansofgw.com/halloween/

Jim (to Melinda): "If you can fight the forces of evil, I think I can do pre-med."

Ghost Rule: Spirits can be visible in photographs because cameras detect a broader spectrum of energy than the human eye.

EP. 3.08 11/16/07
BAD BLOOD
Writer: Teddy Tennenbaum
Director: Peter Werner

When Delia sells a haunted house to a father and his teenage daughter, Melinda must figure out who is haunting the house and why. At first Melinda thinks it must be the wife of the new home owner, but then both father and daughter begin acting aggressively toward each other. Payne and Melinda discover they are being haunted by a pair of ghosts who are forcing the new tenants to reenact a sick game of betrayal, guilt and paranoia that took over their own lives. Melinda must figure out how to release the father and his daughter from the house in order to break the scary spell.

www.fansofgw.com/tos2

Melinda (re. the ghosts' history): "Turmoil, like 'I killed a loved one,' that kind of turmoil?"
Payne: "Okay… I was thinking more like white slacks in November, but I'm sure that would work also."

Melinda: "Your daughter sees ghosts, okay. And I know that because I see them too."

EP. 3.07 11/09/07
UNHAPPY MEDIUM
Writer: Breen Frazier
Director: Fred Toye

A medium comes to Grandview to help a family find their missing daughter. Melinda immediately pegs him as a fraud when he fails to notice a mysterious spirit is attached to him. The medium assures the missing girl's family that she is still alive. However, Melinda discovers that the mysterious ghost attached to the medium is the missing girl. When Melinda shares this news with the medium, he refuses to believe it. For each to prove what they believe to be true, Melinda and the medium agree to work together to find the missing girl and give her family the closure they desperately need.

Melinda: "A lot of responsibility comes with this gift and it's not always just giving people hope — sometimes you have to give them bad news."

Music: 'World on Fire', Sarah McLachlan; 'The First Time', Lifehouse
www.fansofgw.com/quiz

EP. 3.09 11/23/07
ALL GHOSTS LEAD TO GRANDVIEW
Writers: P.K. Simonds & Laurie McCarthy
Director: Fred Toye

Melinda and Jim discover a young girl in the woods who is thousands of miles from home. They bring her into their home and contact her parents, who are on the next flight to pick her up. To Melinda's surprise, the young girl can communicate with the dead. As Melinda teaches the young girl a few tricks of the trade, it becomes apparent the girl is haunted by a combative young ghost who wants help finding his dead parents. The mystery of the ghost's parents leads Melinda back into the world buried beneath Grandview. There, it becomes clear that Gabriel has been using ghosts (including the young ghost's parents) as pawns to recruit earthbound spirits to the dark side.

Music: 'Burn Your Life Down', Tegan & Sara

EP. 3.10 12/14/07
HOLIDAY SPIRIT
Writer: Jeannine Renshaw
Director: Steve Robman

To save Christmas, Melinda must cross over a ghost who is convinced he is Santa Claus and is haunting a workaholic father. The father recently discovered he may not be the biological parent of the young boy he's been raising since birth. After researching several dead-end theories, and with the clock ticking down to the holiday, Melinda discovers the true identity of the Santa ghost and the mystery of his past.

Music: 'Have Yourself a Merry Little Christmas', 'Sleigh Ride', Relient K; 'Oh It's Christmas', Rosebuds
www.youtube.com/watch?v=0Qp84cW27Tw

Payne (to Melinda): "You told Santa he's confused... I guess I know which list you're going on."

Ghost Rule: Ghost visits can be triggered by a birth, death, or special holiday.

Payne: "I never had *anything* written about me. Which is awful. Zip, zero, nothing. Is there anything worse?"

EP. 3.11 1/11/08
SLAM
Writers: Karl Schaefer & Daniel Sinclair
Director: Mark Rosman

Melinda steps into the complex world of high school romance and gossip as she tries to uncover the reason behind a number of hauntings at Ned's new school. Together, they discover that an alumni-from-the-grave is pulling spooky pranks to protect his sister. This involves a complicated love triangle between several members of the most popular clique and a social outcast who's slammed by students online. Melinda must stop the chaos before someone is seriously injured, but the only way to do it is to make the living understand their past for what it is. And to help the ghost understand his sister doesn't need to be protected, she needs to be supported in her chosen lifestyle.

Music: 'Apologize', One Republic; 'Collide', Howie Day
www.lancerslamz.net

Ghost Rule: Ghosts only have on them what they died with.

EP. 3.12 1/18/08
FIRST DO NO HARM
Writer: John Gray
Director: Ian Sander

While trying to rescue two men from a burning building, Jim is forced to abandon one of them as the building collapses. Jim feels guilty about his decision and thinks the ghost of the man he abandoned is haunting him. When Melinda breaks through to the ghost, she discovers 'Jim's ghost' already crossed over and that he's really being haunted by *another* ghost. This one is trying to solve his own murder. Melinda and Jim discover his death is tied to an unusual love story involving a nurse with a suspicious past. The nurse is unaware that she's the true target of the ghost's revenge.

Jim: "Wow, that's a feeling. Just to know you brought somebody a little peace."
Melinda: "Never feel like you don't make a difference or I make more. Sometimes it's the little things you do every single day."

Music: 'New Day's Dawning', The Wilshires

Ghost Rule: Ghosts may appear as a younger version of themselves.

EP. 3.14 4/11/08
THE GRAVESITTER
Writer: John Gray
Director: Fred Toye

Justin Yates is vandalizing Melinda's shop, and Melinda is scared he will reveal her gift to the world on his blog. But when she confronts him, Melinda discovers he has a brain aneurism that could kill him at any moment. *And* he's being haunted by his dead girlfriend, who's turning his life upsidedown. Before Justin's time is up, he needs Melinda's help to right a wrong. Justin believes he can then join his true love in the afterlife. But Melinda knows the ghost of Justin's girlfriend is up to no good.

Music: 'The Moment I Said It', Imogen Heap
www.andshamethedevil.net/

> Melinda: "He saw the ghost of his girlfriend and she told him to come and get her."
> Payne: "That's romantic…
> in a *Dawn of the Dead* kind of way."

Ghost Rule: Sometimes a ghost doesn't initially realize he/she is dead.

EP. 3.13 4/4/08
HOME BUT NOT ALONE
Writers: P.K. Simonds & Laurie McCarthy
Director: Eric Laneuville

Ned thinks his girlfriend might be haunted by her overprotective dead father and it is disrupting their budding romance. When he asks Melinda to check into it, Melinda discovers the girlfriend and her siblings are actually being haunted by the spirit of their over-protective *mother*. On her deathbed, the mother had instructed her kids to cover up her death for fear they would be split up and sent to different foster homes. Melinda must figure out how to sort out this cover-up and still keep the family together.

Delia (re. Ned and his girl-friend): "So what are they doing — are they kissing?"
Melinda: "She just hit him."
Delia: "Thank God."
Melinda: "But it was full of sexual tension."

Music: 'Mercy', Duffy; 'New Day's Dawn', The Wilshires
www.youtube.com/watch?v=MeRMZ_pJT3c

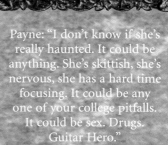

Payne: "I don't know if she's really haunted. It could be anything. She's skittish, she's nervous, she has a hard time focusing. It could be any one of your college pitfalls. It could be sex. Drugs. Guitar Hero."

EP. 3.15 4/25/08
HORROR SHOW
Writer: Jeannine Renshaw
Director: Ian Sander

Professor Payne asks Melinda to set up a family friend with a job, as she's been struggling to pay her way at Rockland U. since losing her scholarship. Payne believes the young woman is having problems because she's haunted, which is another reason he wants Melinda to meet her. Melinda quickly discerns that this friend of Payne's is indeed haunted, and the ghost might be her brilliant, scholarly father. That theory gives way when Melinda is haunted by scenes from horror movies. Melinda discovers the ghost who's doing the haunting was creating a horror film when he died. Now, he's finishing his film from the grave and casting the living as his victims.

Music: 'Capsize', Spencer Tracy

173

EPISODE GUIDE

174

EP. 3.16 5/2/08
DEADBEAT DADS
Writer: Mark B. Perry
Director: Gloria Muzio

Rick reunites with an ex-girlfriend, Nina, who claims she's in Grandview on business. Payne discovers she has a brilliant young son, and after doing the math, deduces the boy may be his child. Nina quickly confirms it. However, Melinda, feeling something isn't right, does some sleuthing and discovers he is being scammed. And his dead wife is jealous. Now, she's back from the grave with a vengeance to make Payne's life a living hell. Melinda must intervene to save her favorite professor, who's caught between his dead wife and his ex-girlfriend.

Payne: "I hate kids. Maybe hate is a strong word, but I have a profound lack of understanding for the need to breed. Besides, kids are just filled with snot."

Music: 'Day Too Soon', Sia

Ghost Rule: Ghosts can go wherever they want and hear everything that is said.

Melinda: "But he just got here and you want me to pretend like he never existed. I mean, don't I have a right to know who my father is, where he's been all these years?"

EP. 3.17 5/9/08
STRANGLEHOLD
Writers: Laurie McCarthy, P.K. Simonds
Director: Eric Laneuville

While trying to figure out the meaning of a dream, Melinda discovers that her father, Tom Gordon, is alive and in Grandview with her half-brother, Gabriel. While searching for clues to Tom's past, Melinda uncovers the murder case of a young boy that he prosecuted. When Melinda visits the victim's family, she learns that the boy's ghost is experimenting with possession — and that her father is being *possessed*. The mystery heightens when the spirit of the murderer, Paul Eastman, turns up and threatens to destroy everything in Melinda's world.

Music: 'Someone You Love', Liz Stahler

www.fansofgw.com/widget/

EP. 3.18 5/16/08
PATER FAMILIAS
Writer: John Gray
Director: John Gray

Melinda bursts into Tom's hotel room, where he has apparently attempted suicide. He is rushed to the hospital in critical condition, but survives. Melinda, assuming that Paul Eastman is seeking revenge for being wrongly convicted, investigates how Tom was possessed when he shot himself. And learns the horrible truth — Tom Gordon is a sociopath and her *real* father is Paul Eastman.

Music: 'It's Amazing', Jem; 'Life Is Beautiful', Vega4
www.fansofgw.com/showcase/

Ghost Rule: The power of love is often strong enough to save even an angry, vengeful earthbound spirit.

Jim: "Now you're gonna tell me some truth, or I'm gonna come back to your room when you're sound asleep, and I'm gonna cut a couple of very important tubes and watch you die for real."
Tom: "But Jim, you're sworn to save lives."
Jim: "That comes in a roaring second compared to saving my wife."

SEASON FOUR

o glad you joined us on this journey through the spirit world. But we're not finished. There's lots more to come in the TV series as well as on the digital media front. The next season promises to be filled with surprises, excitement and ghost rule revelations.

Here, P.K. Simonds teases season four...

There comes a time in any series when life starts to seem just a tad too comfortable. Everyone knows that life throws you curveballs. Life never goes in a straight line. It tests us. So it should do the same thing to the characters we love. That's what life does

to Melinda in season four. Life faces her with what might be the ultimate test. How strong is she? How strong is her faith? How strong is her love?

We all know death is a part of life. No one lives forever. But many shows grow old and die without death ever touching their main characters. Death touches Melinda every day. But how close does it really come? In a season-long storyline that puts Melinda and every relationship in her life to the ultimate test, we explore the many ways *Ghost Whisperer* shows us a world beyond death.

In *Ghost Whisperer*, death isn't always an end. Sometimes it's a new beginning. It certainly is for a new character, played by Jaime Kennedy — a professor of psychology who dies and comes back with powers he never imagined possible. And it is for Melinda too, when death turns her life upside-down. But also gives her second chances she never knew she could have... ✆

ABOUT THE AUTHORS

Ian Sander and Kim Moses are partners in Sander/Moses Productions where they have produced award winning television series, made for TV movies, and feature films for the world's major entertainment outlets, as well as creative content for digital media. Currently they are the executive producers of *Ghost Whisperer* and have directed multiple episodes of the hit series.

Kim and Ian are married and have two sons, Aaron and Declan. They live in a haunted convent built in 1928 in Encino, California. 🐝

www.sandermoses.com

Right:
Kim Moses behind the camera.
Below Right:
Kim Moses directs as Ian Sander watches the monitor.
Below Left:
Ian Sander directing leading lady Jennifer Love Hewitt and David Conrad.